*Individual
Creations*

The Grand Tour

Individual Creations

Flavio Conti

Translated by Patrick Creagh

HBJ Press
Boston

HBJ Press
President, Robert J. George
Publisher, Giles Kemp
Vice President, Richard S. Perkins, Jr.
Managing Director, Valerie S. Hopkins
Text Director, Marcia Heath
Special Projects Editor, Carolyn Hall
Text Editors: Karen E. English, Amanda
 Heller, Victoria Pope
Editorial Staff: Betsie Brownell, Chris Heath,
 Ann McGrath
Project Coordinator, Linda S. Behrens

Architectural Consultant, Dennis J. DeWitt
Text Consultants: Janet Adams, Elizabeth R.
 DeWitt, Perween Hasan
Project Consultant, Ann S. Moore
Design Implementation, Designworks

Rizzoli Editore
Authors of the Italian Edition:
 Dr. Flavio Conti, Paolo Savole, Dr. Gian
 Maria Tabarelli
Idea and Realization, Harry C. Lindinger
General Supervisor, Luigi U. Re
Graphic Designer, Gerry Valsecchi
Coordinator, Vilma Maggioni
Editorial Supervisor, Gianfranco Malafarina
Research Organizer, Germano Facetti
U.S. Edition Coordinator, Natalie Danesi
 Murray

Photography Credits:

Almasy: p. 26 top, p. 27 top/ *Cauchetier:* pp. 9–15, p. 16 top, p. 16 bottom right, pp. 17–19, p. 20 bottom, p. 22, p. 23 top, pp. 24–25, p. 26 center & bottom, p. 27 bottom, pp. 28–32/ *Gode:* p. 46/ *Hassmann:* pp. 73–96/ *M&W Phototeca International:* pp. 41–45, pp. 47–49, p. 52, pp. 106–116/ *Magnum/Marc Riboud:* pp. 121–132/ *Oronoz:* pp. 50–51/ *Photri:* p. 157 bottom, p. 158 bottom right/ *Radici:* p. 169/ *Re:* p. 60 top right, p. 65 bottom/ *Rizzoli:* pp. 57–59, p. 60 left, p. 60 bottom right, pp. 61–64, p. 65 top left, p. 65 top right, pp. 66–68/ *Sheridan:* p. 16 bottom left, p. 20 top, p. 21, p. 23 bottom/ *S. Visalli:* pp. 153–156, p. 157 top, p. 158 top & bottom left, pp. 159–164/ *Zakowski:* pp. 137–148.

© 1977 by Rizzoli Editore-International Division
Copyright © 1978 by HBJ Press, Inc.

All rights reserved. No part of this publication may be reproduced or transmitted in any form or by any means, electronic or mechanical, including photocopy, recording, or any information storage and retrieval system, without permission in writing from the publisher.

Library of Congress Catalog Card Number: 77-94394
ISBN: 0-15-003726-0

Printed in Hong Kong by Mandarin Publishers Limited

Contents

Chateau of Fontainebleau, France   9

The Escorial, Spain   41

Taj Mahal, India   57

The Belvedere, Austria   73

Sagrada Familia, Spain   105

Chapel at Ronchamp, France   121

Taivallahti Church, Finland   137

Guggenheim Museum, U.S.A.   153

Preface
Individual Creations

All men are equal before the law, or so the theory goes. In the history of architecture, some names shine more brightly than others; but architecture is a democratic art honoring individual talent over ancestral titles and inherited reputations. Thus, in this volume the obstinate son of a Swiss watchcase-engraver stands alongside an all-powerful Hapsburg monarch. Here, too, are both the strong-willed offspring of a midwestern preacher and that "Most Christian King" of France who, having lost all but his honor, attempted to regain some of his prestige by building what he intended to be the most magnificent of palaces. He was neither the first nor the last to apply such an enlightened remedy to his problems.

Behind each of the eight achievements in this volume stands the powerful, shaping personality of a single individual—usually the architect, but sometimes a royal client. Each building is marked by the character and effort of its builder, and each testifies to the integrity and perseverance of individual creation. In their own ways, they reflect the spirit of an era and a people, expressed by the ability—and often the sheer obstinacy—of a single man.

No one was more stubborn, nor more able, than Frank Lloyd Wright, who used his talents (about which he had a monumental lack of modesty) to start from nothing and build for himself one of the most brilliant, dramatic, and enduring careers that any architect could possibly hope for. As a young man, he went to Chicago where, through his industry and aptitude, he soon began to make his way in the world. After a few years, he moved on into private practice from the offices of his mentor, Louis Sullivan. By the time he was forty, he was the most famous architect in America. In his middle years it seemed as though he had lost his sense of direction, but the last third of his long life witnessed an unforeseen florescence that even today is not fully appreciated. One of his last and greatest works is the wonderful spiral of the Guggenheim Museum, an immense seashell in reinforced concrete that rose on Fifth Avenue in New York City despite the opposition of the entire city, whose commercial buildings had increasingly come to resemble huge filing cabinets. Wright claimed to love dearly the architects of these buildings, but he added regretfully, "It's a pity I can't say as much for their work." They had not, in his opinion, listened to the voice of truth, the first and only prophet of modern architecture—by which he meant himself. Indeed, Wright seemed at times to regard himself more as god than prophet.

According to Wright, one day he felt that he had to choose between "a false modesty and a healthy pride," and he chose pride. Those who paid the price for this bravura were his clients, whose homes appeared regularly in magazines and books, but who had to allow Wright the first and last say in everything. And Wright was intransigent over the Guggenheim Museum, insisting on building it in the shape of a spiral, which all but eclipsed the pictures it was created to exhibit.

Maybe he was wrong, if the building is considered solely as a museum. But if it is regarded as a spatial experience, his choice is amply justified. As for the pictures, Wright would undoubtedly have countered any criticism by suggesting brusquely that if they did not look good there, then they could always be hung somewhere else.

The work of Le Corbusier, the other master architect of our era, also shows how exalting the "architecture of democracy"—the artistic gift of one free man to other free men—can be. Speaking of his conception of the Chapel at Ronchamp—a vision that occurred to him when he first visited the site, he said:

An idea crystallizes: here in these conditions at the top of a lonely hill, here we must have one all-embracing craft, a team of men working as one in technique and intention, men who are free and masters of their trade. *Bonne chance!*

Poetic rapture ran strong in this Swiss who became more French than Parisian, who eulogized the right angle and took

Cartesian delight in the freedom that came from the rigorous application of mathematics. One critic, writing of Le Corbusier, stated that "only the French should be allowed to make revolutions, because only they really know how to write the necessary manifestoes." The poetic manifesto of the Chapel at Ronchamp was finally realized in stone and cement, steel and glass.

Le Corbusier not only convinces us, he bends us to his will. His Chapel at Ronchamp brought the architectural establishment to its feet, shouting, "scandal!" The so-called experts could not accept that what they disparagingly referred to as a mushroom, a cave, and even a baroque troglodyte was in fact the work of that same fierce polemicist who once peremptorily declared that "a house is a machine to live in." It seemed inconceivable that it had been designed by the same "functionalist" architect who invited his colleagues to admire and imitate the cabins of ocean liners, in which "the most is contained in the least," and who designed his houses with corridors as narrow as those of railway coaches. But the Chapel at Ronchamp is also "functional" in its own way, as a house of prayer. The church on the hill is, as the architect wished, "a place of silence, of prayer, of peace, of inner joy," a place where "all those who climb the hill will be able to find an echo of everything we intended for it." Corbu, as he was popularly known, died in 1965, but his spirit, transmuted into concrete form, still speaks to us from that hilltop in the Vosges.

The Taj Mahal is half a world away in space and immeasurably far in conception and philosophy from the small but monumental French chapel. Strangely enough, the product of the rational, prismatic West is imaginative and unpredictable, while the very symbol of the mysterious and turbulent East is a study in absolute symmetry and geometric grace. Symptomatic of this preoccupation with total symmetry is a large and totally superfluous construction to one side of the Taj Mahal which was built as a counterpoint to the mosque on the opposite side.

The Taj Mahal was erected by Shah Jahan in memory of his wife Mumtaz Mahal, a lament for a lost love. Yet, Shah Jahan himself was no romantic innocent. To gain the throne, he had defeated one of his brothers in open warfare and was indirectly responsible for the deaths of two others, not to mention other sundry cruelties, tortures, and assorted persecutions. Legend has it that, when Mumtaz Mahal was on her deathbed, she asked her husband to erect a monument to her memory and to make its proportions so perfect and its lines so pure that anyone who saw it would feel some small part of the transcendent love that had united their two souls. No witnesses can testify to the truth of this story, but nonetheless the monument was constructed and is one of the most beautiful and melancholy buildings of all time—the triumph, through art, of love over death.

The Escorial, on the other hand, is a monument to death itself, a royal palace built around a royal mausoleum erected by King Philip II of Spain. A good Catholic, and moreover a Spanish Catholic champion of the Counter Reformation, Philip is immortalized in a wonderful portrait by Pantoja de la Cruz. He is shown dressed in penitent black from his hat to his boots, the long chin inherited from his father adorned with a rather skimpy blond beard that falls to his starched lace collar, while his eyes are cold and distant, and his mouth is set in disdain. In his utter dedication to duty, he was dubbed the "first bureaucrat of the empire." Austere and deeply religious, he built the Escorial as a votive act. On Saint Lawrence's Day, August 2, 1557, the Spanish army defeated the French troops at St.-Quentin in Picardy. In gratitude for this victory, the king vowed to erect a monastery to the saint in the heart of his kingdom. Thus, at the precise center of the architectural complex of the Escorial stands a church dedicated to Saint Lawrence, and the plan of the whole building is in the form of a gridiron, the instrument used to martyr that heroic saint.

The Escorial is also perhaps the only royal palace in Europe to contain a monastery—in fact, to be a monastery first and foremost. Not only Philip but also nearly all Spanish monarchs after him are buried in its vaults. If Louis XIV, the Sun King, made his bedchamber the center of France, Philip II made the great Church of St. Lawrence the pivot of his empire. Philip himself—in contrast to his father, Charles V, whose insistence on etiquette and refinement recalls the civilization of Byzantium—was content with a few bare, whitewashed rooms, devoid of any decoration but his paintings. When he died, it was on a simple bed, decorated with one beautiful Flemish tapestry, in the smallest and simplest of his chambers from which he could see the altar of the church as he lay confined to his bed.

The Escorial represents much, but not all, of Spain. It lacks that fantastic, dreamlike spirit that finds expression in the work of another great Spaniard, Antoni Gaudì. Barcelona, the Catalan city that spawned Picasso, is dominated by the most personal and overwhelming of churches: the Sagrada Familia, or Expiatory Temple of the Holy Family. As it now stands, the Sagrada Familia is not so much a church as it is the foreshadowing of a church to come, for Gaudì was only able to build the apse, the crypt, and a single façade. However, about twenty years ago, construction was taken up again in accordance with the plans left by the master. But if Gaudì had lived, he would have undoubtedly modified the plans still further. Gaudí was never content merely to send his drawings along to the building site; he spent his days there, anxiously watching over the construction. No drawing could translate the wealth and beauty of the decorative effects he envisioned: solid masses of stone metamorphosed into flowing vines and leaves, fluid parabolic arches, and intricate tableaux of human and animal figures. An extravagant and fascinating fragment, the Sagrada Familia is the Gothic expression of Gaudí's intensely personal religious fervor and dedication to his craft. Gaudí constructed his extraordinary church in the middle of Barcelona, with the approval and contributions of his fellow citizens, whom he in turn rewarded with one of the most intriguing architectural achievements to have emerged from the depths of the modern consciousness.

Also subtly responsive to the human subconscious is the church recently built—or rather excavated—in Taivallahti Square in Helsinki by Timo and Tuomo Suomalainen, two brilliant young Finnish architects. It is the expression of a rather different, almost subliminal, consciousness. It could even be likened to a kind of "racial memory" of the time when rough rock walls constituted man's only protection from nature. But there is nothing dreamlike or surrealistic in the appearance of this precisely achieved work. The church was excavated from the heart of a rock mass because this was the solution most appropriate to the conditions of the site: in other words, for a rational rather than a romantic reason. Although it cannot be called geometric, it can be seen to follow a logical and mathematical design. But most important of all, the church is conducive to prayer and shows that the language of contemporary architecture can be an affecting means of expression.

Not all buildings achieve such unity and integrity. The work of the first architect of Fontainebleau, Gilles Le Breton, was certainly considered to be less than successful. King Francis I, the king who on one occasion lost everything except his honor, had commissioned Le Breton to remodel—in effect, to totally rebuild—his old royal castle, but he decided that the designs of the master builder were altogether too modest and unassuming for the palace of the "Most Christian King." Le Breton's building followed the fashionable style of the Italian Renaissance, but Francis wanted to be an innovator rather than a conformist.

For artists worthy of his glory, Francis turned to the "home of the arts," the Italy which he had admired so much in his youth and, indeed, had attempted to conquer. Francis was already the patron of the aging Leonardo da Vinci, who spent his last years in a castle by the Loire. To work on his palace, he employed other renowned masters, among them Primaticcio and Il Rosso Fiorentino, as well as a few, such as Vignola, who would later win wide acclaim.

Francis succeeded in his quest. Not until Louis XIV did any French sovereign carve such a niche for himself in the history of art. The group of artists he gathered at Fontainebleau lifted France out of the Gothic era and into the full light of the Renaissance. The works of these artists of the First School of Fontainebleau can tell visitors much about the ruler who took a small castle and transformed it into the setting for a magnificent court.

Many years later, a young lady named Olympe Mancini spent her adolescence at Fontainebleau. Olympe, who was the first love of the Sun King, was to become the mother of a sickly and ill-favored youth named Eugene of Savoy. Because of his ill health and unattractive appearance, Eugene seemed destined for life in a seminary. However, feeling that he had no vocation for the priesthood, he approached the king—who by then had moved to Versailles—and asked to be given a company in His Majesty's army. Ridiculed, he left for Austria, where he offered his services to Emperor Leopold I. He was to become one of the greatest generals in history, *Prinz Eugen, der edle Ritter* ("Prince Eugene, the noble chevalier"), as his troops eulogized him in song. On the battlefield he repeatedly blunted the ambitions of the Sun King. But he was also that rarity in the House of Savoy, an intellectual, alert, and well-educated man, and a close friend of the renowned philosopher Leibnitz. Indeed, Leibnitz admired him so much that he left him all his manuscripts. Eugene was well versed in art and architecture and would intelligently criticize the whole business of war, while personally practicing it as one of the fine arts. He exercised his good taste when he built his summer residence outside Vienna, for he chose one of the best architects of the day, Johann Lucas von Hildebrandt. After giving rigorous instructions, he allowed his chosen man a free hand. This palace, called the Belvedere, was finished by the other preeminent architect of the Austrian Baroque, Bernhard Fisher von Erlach, whose son installed a steam engine in the palace gardens capable of throwing jets of water seventy feet into the air. Thanks to his military capabilities and successes, Prince Eugene, whose name is linked with the battles of Oudenarde and Malplaquet, was finally able to build one of the most beautiful and peaceful of residences.

Such is the way of the world. Architectural masterpieces are not conjured out of a void. But for the individual who has the will power, tenacity, intelligence, and vision, as well as the means, the reward may be Ronchamp or the Belvedere, the Sagrada Familia or the Guggenheim Museum. The rest of us can look on and admire. And this volume is dedicated to precisely that end.

Fontainebleau

France

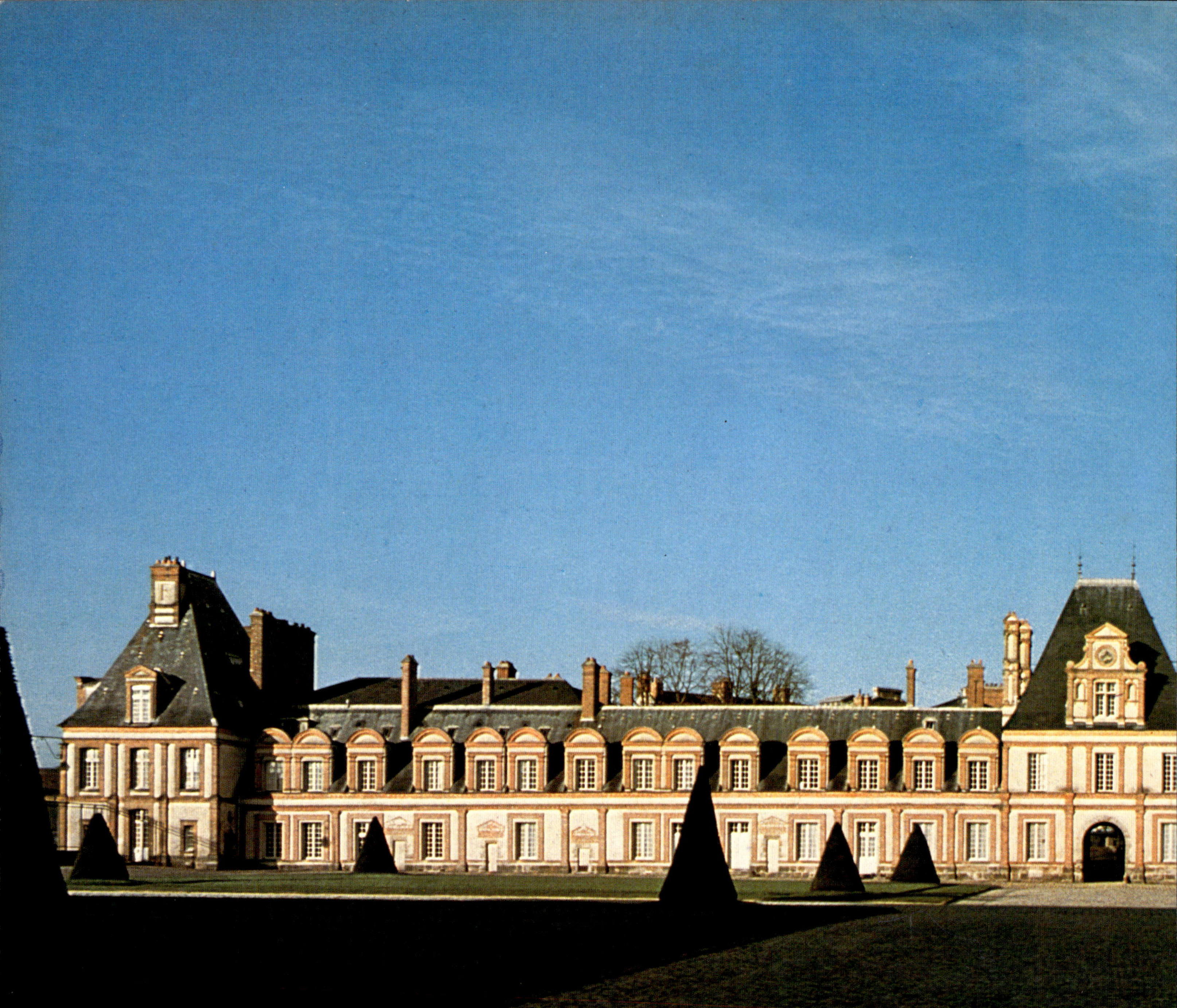

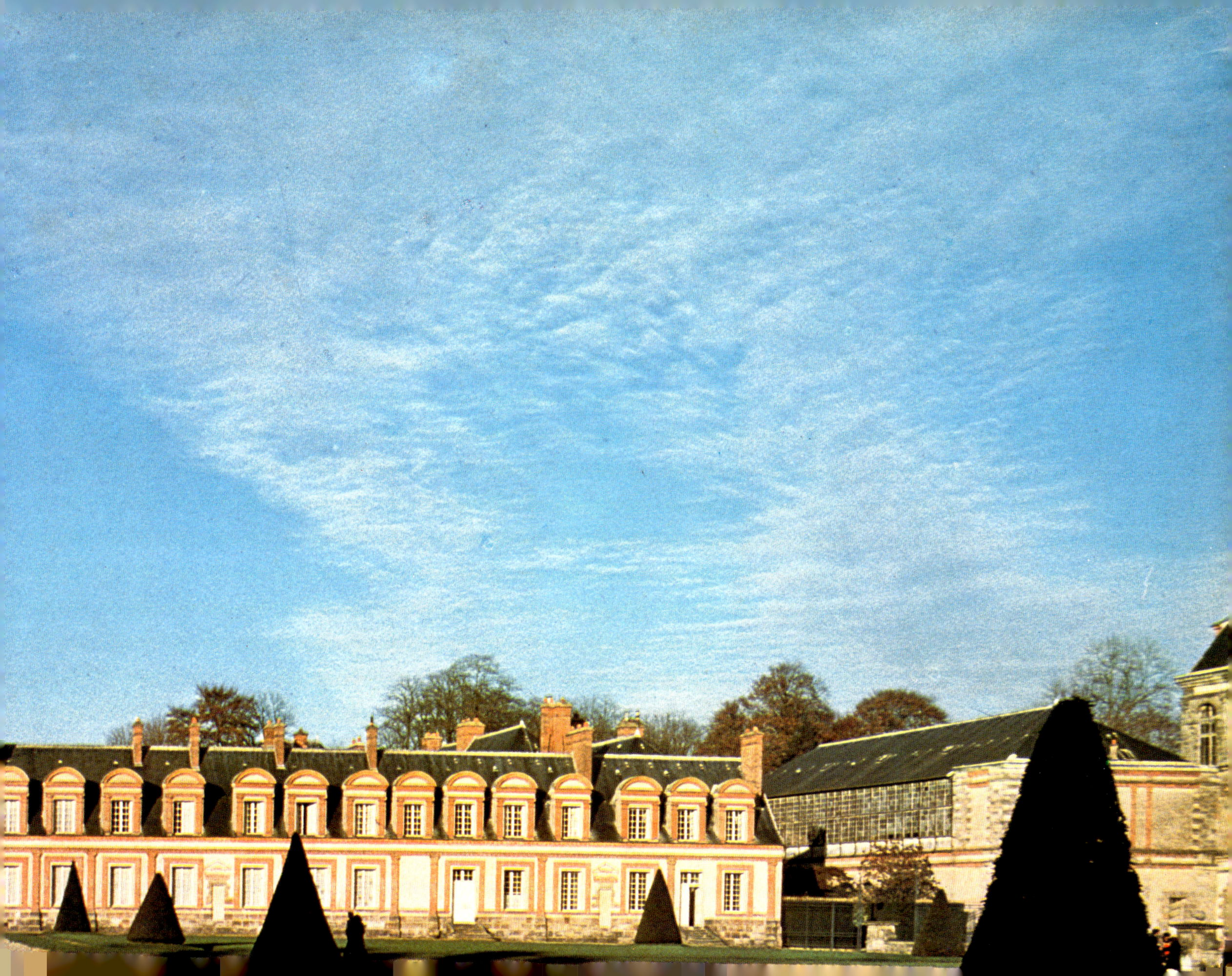

The Wing of the Ministers (preceding page), as it came to be known under Napoleon, was built in a somewhat understated Renaissance style by Gilles Le Breton during the reign of Francis I.

Left and above left, the roof of the central pavilion of the Wing of the Ministers, showing the monogram and the salamander, the heraldic symbol of Francis I.

Above, the Wing of the Ministers. Right, a view of the Wing of the Ministers from the great double horseshoe staircase, completed in 1634 by Jean Androuet Du Cerceau. The staircase—widely imitated in chateaux throughout France—is the central focus of the huge Cour du Cheval Blanc ("Court of the White Horse") which was named for the equestrian statue of Marcus Aurelius that once stood in its center. After his abdication, Napoleon bade farewell to his Old Guard here. Since then, the court has also been known as the Cour des Adieux.

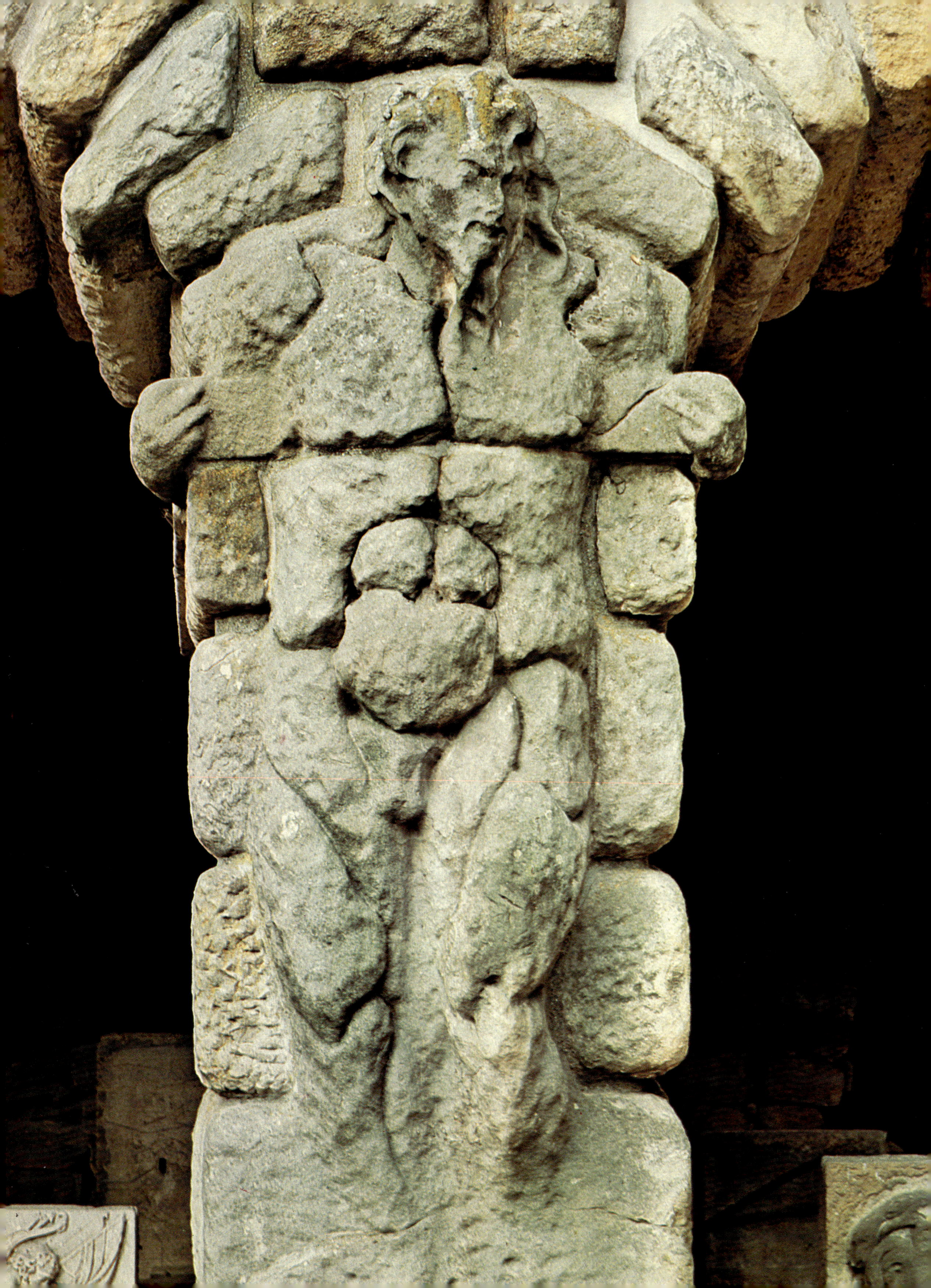

Above, the grotto of the Jardin des Pins ("Garden of the Pines"). This small, typically Mannerist building—often found in Renaissance gardens—dates from about 1543. It was probably designed by Primaticcio; the figures are thought to be the work of Antoine Jacquet. The garden was laid out by the Italian for Francis I. Facing page and right, details of the grotto, showing the figures carved in grès, a local sandstone that, though particularly difficult to work, was widely used at Fontainebleau.

The Porte d'Orée (above) is one of the oldest parts of the palace. Commissioned by Francis I in 1528, it was constructed by Gilles Le Breton before the king began to rely upon Italian architects. Its design is modeled after the façade of the ducal palace in Urbino. The Porte d'Orée, the original entrance to the chateau, leads to the Cour Ovale ("Oval Court"). Left and below, details of the lower portal.

The irregularly shaped Cour Ovale (above right) was constructed by Francis I on foundations of the original castle. It is primarily the work of Gilles Le Breton but was also worked on by Serlio and Philibert Delorme. Some alterations were made to the courtyard during the reign of King Henry IV.

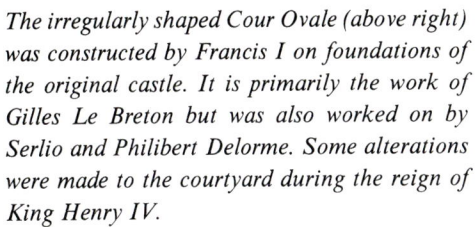

Immediately above, the portico attributed to Serlio.

Center and right, the entrance to the staircase named after Francis I, surmounted by a bust of Francis I flanked by classical gods.

Among the most beautiful works at Fontainebleau are the decorations (below and right) carried out under the direction of Il Rosso Fiorentino and Primaticcio, two Italian artists employed by Francis I. The supreme example of their achievement is probably the bedchamber of the Duchesse d'Etampes. Typical features are the eighteen slender stucco female figures that support the plaster frames of the frescoes. The frescoes themselves represent the history of Alexander the Great. This room was drastically altered during the reign of Louis XV, when Gabriel converted it into the top landing of a ceremonial staircase. Although the staircase itself is splendid and the original decorations remain, the space has been irremediably changed.

Left, a great mask of Hercules on a doorway.

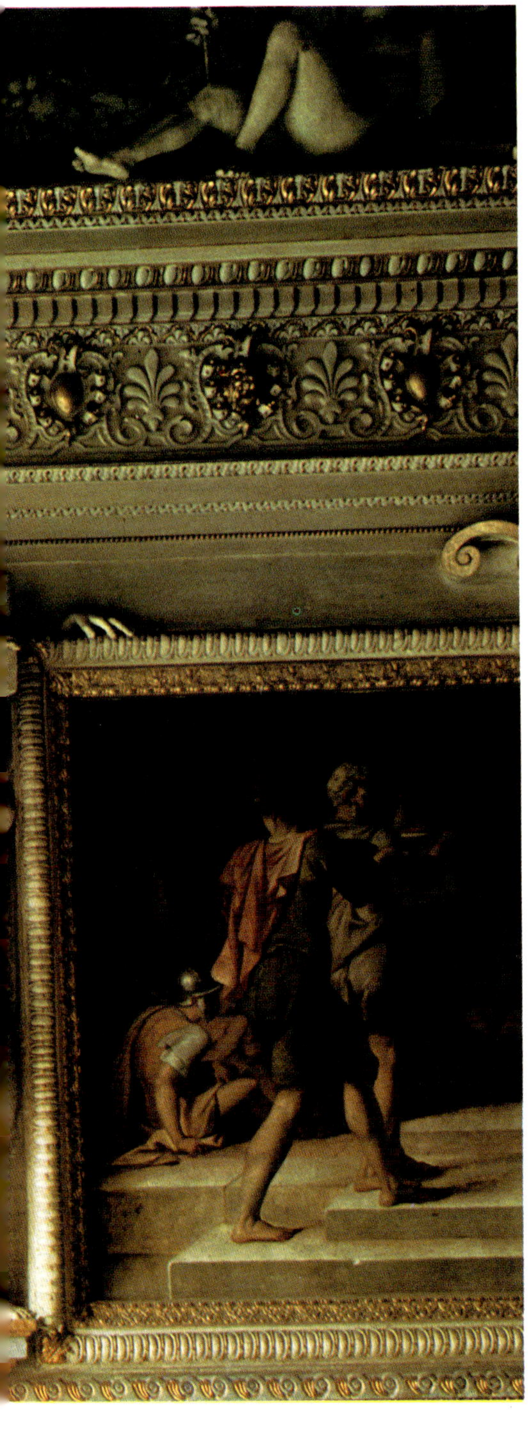
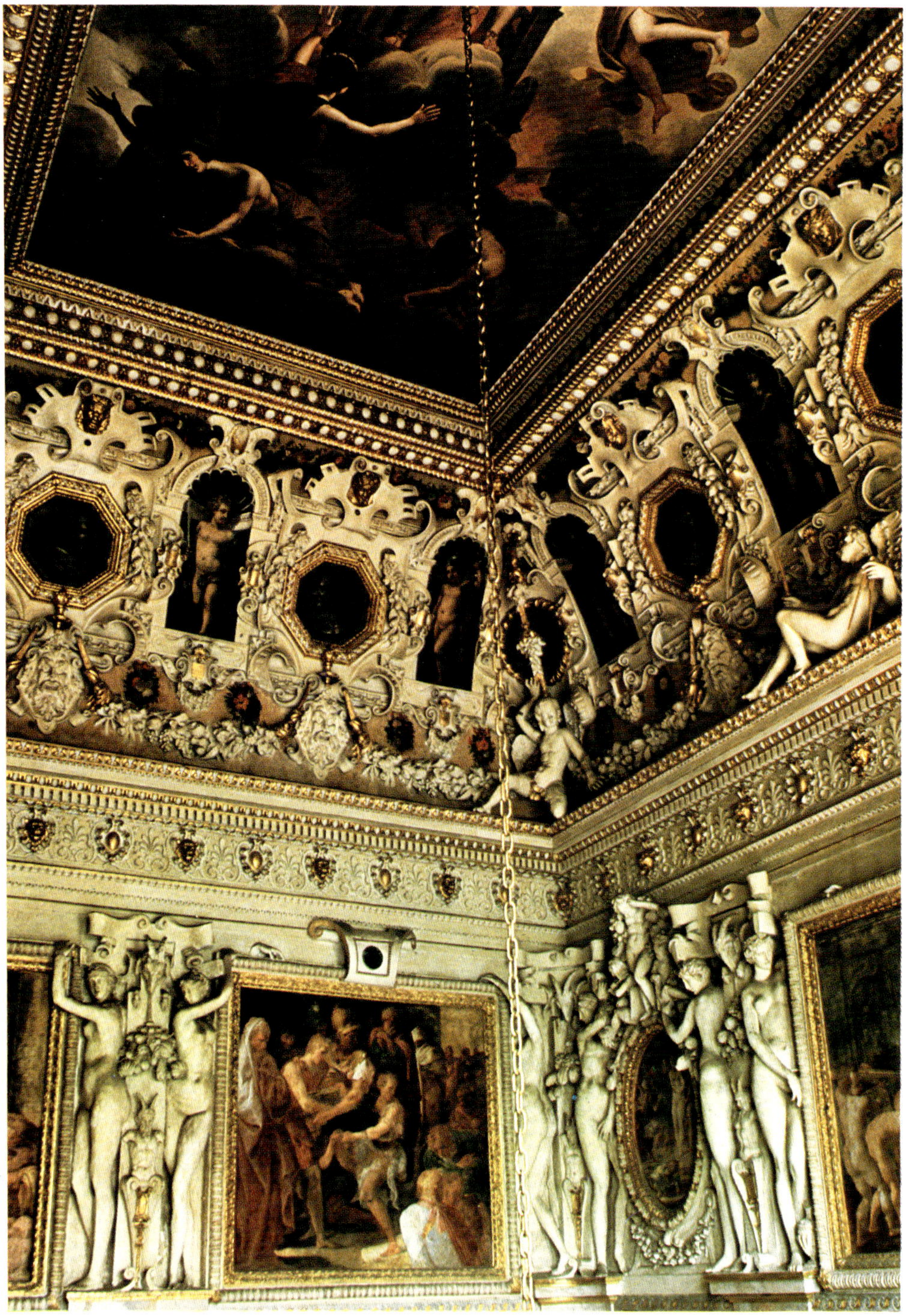
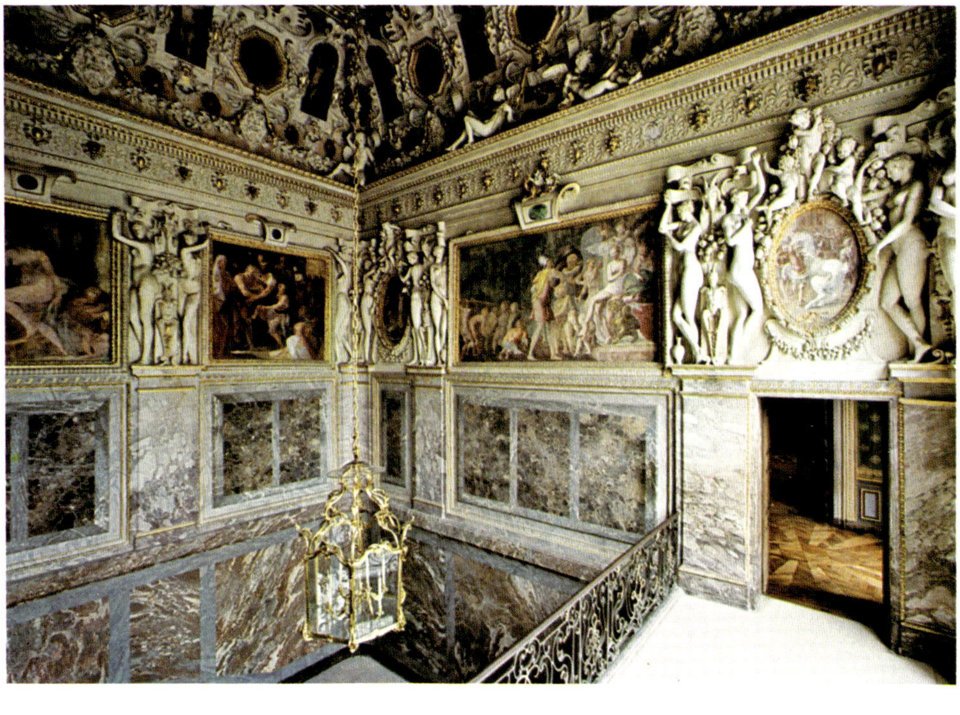

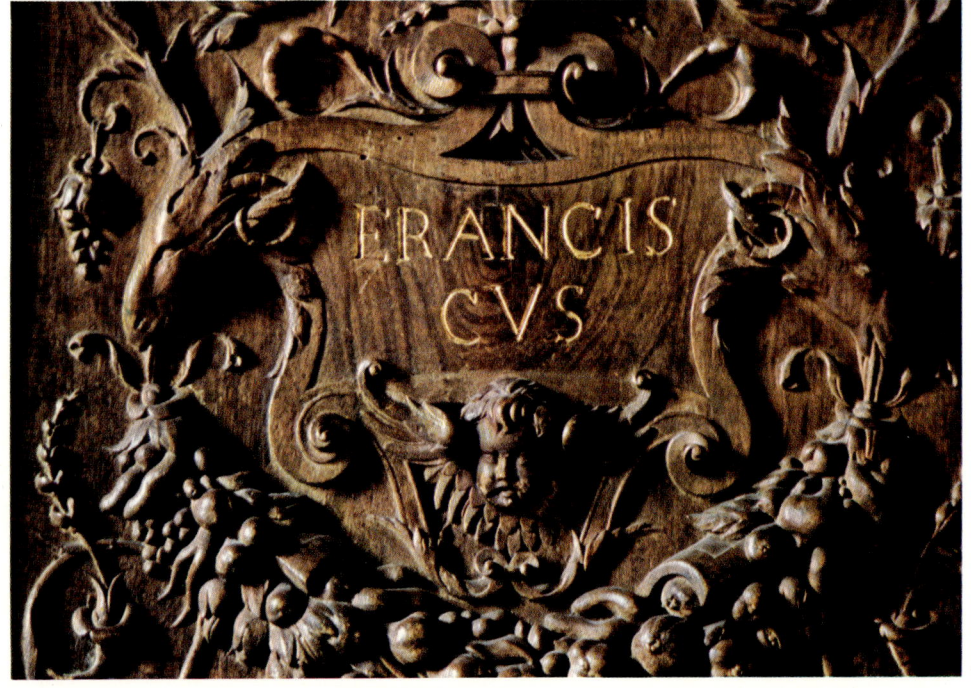

The Gallery of Francis I (facing page) is the showpiece of Fontainebleau. The gallery, a forerunner of the famous Hall of Mirrors at Versailles, is the most complete and significant achievement of the First School of Fontainebleau, the group of artists who introduced the art of the Italian Renaissance into France. The building itself is the work of Gilles Le Breton, but the splendid interior, a masterful blend of frescoes, stucco, and woodwork, is the creation of Il Rosso Fiorentino, Primaticcio, and their pupils. The overall theme of this decorative work (above and left) is the glorification of the king, whose monogram and name are used as motifs throughout.

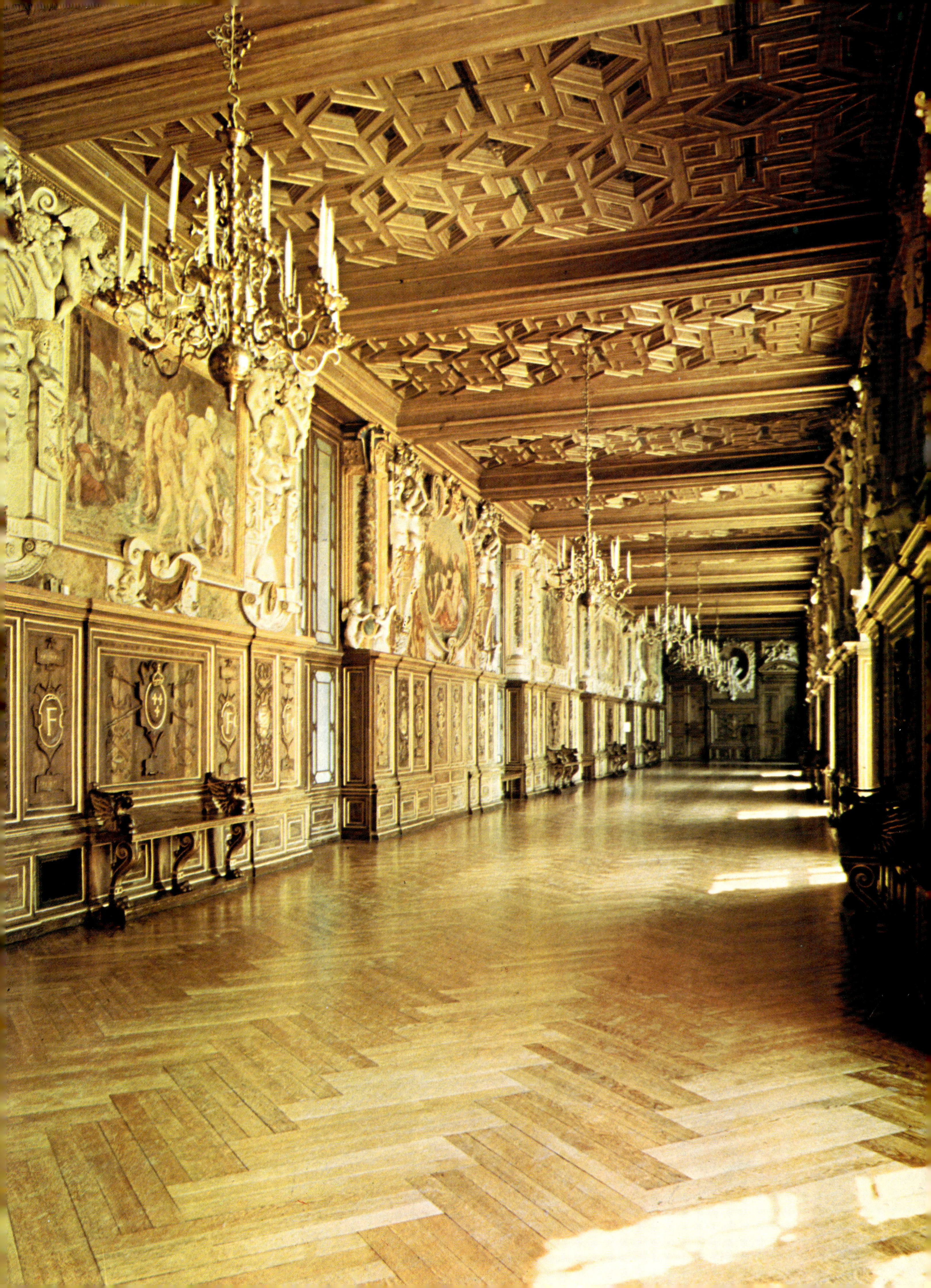

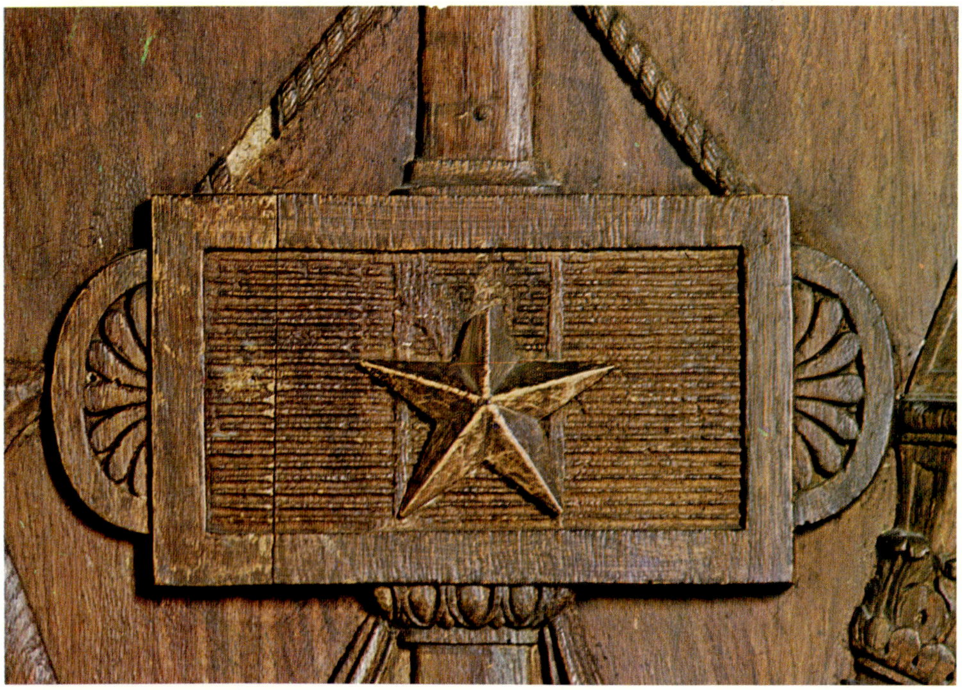

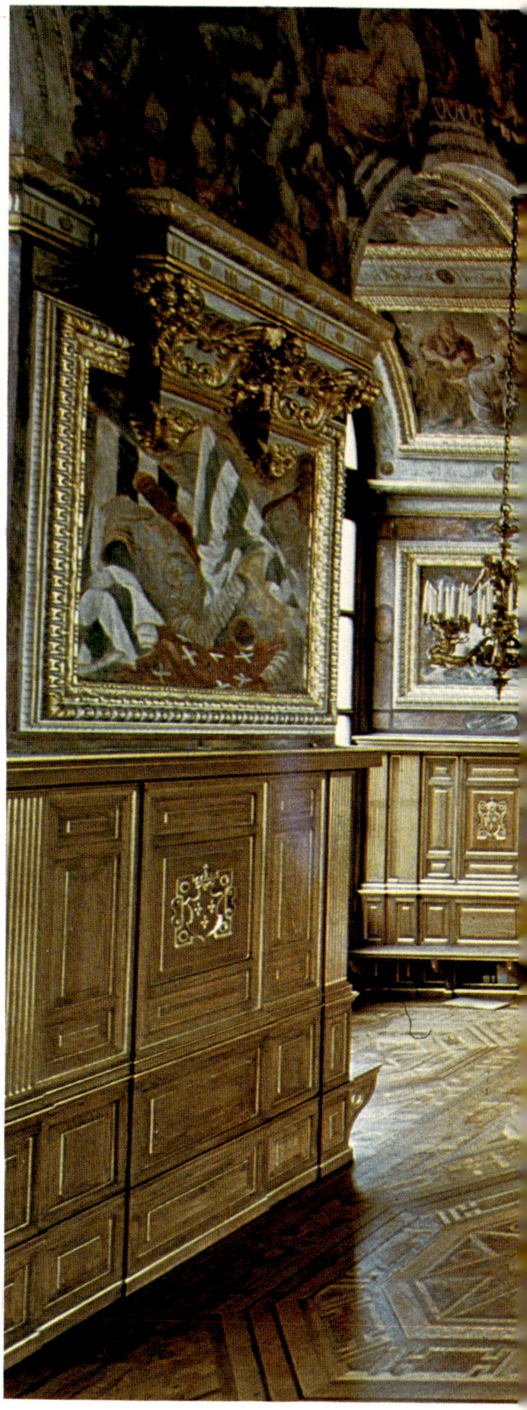

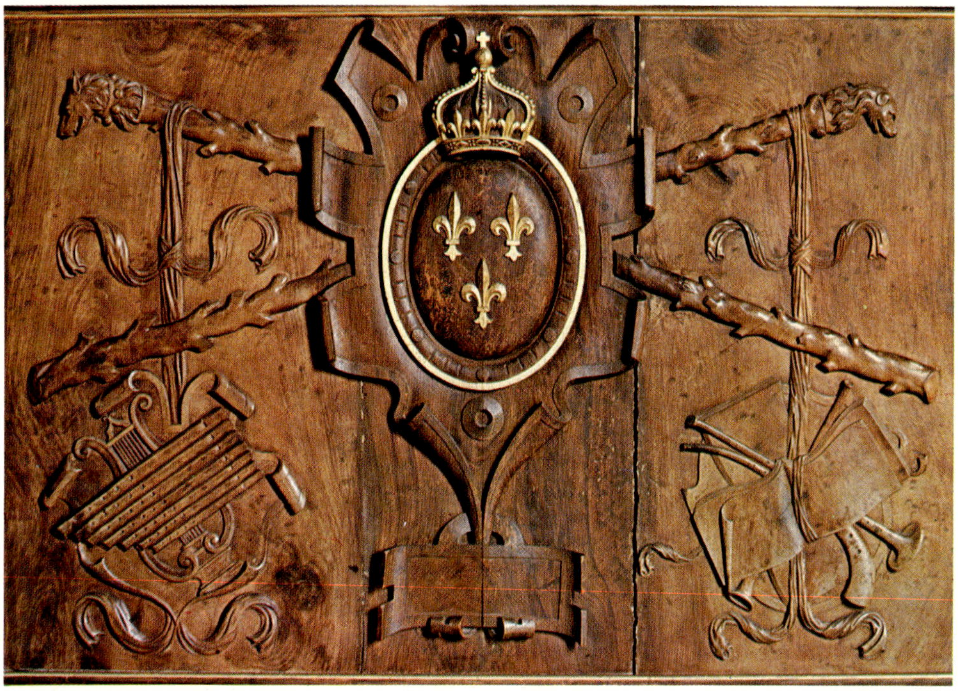

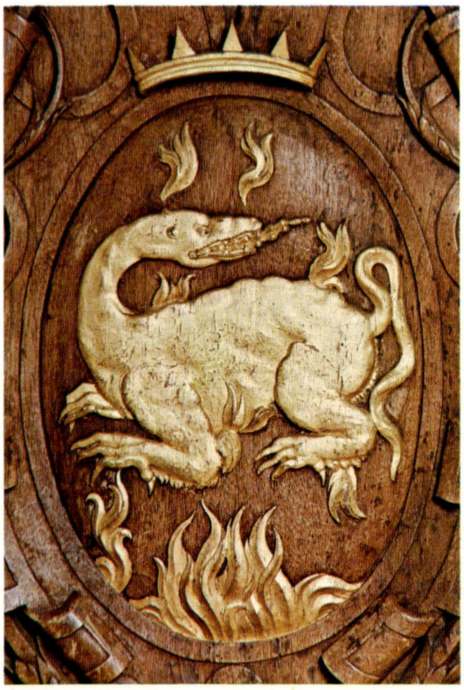

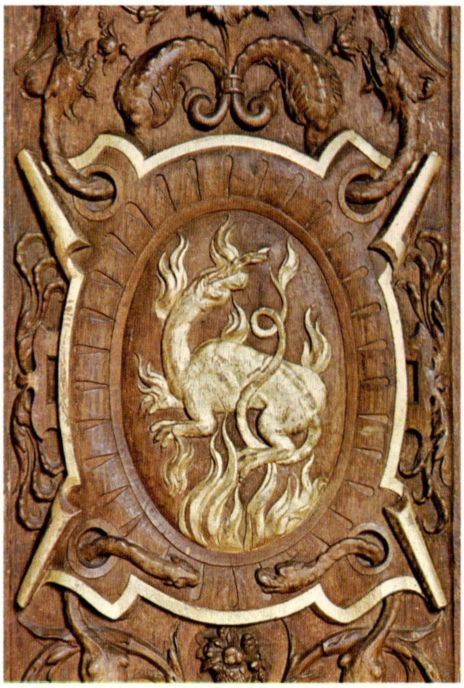

The decorations of Fontainebleau bear witness to the passage of history. This door (above left) originally bore Napoleon's initial, but during the Restoration it was replaced by a star.

Left center, the arms of the kings of France. Under Francis I, Fontainebleau was the chief royal residence outside Paris, but later it became a hunting lodge and secondary residence.

Bottom, the salamander, the personal symbol of Francis I, who was the first of the great builders of Fontainebleau.

Above, the great ballroom, with (right) a fireplace executed by Guillaume Rondelet in 1556. The ballroom was designed by Le Breton and subsequently decorated by Philibert Delorme, who filled the original open arches with huge windows. The paintings are mythological scenes by Niccolò dell'Abbate after designs by Primaticcio.

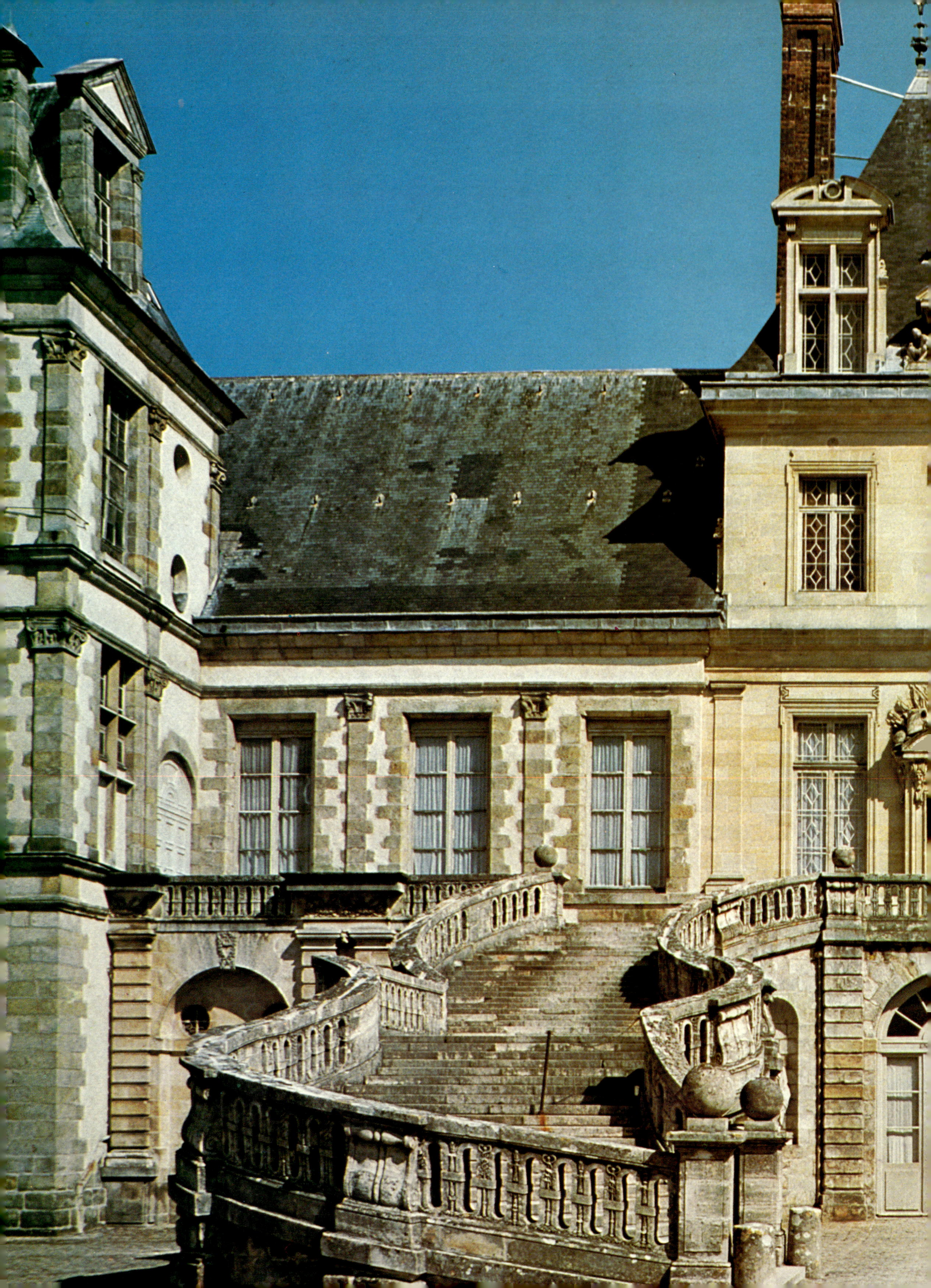

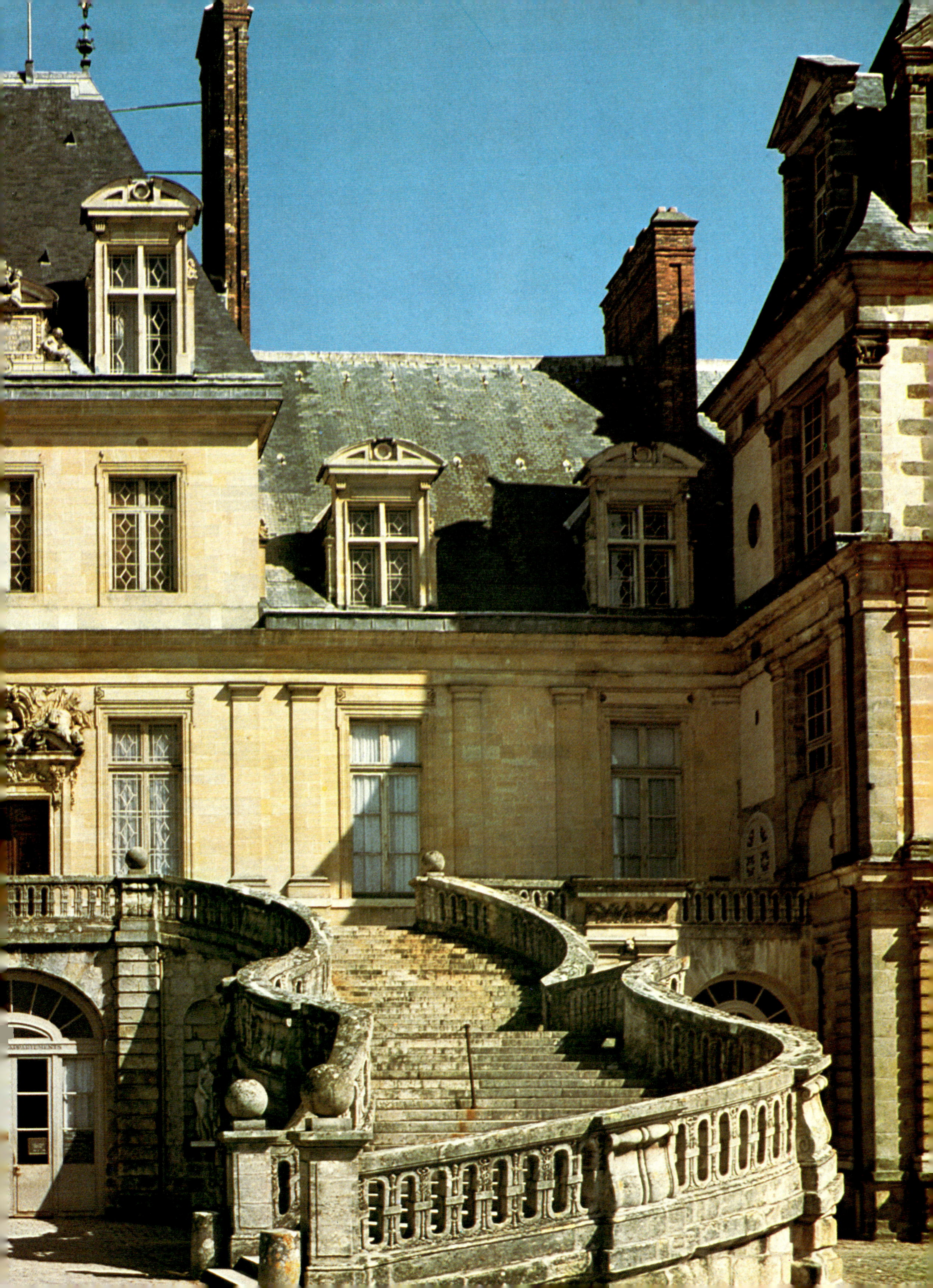

Preceding page, the dramatic double horseshoe staircase, leading from the Cour du Cheval Blanc to the Gallery of Francis I.

This page, views of the staircase and of the courtyard. Originally built in about 1540 as a place for tournaments, festivities, and ceremonies, the courtyard was substantially altered by Napoleon I. During his restoration of the chateau after the Revolution, Napoleon demolished the buildings on the side of the courtyard opposite the staircase.

Far right, the Pavilion of Arms.

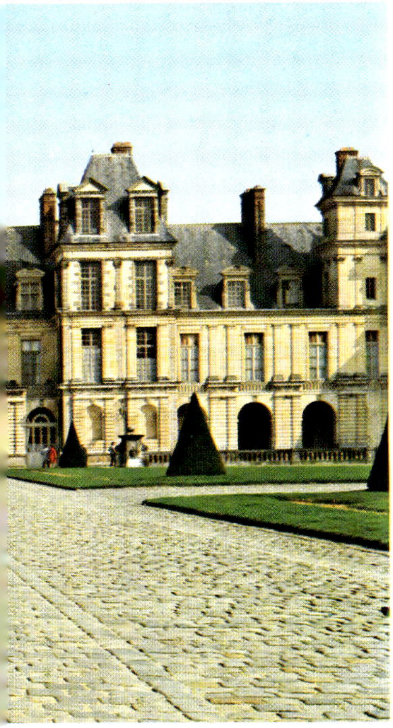
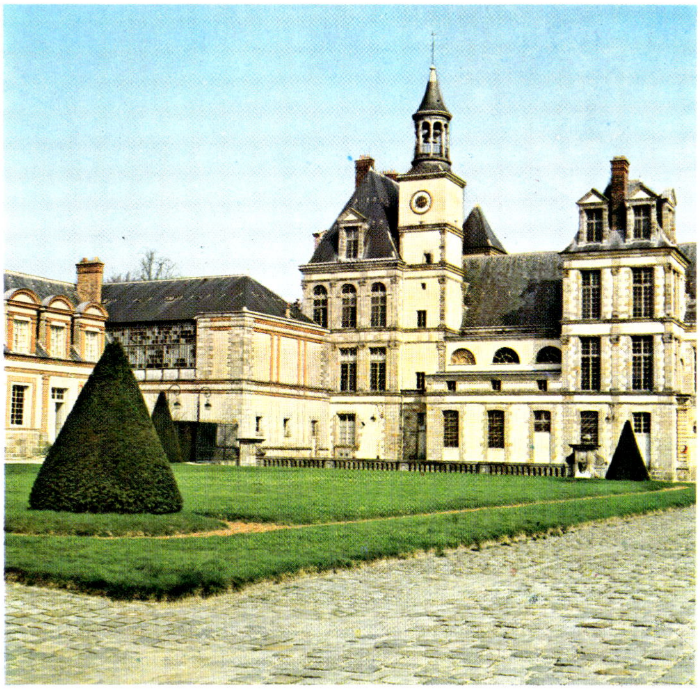
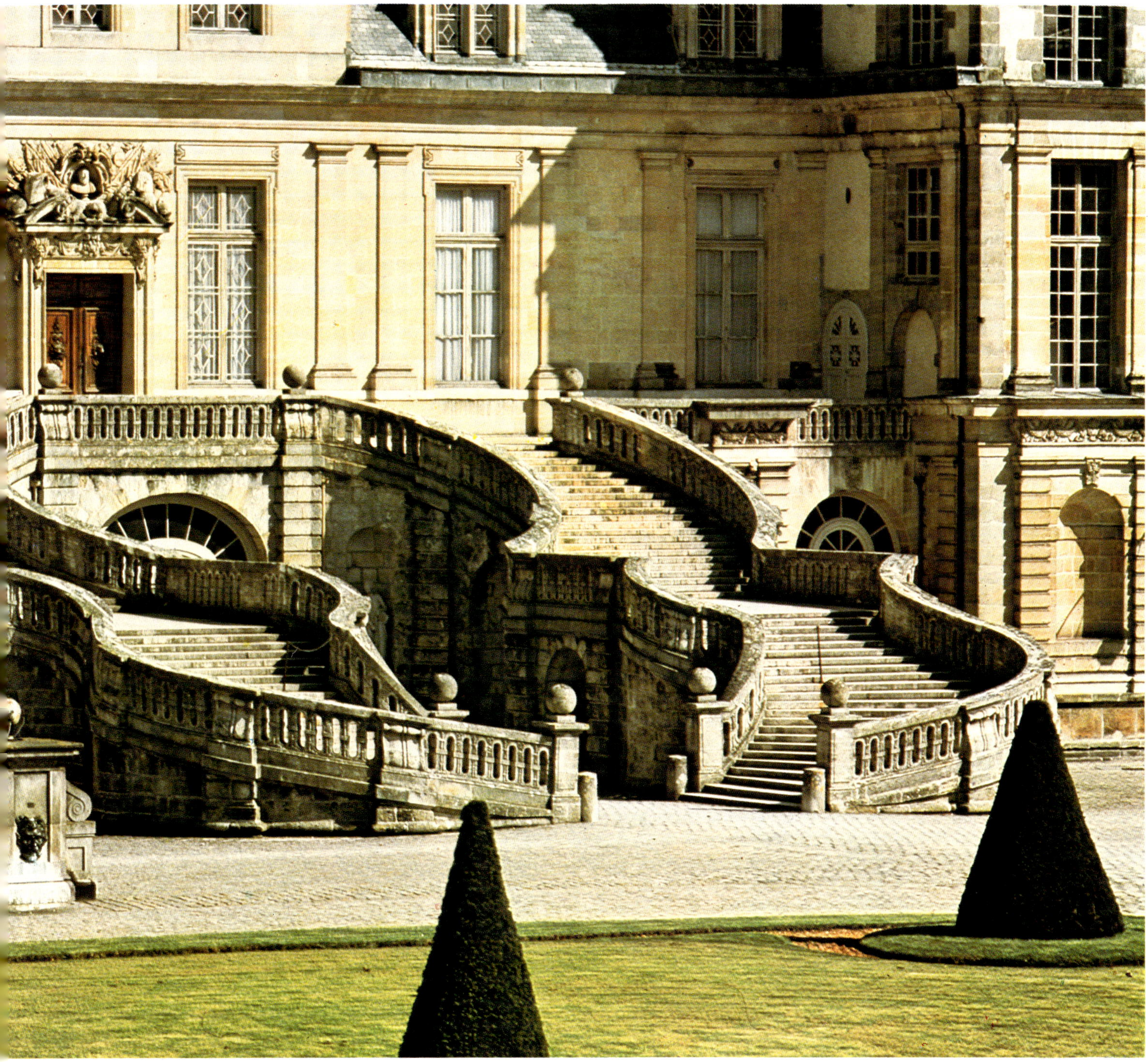

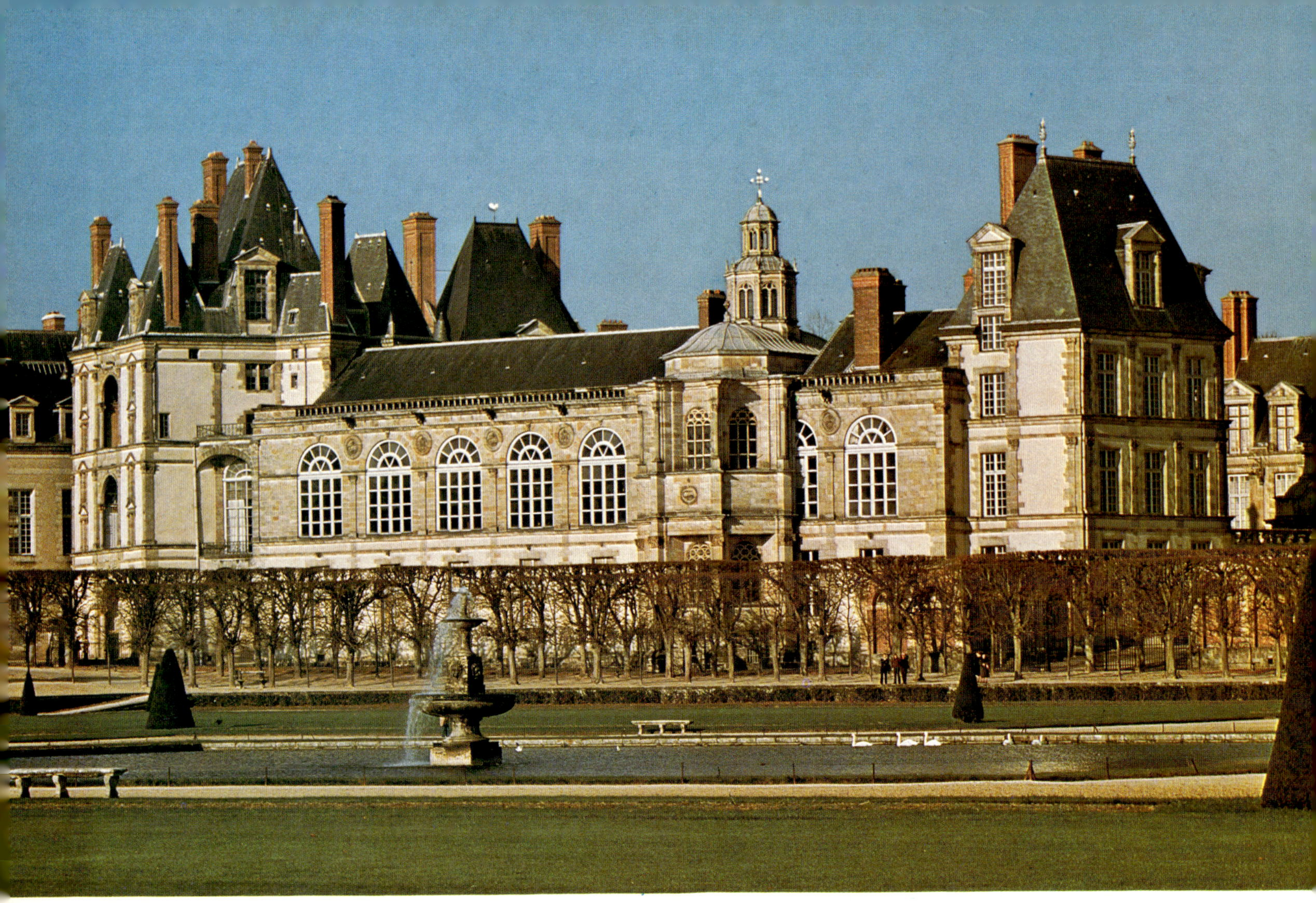

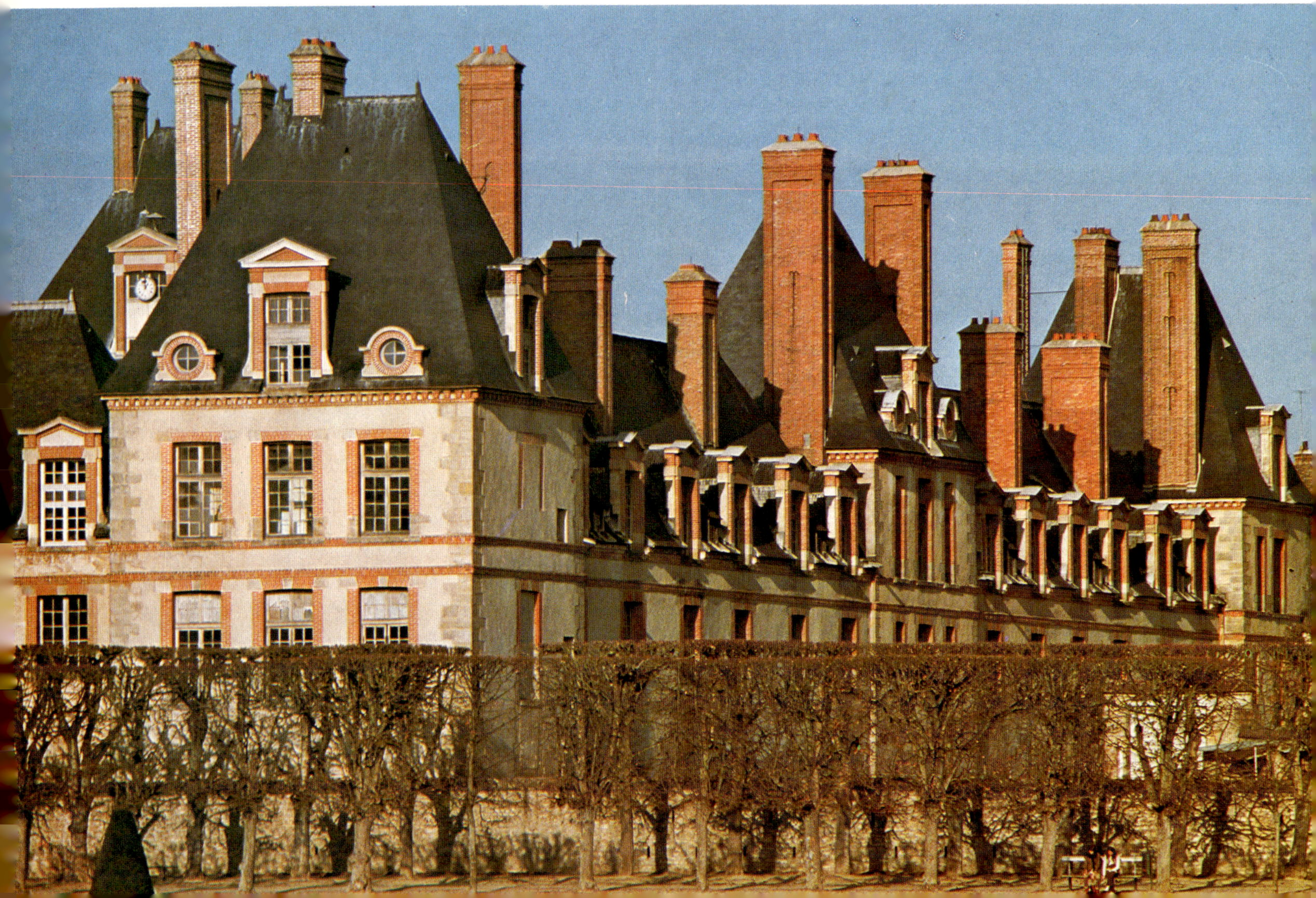

Left, the Porte d'Orée (to the rear left in photo) linked by the arched windows of the ballroom to the Chapel of Francis I, beyond which is the Pavilion of the Dauphin. The variety of brick chimneys provides a picturesque quality to the offices and service buildings on the south side of the Cour Ovale (below left). These wings were created by the architect Rémi Collin for Henry IV. The simple, almost rustic, style is well suited to their function.

Right, the Grand Pavilion, overlooking the Carp Pool. Completed in 1748, it reflects the coming maturity of French Neoclassic architecture.

Above, the Carp Pool and the Cour de la Fontaine. On the near side of the court is the Grand Pavilion, or Wing of the Queen and of Pope Pius VII. On the far side is the Ancienne Comédie, so called because it once contained a theater commissioned during the reign of Louis XV but destroyed in 1856. It is also known by its previous name, L'Aile de la Belle Cheminée, which derives from a huge fireplace once decorated with a life-size equestrian statue of Henry IV. At one time the Carp Pool was embellished with a little temple, but has long since been demolished.

Many of the statues commissioned for Fontainebleau—including Cellini's Nymph of Fontainebleau, originally intended for the Porte d'Orée—have been removed. Others, like the equestrian statue from the Cour du Cheval Blanc or the statue of the Tiber which once stood in the Parterre du Tibre, have been destroyed.

Left, detail of the fountain of Diana (ca. 1603) by Barthélemy Prieur, in the north garden. Originally, four bronze dogs surrounded the statue of the huntress. Right, a seventeenth-century bather along the Great Canal. Far right, a decorative sphinx.

Following page, the Great Canal in the park, constructed in the time of Henry IV.

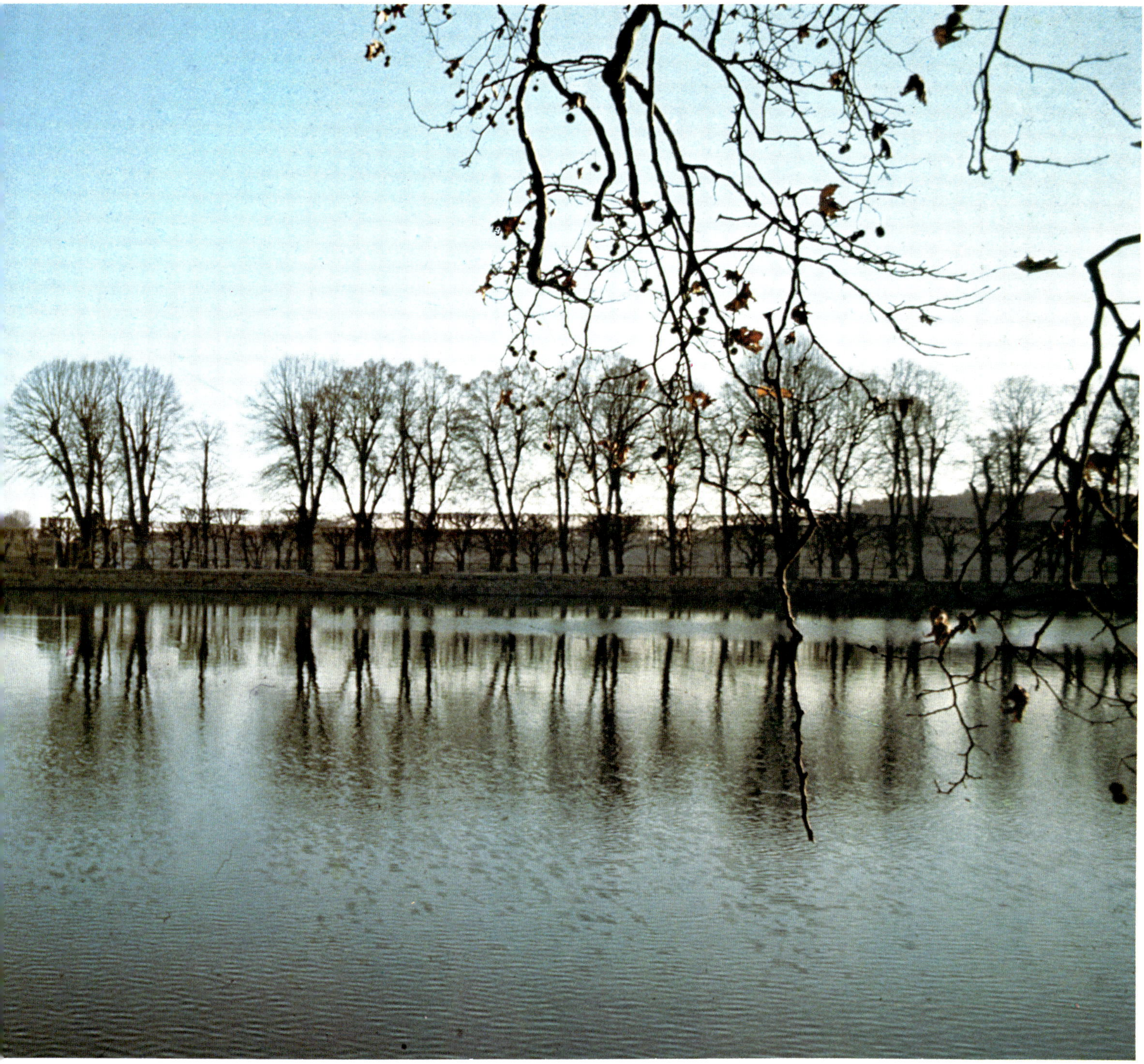
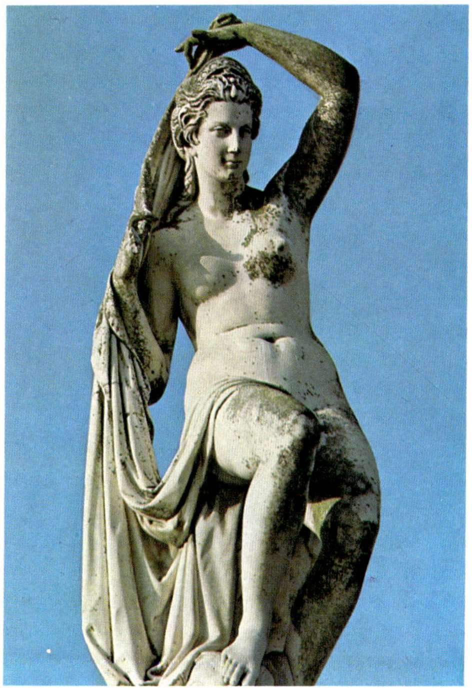
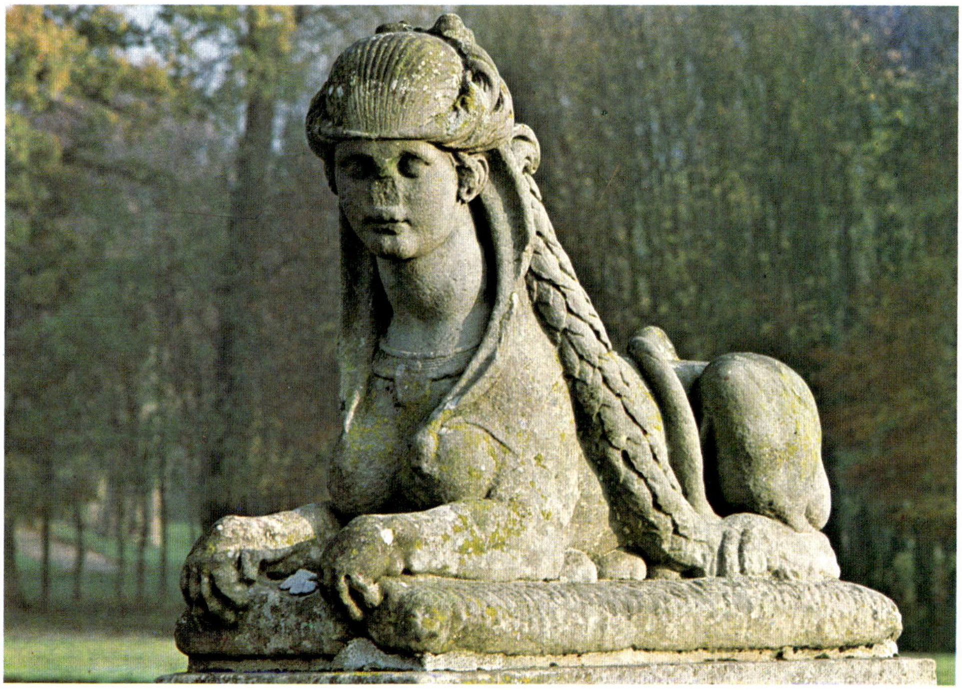

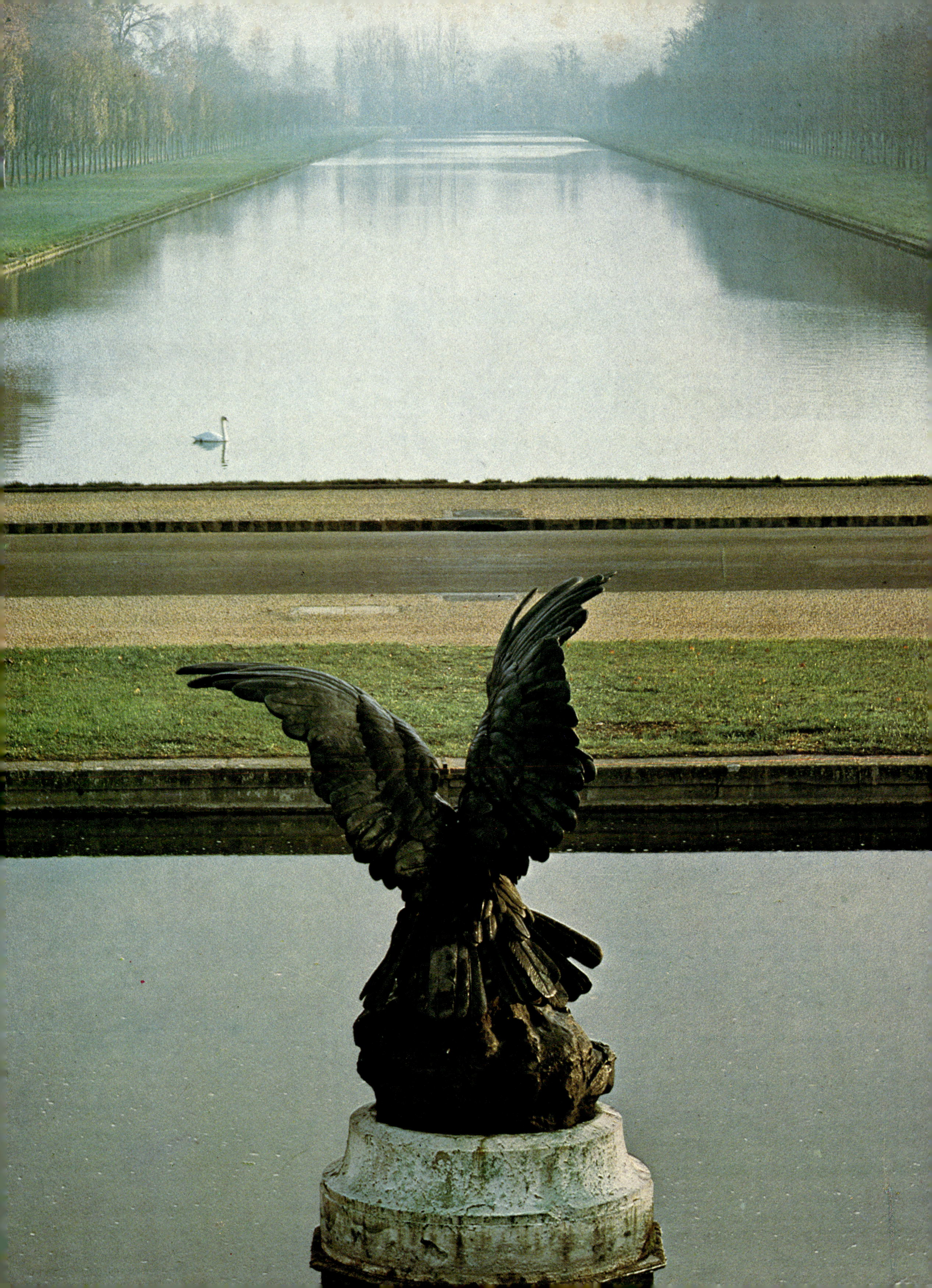

Chateau of Fontainebleau France

The Chateau of Fontainebleau is steeped in history and legend. Napoleon called it "the true residence of kings, a house that belongs to the centuries." Tradition holds that even the fish in the Carp Pool (Étang des Carpes) are hundreds of years old. Unfortunately, this story is more poetic than precise. The royal carp survived the Revolution and prospered under the Empire but fell victim to the Restoration. They finished up on the table of the generals who, in 1815, reinstated the Bourbons on the French throne. The pool was restocked, but a similar fate befell the second dynasty of carp. They were devoured by the high command of the Wehrmacht during World War II.

An eighteenth-century view of the chateau and the parterre, with the canal in the background.

Fontainebleau dates at least from the reign of Louis VII. A document dated 1137 bears the legend *"apud fontem Bleaudi in palatio nostro"* ("in our palace near the spring of Bliaud"). This palace was probably a tower erected by the king's father, Louis VI. Some scholars claim that the spring of Bliaud was also known as *belle eau* ("beautiful water") and that from this spring Fontainebleau received its name.

Louis VII added a chapel to the original tower and dedicated it to the Virgin and to Saint Saturnin. The chapel was consecrated in 1169 by Thomas à Becket, the archbishop of Canterbury, who was at the time a political refugee in France. Only a year after consecrating King Louis' chapel at Fontainebleau, Becket returned to Canterbury, where he was murdered in his cathedral.

Becket's was the first of many famous names to be linked with Fontainebleau. At the start, though, the willfulness of an anonymous peasant had a considerable influence on the chateau. In fact, the site had to be changed when he refused to sell his field, which was within the area chosen by the royal architects. Louis VII must have been a remarkable king, for instead of exercising the usual prerogative, he had the "illegal" chateau torn down. At least that's how legend would have it. According to a contemporary account, he even went so far as to declare: "The peasant has a right to his property before God, and above that of the king himself."

Despite this early setback, the castle grew. In 1359, Louis IX—later canonized Saint Louis—added to the original tower and built an abbey for the monks of the Holy Trinity. In succeeding years, the kings of France hunted frequently in the already famous forest of Fontainebleau and used the castle as a royal hunting lodge and palace. Some, such as Philip IV (Philip the Fair), were born and died there. Isabella of Bavaria added the series of buildings that today form the foundations of the Cour Ovale ("Oval Court"). Isabella hated her son Charles VII so much that she falsely claimed to have committed adultery for the perverse pleasure of calling him a bastard. Charles VII—whose appellation changed from "the Indecisive" to "the Victorious" when Joan of Arc had him crowned at Reims in 1429—understandably disliked his mother's chateau and allowed it to fall into decay.

The flamboyant and sophisticated king Francis I put Fontainebleau back on the map and made it the magnificent forerunner of Versailles. Born the Comte d'Angoulême in 1494, Francis succeeded his cousin and father-in-law Louis XII who had no male heirs. The pope gave Francis the title of "Most Christian King," a title that later became hereditary for French monarchs. Francis celebrated his nomination by making an alliance with the Muslim Turks to the detriment of the Holy Roman Emperor. When defeated at Pavia in northern Italy, in one of the most disastrous battles in French military history, he became famous for his message communicating the news to his mother: "Madame, all is lost except honor...."

The defeat meant two years of imprisonment in Madrid for Francis. But no sooner had he been released—leaving behind, as was customary among warring medieval rulers, two young sons as hostages—than he resumed the struggle against his bitter enemy, the Hapsburg emperor, Charles V. Francis was well aware that the power of a king was demonstrated not only by military strength abroad but also by a splendid court at home. During his military campaigns in Italy, which was then the center of Renaissance civilization, he had learned to appreciate artistic excellence. He was determined to spare no expense in enlarging and decorating his own palaces.

Fontainebleau was not the king's only building venture, but it was the most luxurious, the most famous, and the dearest to his heart. In 1528, after returning from his wretched imprisonment in Spain, the king adopted it as his favorite residence. He commissioned the Parisian master builder Gilles Le Breton to rebuild the existing medieval castle, saving little more than the foundations. In fact, the foundations of Queen Isabella's medieval structures determined the form of Le Breton's irregular Cour Ovale. The buildings around the court still remain at the core of the whole complex.

Despite his reputation as an accomplished Renaissance architect, Le Breton was more a master builder in the medieval tradition that was then still very much alive in France. Francis probably had rather vague notions about the rationale behind the new Italian style, which he interpreted more as a set of rules than as a philosophical movement. Thus, the careful proportions of the Porte d'Orée, the great "golden" entrance portal to his Fontainebleau, show an understanding of the aims of Italian Renaissance architecture. The tall roofs, however, that complete the composition are unequivocally French and medieval in spirit. This portal takes its name from the gilt ornament added by the Italian Francesco Primaticcio in 1535 to

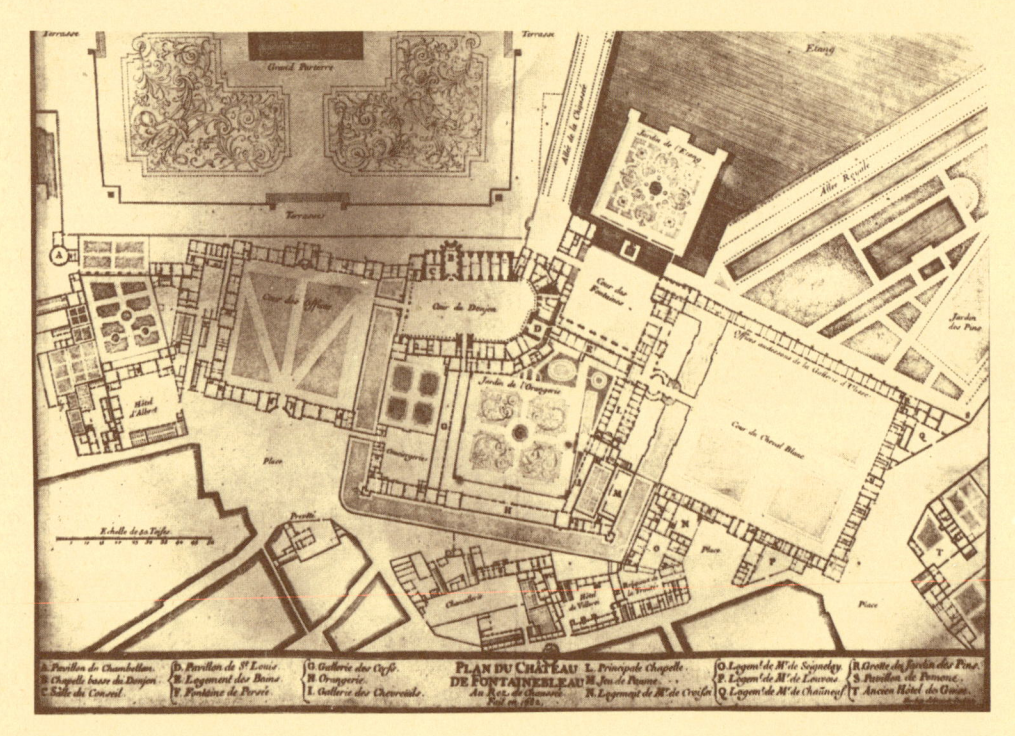

Above, a detailed plan of the chateau, made during the ancien régime. Notice the moat that once surrounded the central complex of buildings, even cutting through the Cour du Cheval Blanc, and the square island, since removed, in the Carp Pool.

Right, a plan for the improvement of the façade of the Cour de la Fontaine. It was never used.

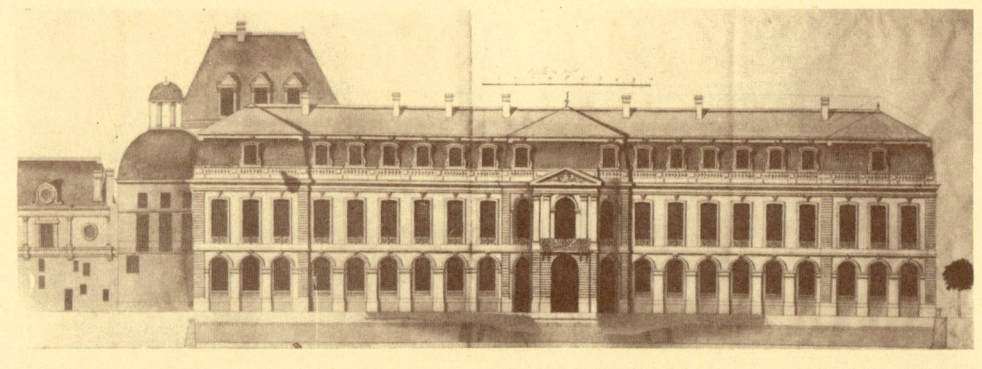

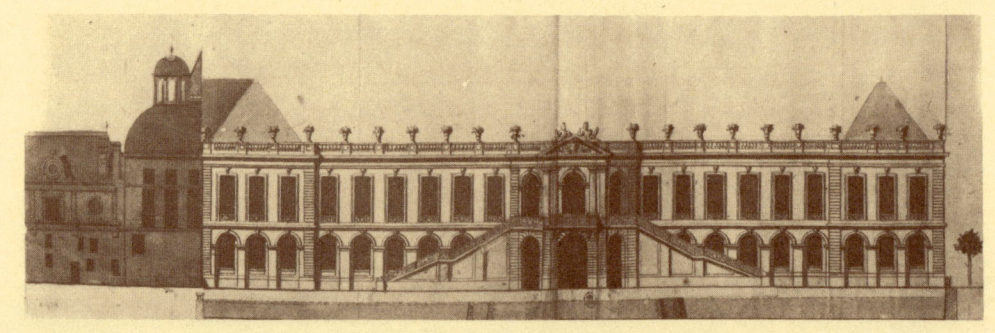

Above, a meeting between Louis XIV and Cardinal Chigi at Fontainebleau in 1664, as depicted in the Gobelin Tapestry by Le Brun.

Left, Louis VII, and far left, Francis I, the king who made Fontainebleau into a Renaissance masterpiece.

1536. Its form, which consists of three porches, one above the other, appears to be based rather freely on the then renowned ducal palace at Urbino. But in several details it displays an awkwardness common to Le Breton's buildings. The sills of certain windows, for example, rest oddly on the pediments of the windows below them.

Le Breton did preserve in this part of the palace the original twelfth-century keep, or tower, which was the residence of the chatelain, or master of the palace. To it he added in 1531 a long gallery, now known as the Gallery of Francis I. It connected the Cour Ovale with the abbey founded by Saint Louis. The monks, however, were soon evicted from their quarters to make room for a huge courtyard which was surrounded by two-story buildings and eventually became the scene of tournaments and pageants. This splendid courtyard, the Cour du Cheval Blanc ("Court of the White Horse"), was so named for a plaster cast of a famous Roman equestrian statue of Marcus Aurelius.

But Le Breton's work did not satisfy Francis. He wanted the exteriors of his palace to achieve the same standard of excellence as the interiors. As early as 1530, Francis I had employed a noted Florentine artist, Giovanni Battista Rosso (called Il Rosso, "the Redhead") to work on the interiors. He was joined two years later by his countryman Francesco Primaticcio, to oversee the decoration and internal arrangement of the new buildings. They were aided in this by others, notably Niccolò dell'Abbate, Francesco Pellegrino, Jean Cousin the Elder, and Geoffroy Dumoûtier. They formed the nucleus of a group of artists that became famous as the First School of Fontainebleau.

The work of these artists is exceptional. Although the Gallery of Francis I is unremarkable on the outside, the interior is a marvelous example of decorative art. With paintings by Primaticcio and woodcarvings by Scibecco da Carpi, it has been compared to the more famous Hall of Mirrors at Versailles.

Above, an eighteenth-century view, looking from the Cour de la Fontaine toward the Wing of Louis XV, which was not completed.

Above, Catherine de Médicis, whose apartments were replaced by the Wing of Louis XV, and her husband, Henry II (right).

At that time, the royal picture collections in France included many Italian masterpieces, including the *Mona Lisa* and works by Raphael and Andrea del Sarto. Experience with the work of the greatest Renaissance artists had created a refined taste for the style. Inevitably, in 1540 the king looked to Italy for an architect to replace Le Breton who would then be demoted to a more technical post.

His choice was Sebastiano Serlio, a Bolognese who had studied with Peruzzi in Rome and then pursued a career in Venice. Serlio is noted for helping to popularize the so-called Palladian window—an arched central window flanked by two smaller flat-topped windows. As it turned out, Serlio did not leave a significant personal stamp on the construction at Fontainebleau—apart from the Cour Ovale, where there is a portico named after him. Nevertheless, his arrival in 1540 coincided with the beginning of drastic Italianization at Fontainebleau. That year, Primaticcio left for Rome to make a series of plaster casts of classical sculptures for the French chateau. On his return, he installed a foundry at Fontainebleau, where the architect Giacomo da Vignola began his career by helping to cast the statues in bronze. Another arrival at the court was Benvenuto Cellini, who fashioned a beautiful gold saltcellar for the king as well as the famous *Nymph of Fontainebleau*. This statue, intended for the Porte d'Orée, ended up instead on the portal of the Château d'Anet—a gift from Francis' son, Henry II, to his mistress Diane de Poitiers.

Also dating from the reign of Francis I are the splendidly decorated Galerie d'Ulysse and the bedchamber of the Duchesse d'Etampes, which was later converted into the upper end of a monumental staircase. In addition, an Italian-style garden was begun, and workshops for weaving tapestries were opened.

The death of Francis I in 1547 did not end the construction. Only the architect was changed. The Frenchman Philibert Delorme, who enjoyed the patronage of Diane de Poitiers, was appointed. Under Delorme's direction, the arches of the ballroom (originally an open loggia) were enclosed with huge windows. Delorme was an exceptionally talented architect, but on Henry II's death in 1559, he, too, was replaced. Primaticcio was chosen to succeed him, not only because of his artistic ability but also because he enjoyed the favor of the Italian Catherine de Médicis, who had become regent for her son Charles IX.

The Heyday of the Chateau

For nearly thirty years there was no more building at Fontainebleau, as the wars of religion took priority over work on the chateau. Finally, Henry of Bourbon emerged victorious from these wars and was crowned King Henry IV of France in 1589. He proceeded to belie his Gascon heritage with its tradition of miserliness by spending two and a half million livres on embellishing and enlarging Fontainebleau. As Henry said of himself: "I do three things that sit ill with avarice: I make war, love, and palaces." History bears out this characterization. Henry was an acknowledged military hero, and his mistresses included Gabrielle d'Estrées and the young Henriette d'Entragues.

The amount of money Henry lavished on Fontainebleau was a trifle compared to what his grandson Louis XIV was to spend at Versailles. Nevertheless, it was the largest sum spent by a French king on a chateau up to that time. Henry IV increased Fontainebleau to its present size. He altered the Cour Ovale and dug the Great Canal in the park. He also designed the Carp Pool and modified the Cour du Cheval Blanc. His French and Flemish artists—including Martin Fréminet, Ambroise Dubois, Antoine Caron, and Toussaint Dubreuil—are now known as the Second School of Fontainebleau.

The palace at the time of Henry IV centered around the Cour Ovale and the large, rectangular Cour du Cheval Blanc. Henry also added a new rectangular court at the end of the east wing and a block of service buildings around the Cour des Princes, one of the short sides of which abutted on the Cour Ovale.

This period was the splendid heyday of Fontainebleau. In 1601 the heir to the throne, the dauphin—later Louis XIII—was born at Fontainebleau. In 1606 he was baptized at the new outer main gate of the chateau. The gateway has since been known as the Porte Dauphine, or the Baptistery, in honor of the event.

Louis XIII and his wife, Anne of Austria, spent long periods at the chateau, using it as their main residence outside Paris. However, under Louis XIV, the Sun King, it was relegated to second rank by the new architectural wonder at Versailles. Fontainebleau was used for only a month or two each autumn during the hunting season. In 1657, during one of these sojourns, the chateau was the scene of a scandalous murder. Christina of Sweden, the Protestant queen who had given up her throne to become a Catholic, was a guest at the palace when she found out that her Italian lover, Giovanni Monaldeschi, had been unfaithful to her. She had him assassinated in the Gallery of Stags—presumably a deliberate allusion to cuckoldry. This immense hall, built during the reign of Henry IV, owes its name to hundreds of pairs of antlers, the trophies of many royal deer hunts, along its walls. Louis XIV, whose own enemies had been known to disappear suddenly without a trace, declared that the business struck him as being "in very bad taste," and it was soon arranged that Queen Christina leave France.

Ninety years later another famous person was to offend the court with his bad taste. The culprit was François Marie Arouet, better known as Voltaire. In Oc-

Far left, Francis II. Left, Henry IV, first of the Bourbon kings. Below, one of the magnificent ceremonies of the time, the entry into Paris of Cardinal Farnese. Fontainebleau was often the scene of such spectacles.

Above, the Great Canal of Fontainebleau, a precursor of the canal at Versailles.

tober 1757, he was received at Fontainebleau along with his protectress of the time, Madame de Châtelet. This lady had a single passion—gambling. She indulged this passion at the table of the queen and soon lost a considerable sum, part of which she had borrowed from Voltaire. Livid with rage, the writer whispered to her: "But don't you realize you're playing with rabble!" Though his judgment was uttered in a whisper, and in English at that, it was no less harsh for being true. Cheating was the norm at the French court. Only a swift flight in a coach saved the philosopher and his lady from the wrath of the queen herself.

The kings who succeeded Henry IV made unfortunate changes in almost every part of the chateau. Louis XIII's architect, Jean Androuet Du Cerceau, placed within the Cour du Cheval Blanc a great, if excessively exuberant, staircase in the form of a double horseshoe, which was widely imitated throughout France. Most of the other changes were artistically less successful. For example, the apartment in the Porte d'Orée commissioned by Louis XIV for his mistress Madame de Maintenon was decidedly a mistake. Then, under Louis XV, the architect Jacques-Ange Gabriel rebuilt the right wing of the Cour du Cheval Blanc and erected a large pavilion in the Cour de la Fontaine. Worst of all, following orders from the king, Gabriel destroyed the Baths of Francis I and the Galerie d'Ulysse, and he altered the bedchamber of the Duchesse d'Etampes to make way for the top landing of a great ceremonial stairway.

During the reign of Louis XVI, a new wing was erected adjacent to the Gallery of Francis I, blocking half its windows. Other alterations to the chateau were made in honor of a visit by his queen, Marie Antoinette, in 1786, but the Revolution was imminent, and because of the widespread confusion of the times, she never actually saw them.

During the Revolution, the chateau, now called a "nest of tyrants," was stripped of its valuable furnishings and decorations, which were then sold. ("The Revolution has destroyed little," observed one commentator, "but it has stolen a lot.") The empty building was used partly as a prison and partly as a school. Therefore in 1804, when Napoleon Bonaparte, newly crowned emperor, decided to use Fontainebleau as his residence, it was necessary to restore and furnish virtually the entire palace. Ironically, the revolutionary general proved to be more conservative than the kings whose home he had inherited. Whenever possible, he respected the decorations of his predecessors. Only the gallery overlooking the Jardin de Diane ("Garden of Diana") was rebuilt in the style of the empire, while the king's bedchamber became the throne room.

His two most important modifications were external. First, the military-minded Napoleon turned the Cour du Cheval Blanc into a parade ground by demolishing its western side, which was then replaced with iron railings. The second change, although attributed to Napoleon, was almost certainly commissioned by his wife Joséphine de Beauharnais.

Empress Joséphine had two passions: her husband and the study of botany. There was no connection between the two, though when she died, the Bourbon police published an obituary that read:

The death of Mme. de Beauharnais has caused general mourning. Desperately unhappy during her husband's reign, she sought refuge from his brutality and neglect in the study of botany.

She used her first passion to satisfy the second. From 1809 to 1812, the western part of the garden of Fontainebleau, which contained the ancient spring of

Above, the Carp Pool, with the Cour de la Fontaine in the background.

Left, Christina of Sweden, who had her unfaithful lover murdered at Fontainebleau.

Below left, Madame de Montespan and below right, Comtesse Du Barry, two of the royal favorites whose stories are linked to the chateau.

"beautiful water," was transformed by the architect Heurtaut into a romantic English garden.

Fontainebleau is justly famous for the range of styles of its gardens, which records more than three centuries of fashions in landscaping. There is Napoleon and Joséphine's Jardin Anglais; the Carp Pool of Henry IV (later embellished by Napoleon with a pretty Neoclassic temple on an island); a fine Italian garden (the parterre laid out for Henry IV); and a large park in the French style, designed by Louis XIV's great landscape gardener André Le Nôtre. There is also the elegant Jardin de Diane, named for its statue of the goddess.

A Decline in Political Prominence

Napoleon did much more than restore the appearance of Fontainebleau. Under him the palace was the scene of several historic political confrontations. There, in 1804, Napoleon welcomed Pope Pius VII, who had come to crown him. And there, eight years later, Napoleon imprisoned the pope after His Holiness had not taken kindly to the suggestion that he become a sort of private chaplain to the Master of Europe. Finally, after more than a year of incarceration, the pope acceded to the emperor. On January 25, 1813, he agreed to a concordat, by which he relinquished his temporal powers—but for a very short time, as it turned out.

It was at Fontainebleau, too, that Napoleon abdicated in 1814 from the thrones of France and Italy. (The little round mahogany table at which he wrote can still be seen in the former library of Louis XVI, now known as the Abdication Chamber.) The Russian steppes had swallowed the Grand Armée; the allied armies were converging on Paris. Napoleon's marshals, his relatives, and his friends were abandoning him. Even his attempt to commit suicide had failed. Banished to Elba, he bade an emotional farewell to his faithful Old Guard on April 20, 1814, in the Cour du Cheval Blanc. Since that day, the courtyard has been known as the Cour des Adieux.

After the Restoration, Louis XVIII and Louis Philippe initiated some mediocre restorations that are still partially evident. But with the departure of Napoleon, Fontainebleau's six hundred and fifty years of political prominence were ended. The glorious old palace still stands, however, a magnificent expression of France's artistic, cultural, and political heritage. It looks today much as it did on that windy April day in 1814 which—save for Waterloo—marked the conclusion of its last epic adventure that had spilled the blood of Europe and had set that continent moving down a path it has followed ever since.

Above, Pope Pius VII and (center) Napoleon Bonaparte. A dramatic confrontation between them at Fontainebleau resulted in Napoleon taking the pope prisoner.

Below, an eighteenth-century view of the Cour Ovale.

The Escorial

Spain

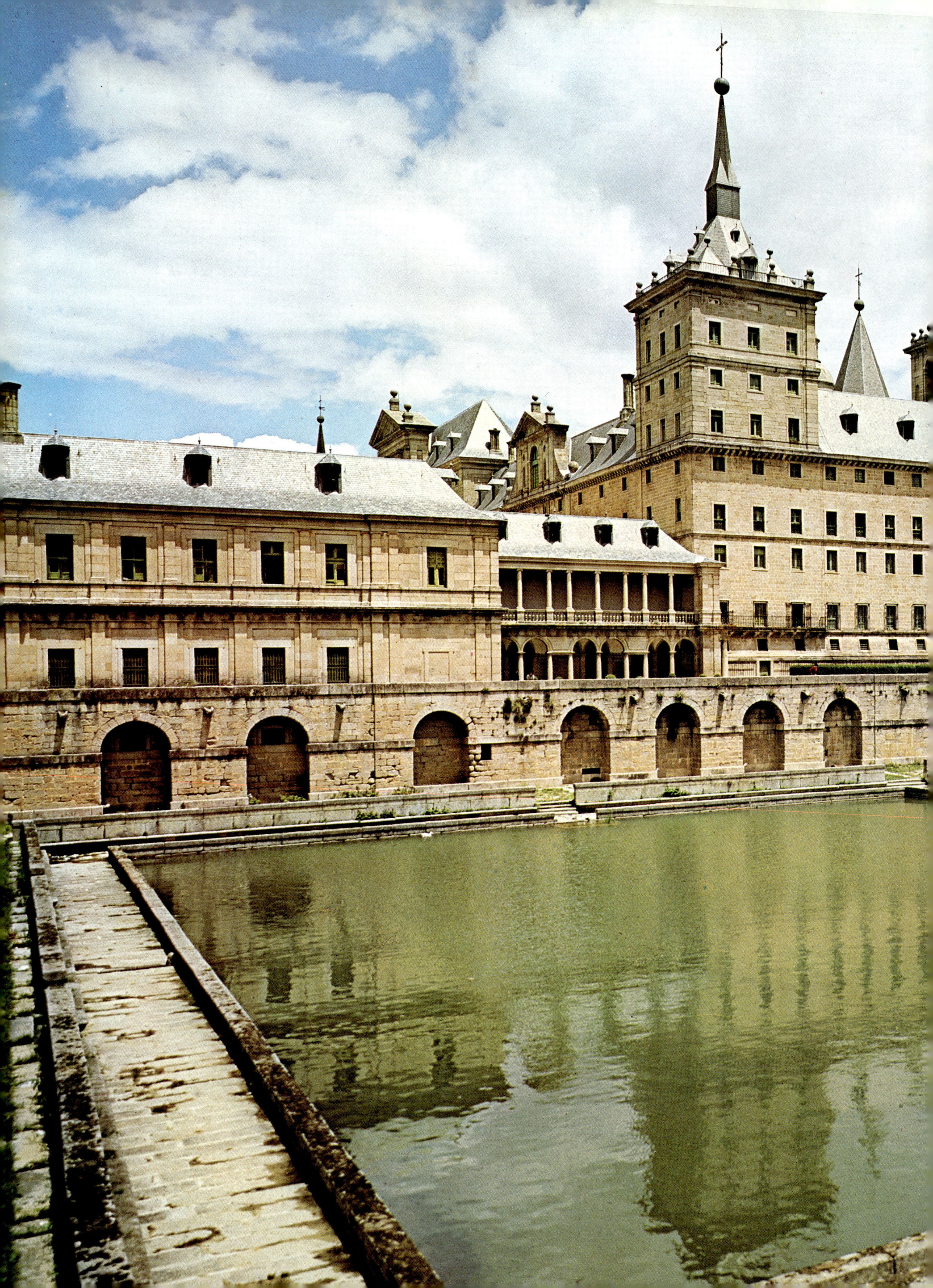

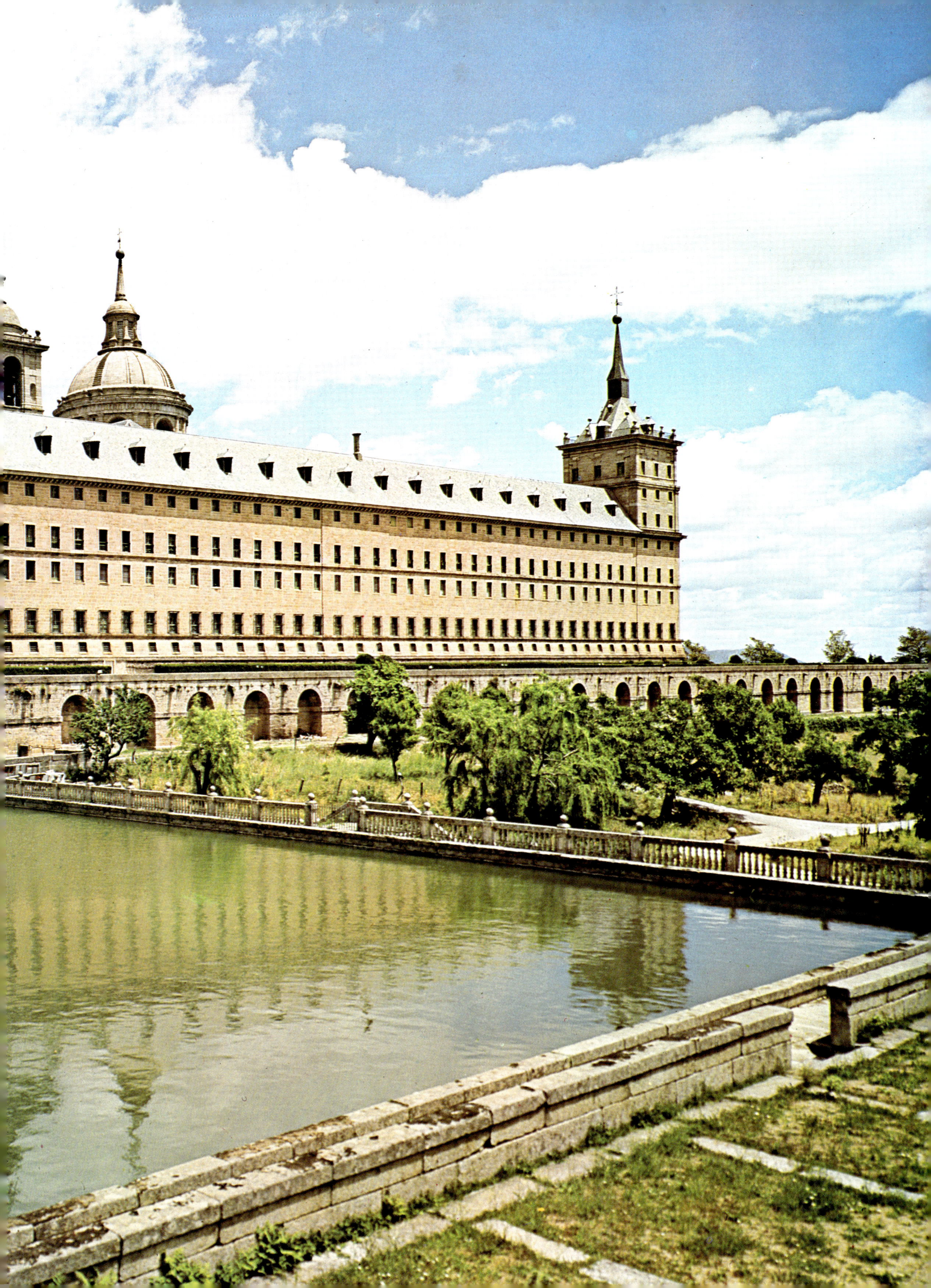

Preceding page, reflected in a reservoir, the southern façade of the Escorial, which overlooks the slopes of the Sierra de Guadarrama. To the left is the Convalescents' Gallery.

Above and left, the main façade of the monastery, facing west, attributed to Juan de Herrera, who began working on it in about 1576. The façade marks the introduction of the Baroque in Spanish architecture.

Far right, the two niches above the main entrance, containing a statue of Saint Lawrence and the arms of Philip II surmounted by the royal crown.

Right, the symmetrical northern façade. The four square towers at the corners of the palace (seen also above right) are reminiscent of an alcazar, or Moorish fortress.

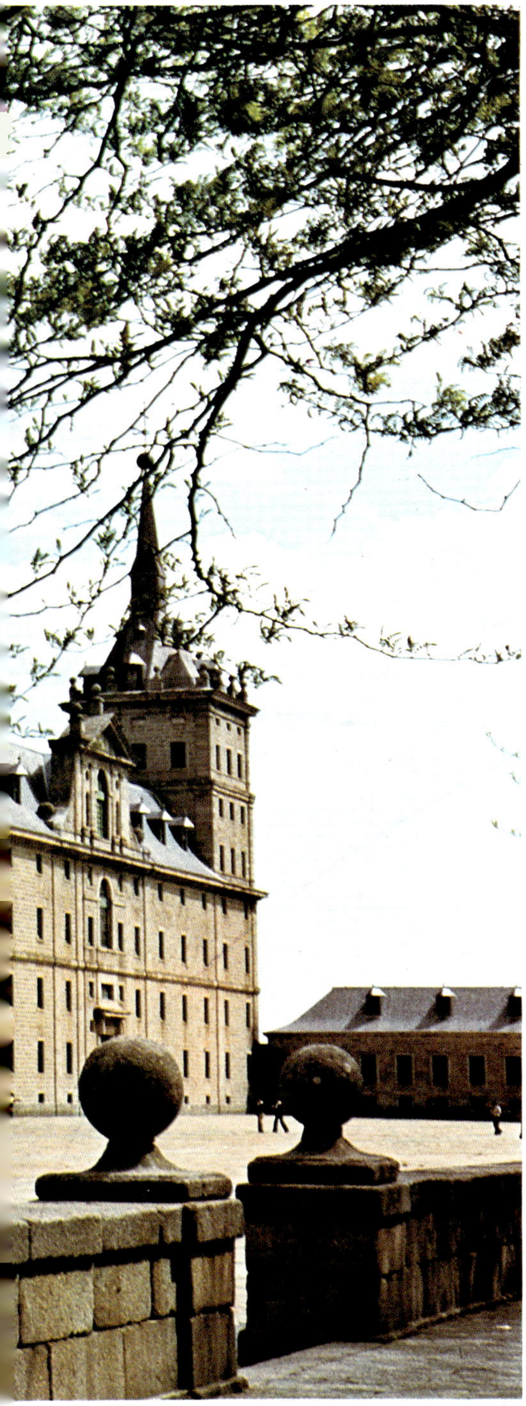
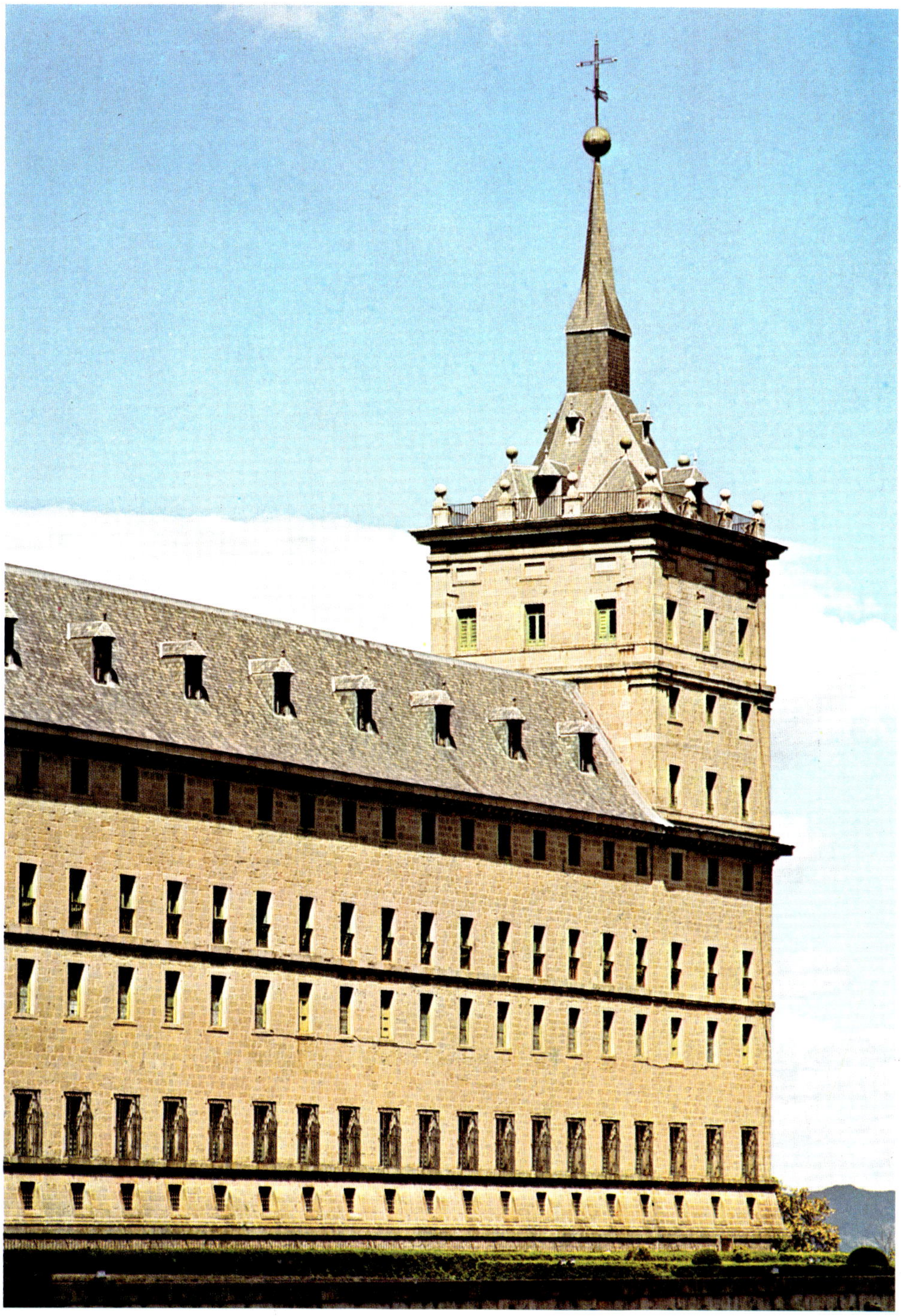
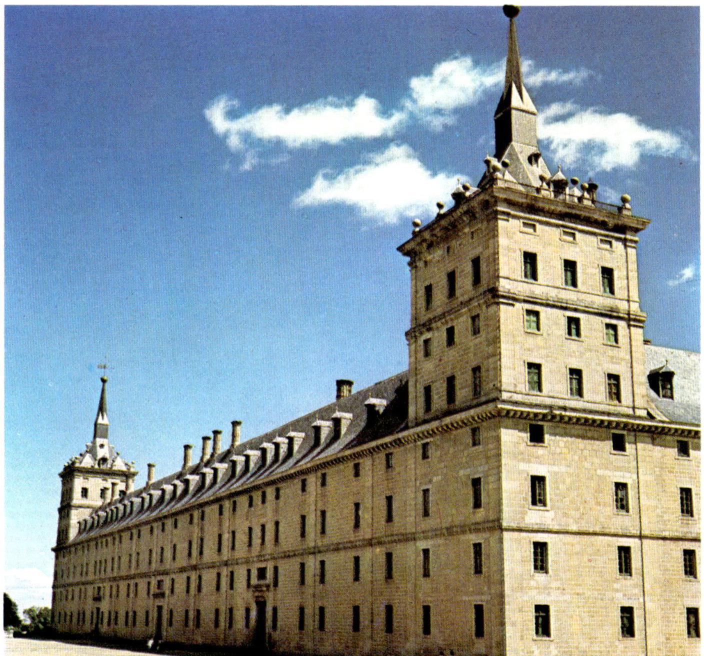
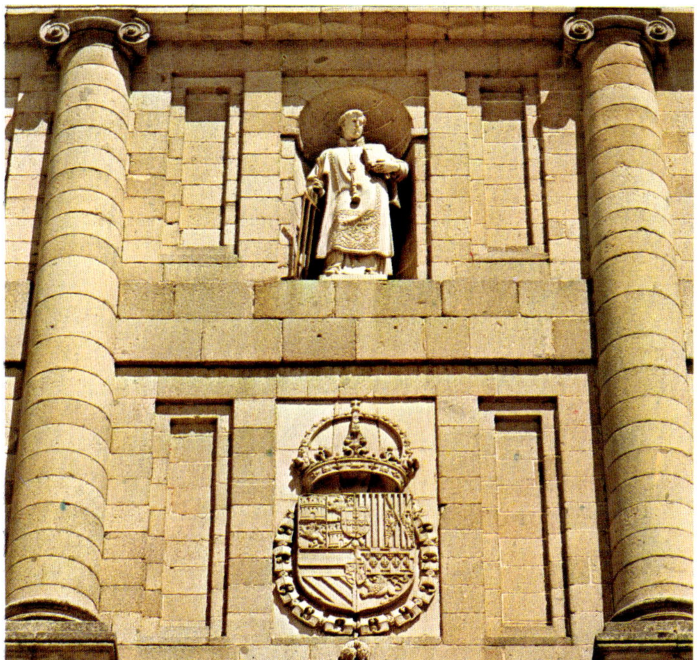

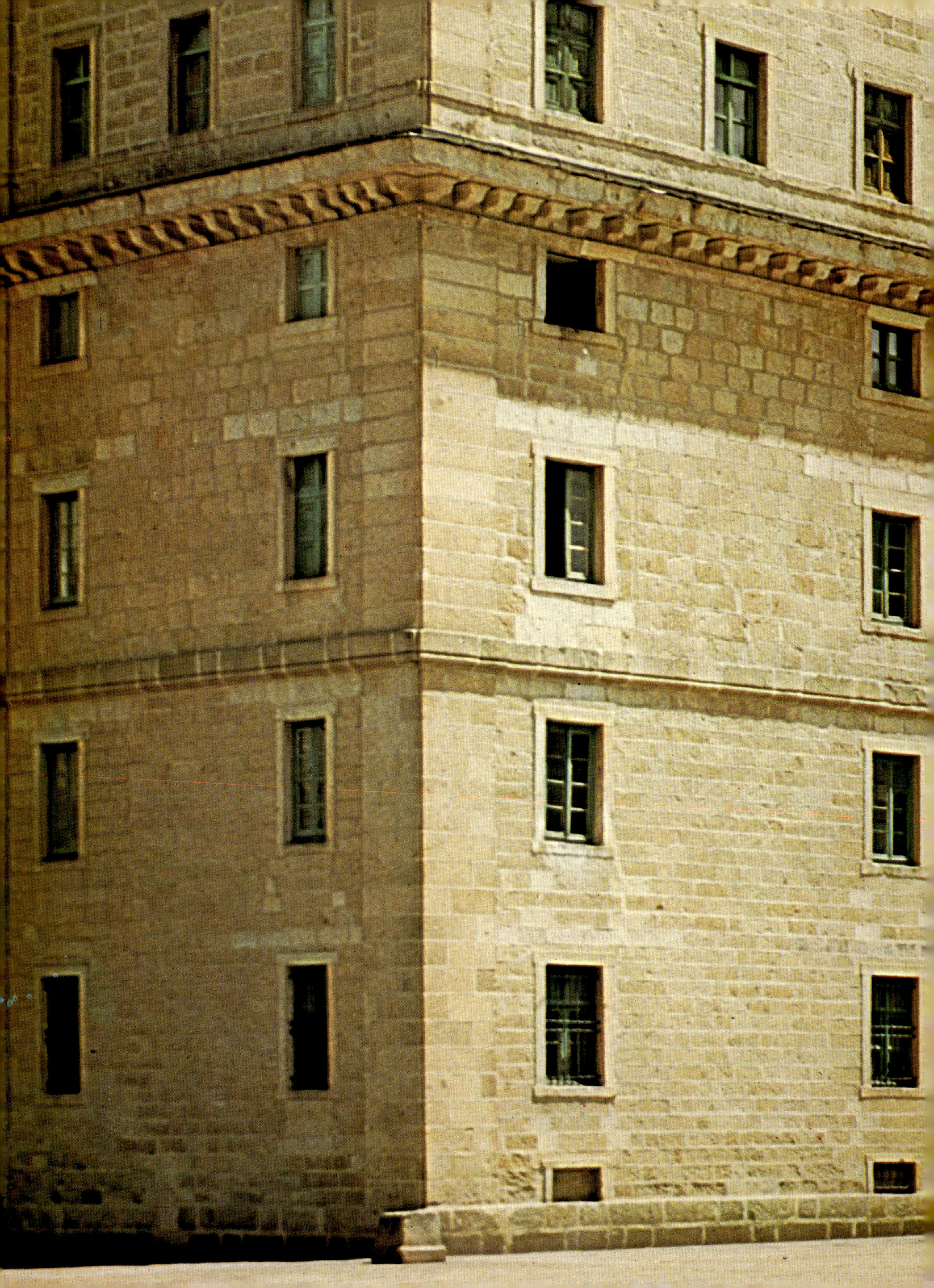

Facing page, one of the four corners of the Escorial. The mighty square corner towers reflect the austere, rigidly geometric concept on which the design is based.

Above, the Renaissance dome and one of the bell towers of the church seen above the dormered southern façade.

Below left, the statues of David and Solomon in the Patio de los Reyes ("Court of the Kings"). The work of a sculptor from Toledo, Juan Bautista Monegro, they are made of granite except for their marble heads and hands. The scepters, crowns, and insignia, in fire-gilt bronze, are the work of Sebastian Fernandez.

Below right, the southwest tower, which looms above the upper level of the Convalescents' Gallery. The gallery is called the "smile of the Escorial" because it has the effect of enlivening the otherwise somber façade.

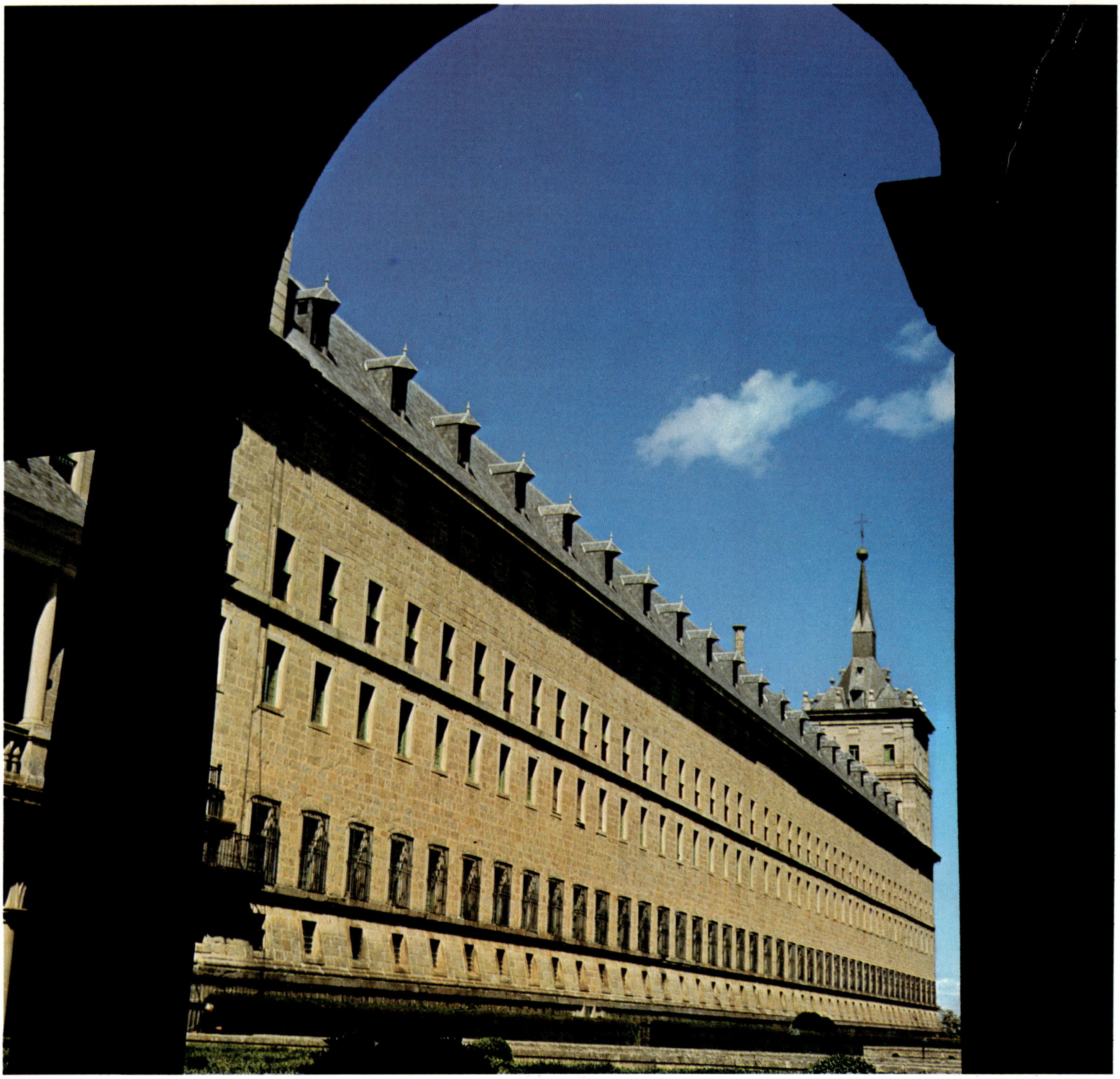

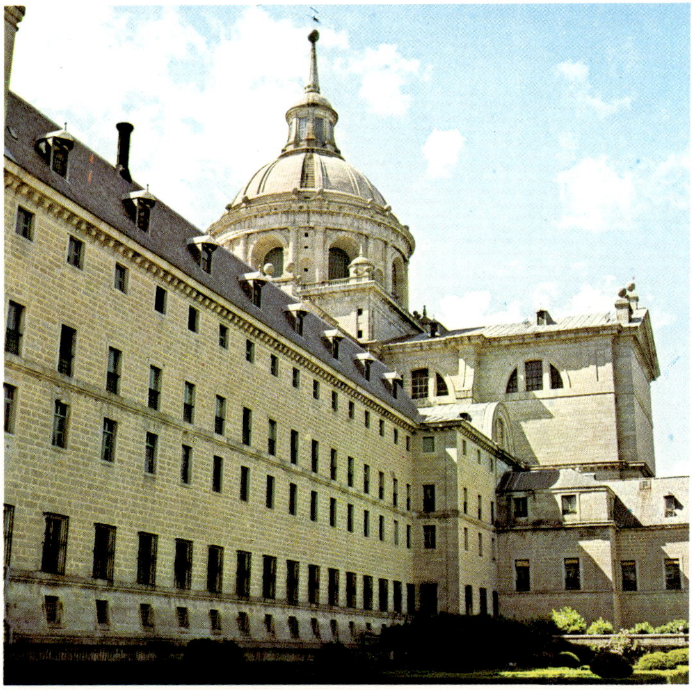

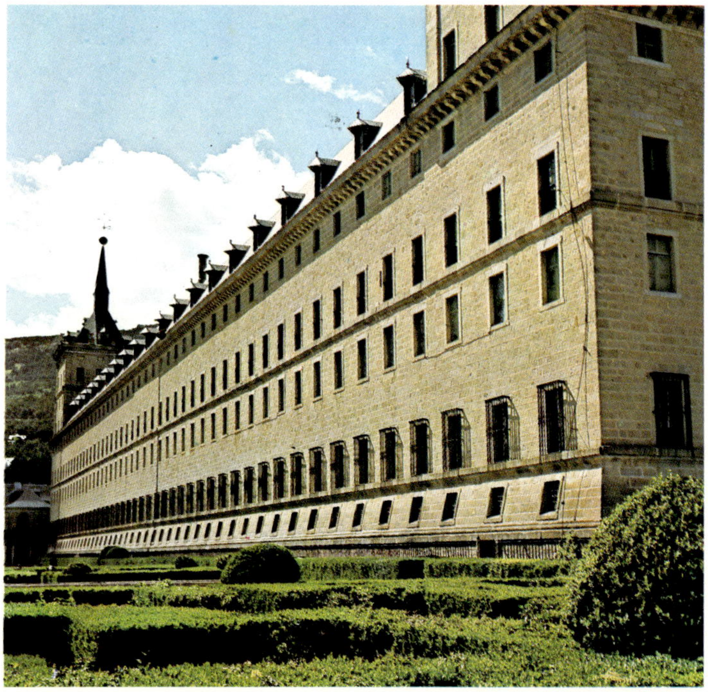

Facing page, above and below right, the southern arcade of the palace, characterized by a strict geometric restraint. Below left, the apse of the basilica, which protrudes through the eastern façade of the Escorial. On this one side at least, the dignified serenity of the exterior is relieved both by the fragmented blocks of the royal apartments surrounding it and by the relative richness of the dome. The dome, normally obscured by surrounding buildings, can only be seen properly from this point.

Above, the lower arcaded loggia of the Convalescents' Gallery. Its upper loggia (right) overlooks the gardens and the surrounding countryside.

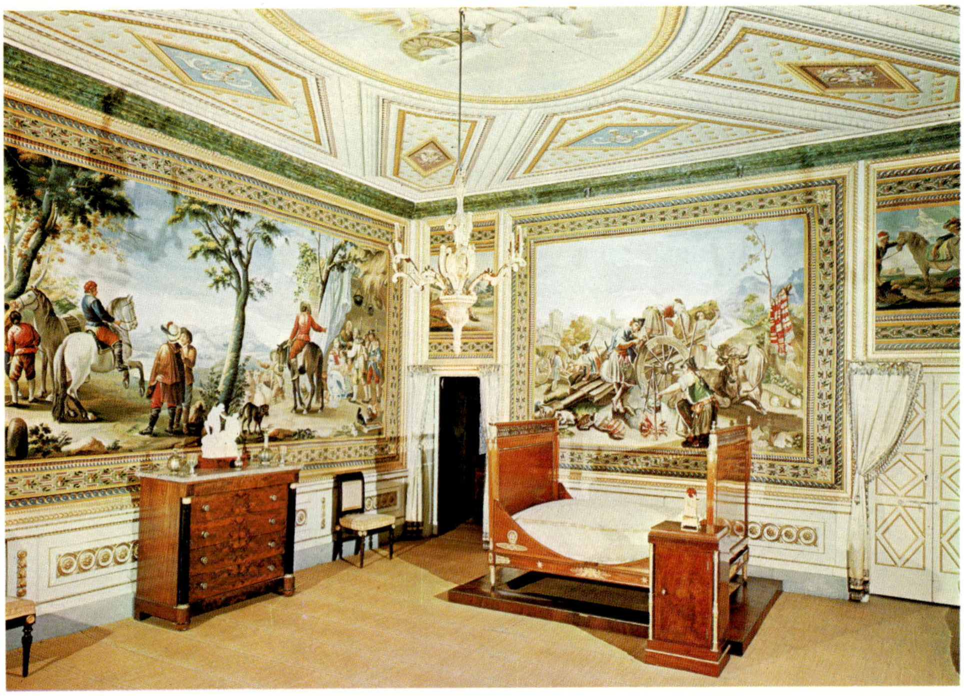

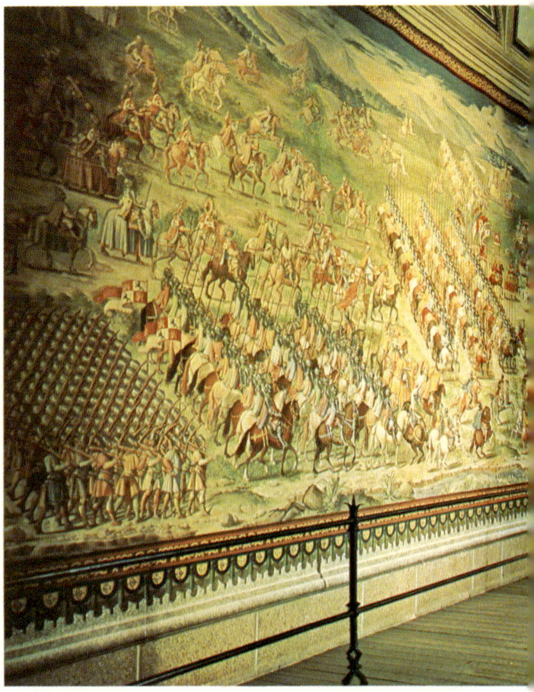

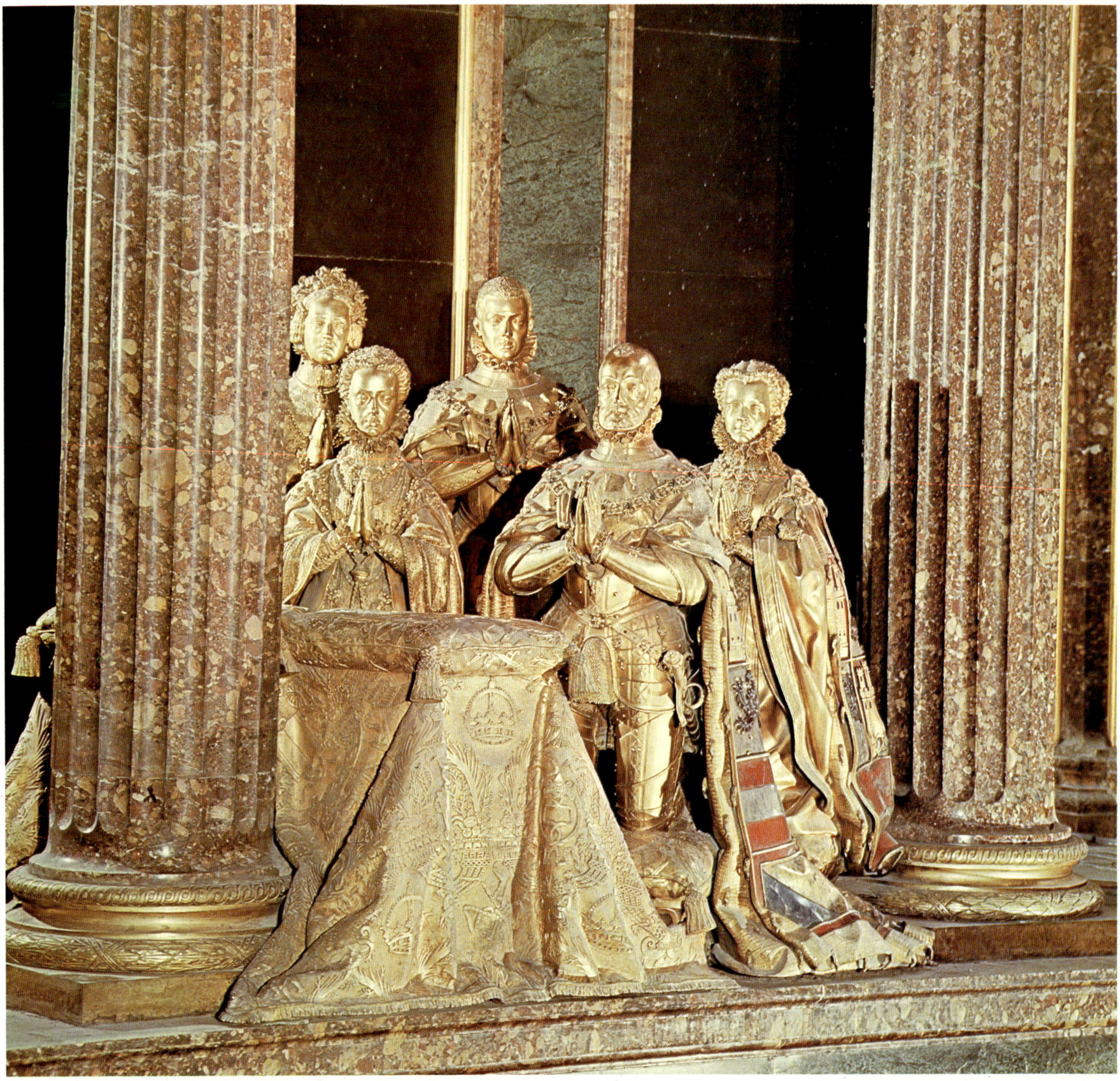

The interior of the Escorial is austere, as befits a building planned as a monastery. But it also contains rooms of singular beauty. Above center, the great Gallery of the Battles. Above right, the Rubens Room; Rubens made the cartoons for the tapestries on the walls. Below, the hall containing Charles V's campaign stool, which was used as a throne by his son Philip II. Above left, the bedchamber of King Charles IV of Spain.

Below right, the richly evocative Pantheon de los Reyes. Here, one above the other, lie the marble sarcophagi containing the remains of the Spanish sovereigns and their queens. Above the Pantheon in the church proper are two remarkable groups of sculptures, one portraying Philip II and his family (left), the other representing Charles V and his family.

Following page, view of the Escorial and the surrounding country of the Sierra de Guadarrama near Madrid.

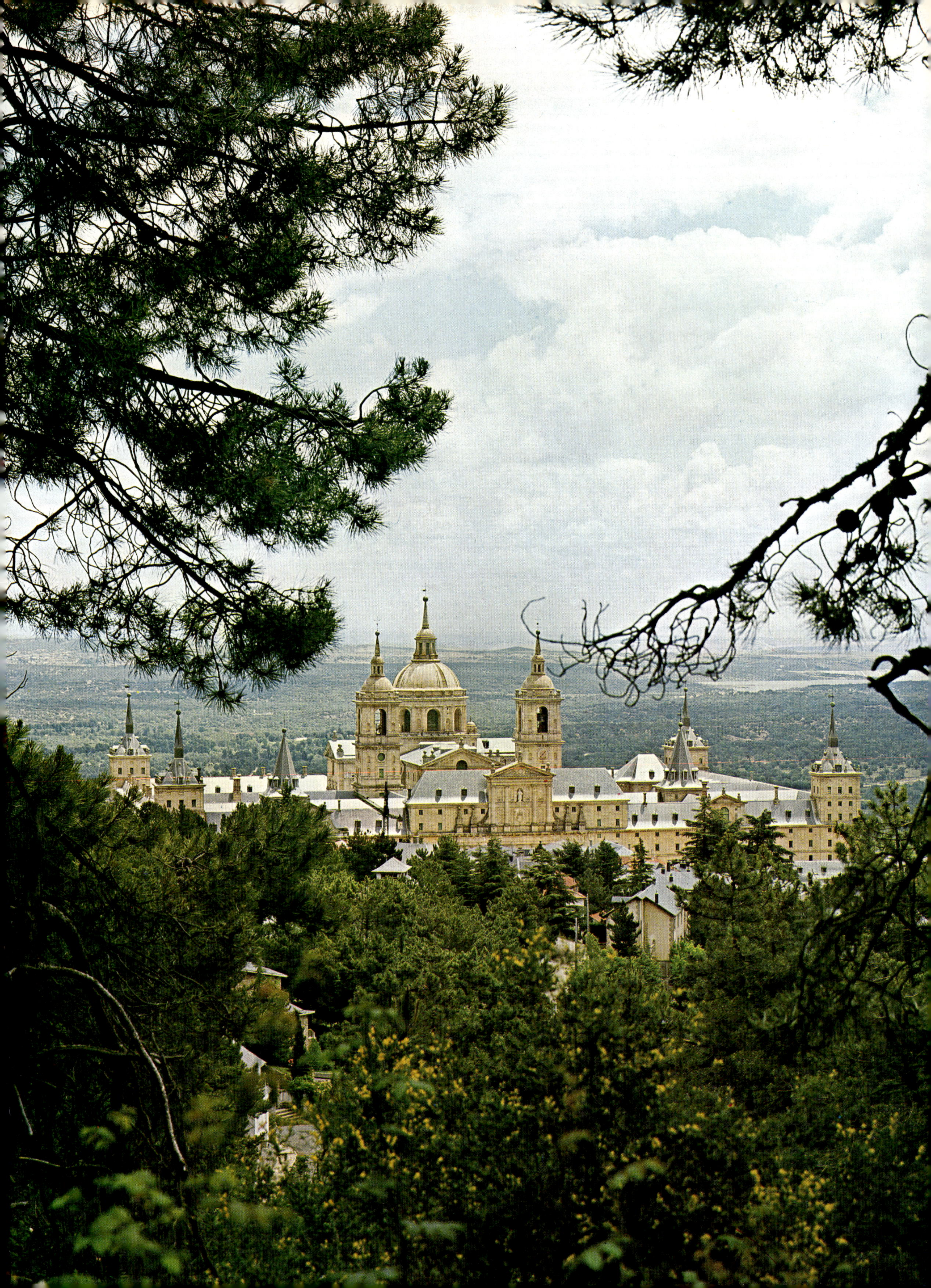

The Escorial Spain

On Saint Lawrence's Day, August 2, 1557, the troops of King Philip II of Spain achieved a long-awaited victory. They defeated the French forces at St.-Quentin in Picardy. Hardly a year later, Philip's father, the emperor Charles V who had abdicated in his son's favor, died leaving a modest request: that his son build him a burial place. However, Philip conceived a grander idea—to construct a monument to honor both his father and Saint Lawrence, and also the vast Spanish empire itself.

Planning began immediately. On April 23, 1563, Philip laid the foundation stone of the Escorial. This somber complex was to serve as a church, a royal palace, a monastery to which he could retreat (Philip's contemporaries called him "the throned monk"), and a mausoleum for the kings of Spain. Philip chose a site in the harsh country of the Sierra de Guadarrama, near Madrid. Here, among mountains as austere as the character of the king himself, among forests abounding in streams and game, he built the Escorial, one of the most formidable of all Spanish buildings.

It has been said that the Escorial was an attempt to "baptize the Renaissance." The style of the Escorial echoes the classical spirit of the time, epitomized by the work of the Italian architects Bramante and Vignola. The Escorial also incorporates the influence of the medieval religious beliefs that prospered in Spain until the end of the eighteenth century.

Juan Bautista de Toledo, a relatively unknown architect, was appointed director of works. On his death in 1567, he was succeeded by Juan de Herrera, an expert in stonework from the valley of Trasmiera, where this art had been cultivated for generations. Carpenters, goldsmiths and metalworkers, miniaturists, sculptors, painters, masons, and organ builders were called in from all over Europe. In time, the site virtually became a school of the fine arts.

Though many had a hand in the construction of the Escorial, the genius governing the project was that of the king himself. Philip followed with close interest every detail of the design and construction, always inspecting, correcting, and improving his architects' plans. By contemporary standards, the work was done quickly. The Escorial was completed in 1584, twenty-one years after the work was begun. The church was consecrated on the eve of Saint Lawrence's Day in 1586.

The Escorial is characterized by its absolute unity, by the geometric symmetry of its construction, and by the austerity of its design and appearance. Its overall conception reflects the severity of Philip's own character. Few decorative elements soften the stern aspect of the building. The general layout and the details are rooted in an exact, almost obsessive, mathematical logic. In fact, the only ornamentation lies in the details of the restrained moldings, in the play of the proportions, and in the careful choice of the materials that are worked with the utmost mastery.

The ground plan is an enormous gridiron covering 500,000 square feet. Philip himself is thought to have been responsible for the gridiron plan, which supposedly symbolizes the grill on which Saint Lawrence was roasted alive. But the plan

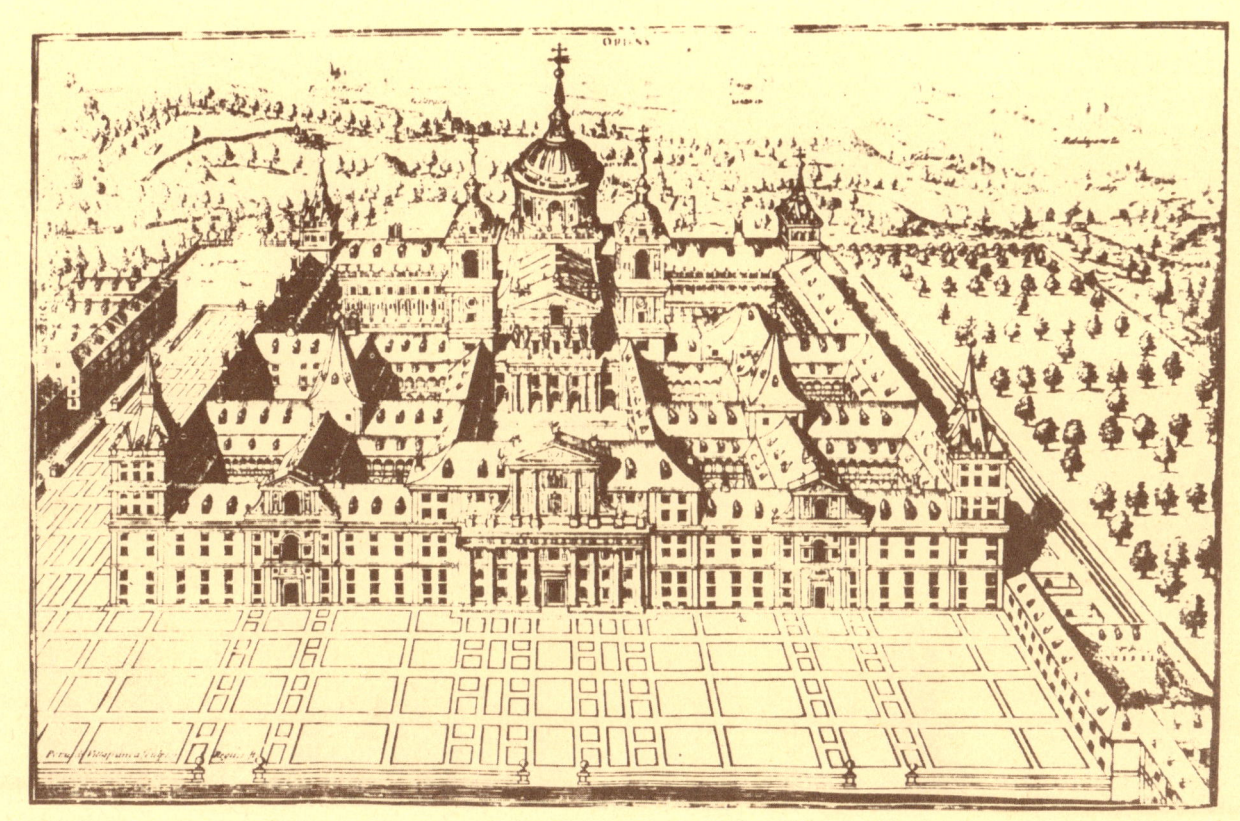

Above, a portrait of Philip II by Titian.

Left, a view of the Escorial in a sixteenth-century print. The gridiron pattern divides it into sections facing spacious courtyards.

54 · Individual Creations

Right, longitudinal and cross sections through the church.

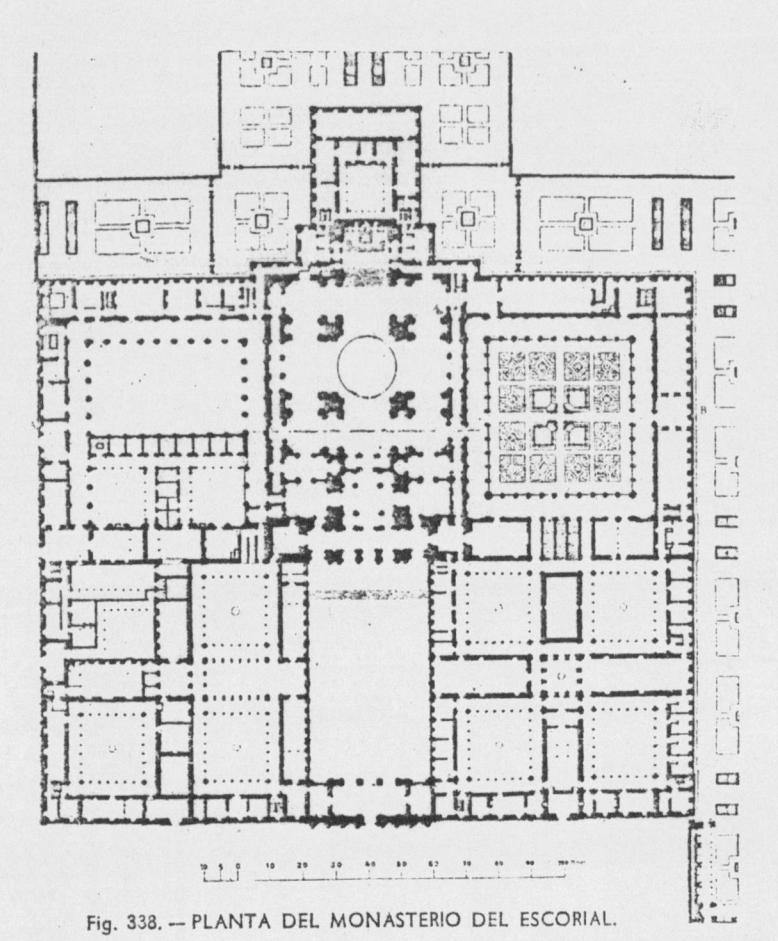

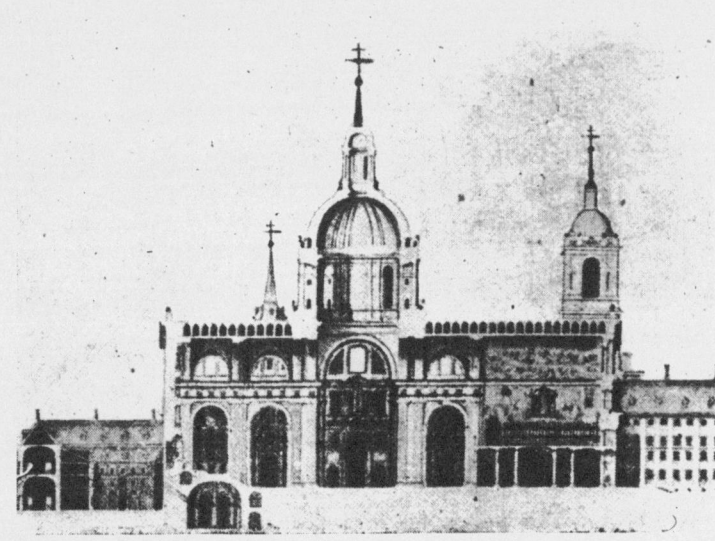

Fig. 338. — PLANTA DEL MONASTERIO DEL ESCORIAL.

Above, floor plan showing how the Escorial is laid out in the form of a gridiron, the instrument used to martyr Saint Lawrence. In the center is the church, in the form of a Greek cross; to the right is the Patio of the Evangelists; to the left, the royal palace of the Bourbons; bottom center is the Patio de los Reyes. At the bottom left is the school; bottom right is the library and Convalescents' Gallery.

is also practical since it helps differentiate the spaces devoted to the diverse functions of the buildings: the royal palace, the church, the monastery, and the schools. The church, of course, stands at the center of the complex. Its imposing dome, which owes much to the work of Donato Bramante, dominates the linear and symmetrical elements that compose the rest of the building.

The Escorial also reveals certain Arabic and northern European aspects. The massive structure with its four square towers, for example, may be considered the last of the alcazars, the Arab fortresses that often crowned the tops of the sierras. On the other hand, the steep roofs of the towers recall the roofs of Flanders and Burgundy, which were at that time domains of the king of Spain.

The façades, impressive with their relentless rows of identical windows set in smooth walls, vary in interest. The three great doors of the western façade lead to the three principal divisions of the building: the monastery to the south; the school, symmetric to it to the north; and the complex of church and royal palace in the center and rear. An extension of the southern façade is the Convalescents' Gallery, the only external loggia of the Escorial. The gallery, situated near the infirmary and sheltered from the cold mountain winds, was used as a solarium by convalescing monks.

At the heart of the immense palace, the Church of St. Lawrence occupies a position in the Escorial equivalent to that of the king's bedchamber at Versailles. The original design for the church is attributed to the Italian architect and engineer Paciotto da Urbino, whose drawings are thought to have been interpreted and revised by Herrera.

The church itself is in the form of a cross with enormous frescoed barrel vaults. In customary Spanish fashion, the choir is situated not at the end of the church but on a raised platform in the nave. As a result, from the outside the church appears to form a Latin cross, with the nave longer than the apse and transepts. Yet, from the inside it seems to be a Greek cross, with all four arms stretching an equal distance from the dome.

In front of the church, immediately inside the central gate of the Escorial, is a large courtyard called the Patio de los Reyes ("Court of the Kings"). This courtyard is named for the six large statues of Old Testament kings that overlook it from the façade of the church.

The Escorial • 55

Philip II usually showed excellent discrimination in his choice of artists, although his appointment of Luca Cambiaso to fresco the vaults of the church proved unfortunate. He had originally selected the Venetian Paolo Veronese. When Veronese declined the invitation, Philip had to settle for the Ligurian Cambiaso, who had a good reputation as a perspective painter. But the middle-aged Cambiaso's ceaseless amorous entanglements robbed him of time and energy, making it impossible for him to devote sufficient attention to the king's palace.

Ironically, it was the dull and sickly Charles II, last of the Spanish Hapsburgs (he ruled from 1665 to 1700), who eventually discovered a more capable artist to fresco the Escorial. His choice was Luca Giordano of Naples, one of the leading decorative artists of the day. He was nicknamed *Luca Fa Presto* ("Speedy Luke") because of the incredible swiftness with which he carried out his commissions.

If Philip was disappointed with Cambiaso, he was, on one occasion, terrified by his architect Herrera. Extremely skillful in the use of stone, Herrera would sometimes try his expertise to its limits. For example, in the monastery he built a choir that stood over an almost flat granite arch, and on the keystone of the arch he calmly placed an extremely heavy lectern of marble and bronze. The king did not trust the stability of the structure and insisted that the arch be supported by a sturdy column. After that, whenever he passed beneath the arch, Philip was reassured by the presence of the mighty support. But the column was actually nothing but papier-mâché. When construction was fin-

Above, the interior of the church in an eighteenth-century engraving by Alegre. It is Holy Week, and hundreds of candles have been lighted before the main altar.

Right, Pellegrino Tibaldi, one of the first architects to work on the monastery. Center, Juan de Herrera, perhaps the best known of the architects of the Escorial. Far right, a portrait of Father José de Siguenza, poet and historian, whom Philip II considered to be "one of the wonders of the Escorial."

A corridor in the main cloister of the Escorial, depicted in an eighteenth-century engraving. The building still contains the library begun by Philip II, which holds a collection of 4,742 rare manuscripts and over 40,000 printed books.

ished, Herrera had it demolished before the very eyes of his uneasy sovereign.

The king entrusted the Italian sculptors Leone and Pompeo Leoni with the numerous religious and funerary statues. Two groups of their figures, those of the families of Charles V and Philip II, can be seen in the Church of St. Lawrence. Only Mary I of England, Philip's third wife, is not represented.

Over the high altar is a beautiful crucifix by Domenico Guidi, a fine work in gilded bronze dating from the seventeenth century. Directly under the altar is the Pantheon de los Reyes, designed by the architect Giovanni-Battista Crescenzi to serve as a royal mausoleum. Nearly all the kings and queens of Spain since the time of Charles V lie in the great Pantheon, which is built of polished marble accented with gilt bronze. However, the monarchs were not laid to rest in the Pantheon immediately after they died. They were first left for ten years in a sort of anteroom to the place of eternal rest, a vile-smelling place known as *el pudridero*. Though the monarchs of Spain believed themselves to be the most powerful on earth, this resting place reminded them that they were nothing but dust, that the pomp and splendor to which they were born was a gift of divine grace and ultimately transitory, a mere vanity.

The Escorial is, nevertheless, a repository for a vast accumulation of treasures gathered over the centuries by the kings of Spain. The riches include a matchless collection of water colors by Dürer and another of early printed books. There is also a picture gallery representing centuries of European painting; a priceless collection of holy relics; and an immense library of Islamic manuscripts, collected by Philip III, who was pitiless in his persecution of the Moriscos, those Arabs who had converted to Christianity.

Unlike the later embellishments of the Escorial, the rooms of Philip II are plainly and modestly whitewashed, decorated by equally modest blue Talavera tiles. Even the furniture is humble. All the pictures in his rooms, however, are the works of great masters. Enfeebled and withdrawn, Philip II, the true architect of the Escorial, died on September 13, 1598, in these austere surroundings.

As Spain entered the modern age and the medieval notions of royal power gave way to less rigorous attitudes, the Escorial declined in importance. Under the Bourbons, it remained the official royal residence, but the rulers abandoned it as often as possible for the less gloomy palaces of Granja or Aranjuez. The Escorial came back into favor during the reign of Charles III in the late eighteenth century, when the Age of Reason reinstated a taste for classical restraint.

Charles III had been Duke of Parma and king of Naples before becoming king of Spain. He had been in Naples when the city of Pompeii was discovered, an event depicted in the tapestries in his apartments. If this philosopher-king ruled during the Age of Reason, he also ruled during the "age of bureaucracy." In fact, he considered the vast Escorial far too small to accommodate all his functionaries. He, therefore, commissioned his architect Juan de Villanueva to add two annexes to the huge complex: the *casita* of the prince and *casita* of the infanta. The two additions, built two hundred years after the main building, fit in perfectly with the original complex because Villanueva, like most Spanish architects of his time, was sympathetic to many of the ideas of Philip and Herrera.

The Escorial was a model for Spanish architecture for more than a century after it was built. But this austere royal monastery cannot be said to be typical of all Spanish architecture. Standing at the administrative center of Spain and its empire, at the heart of a dominion which stretched from America to Asia, the Escorial is an assertion of the essential European heritage and character of the Spanish people. But above all, it is a personal building, the perfect artistic expression of the soul of Philip II.

Taj Mahal

India

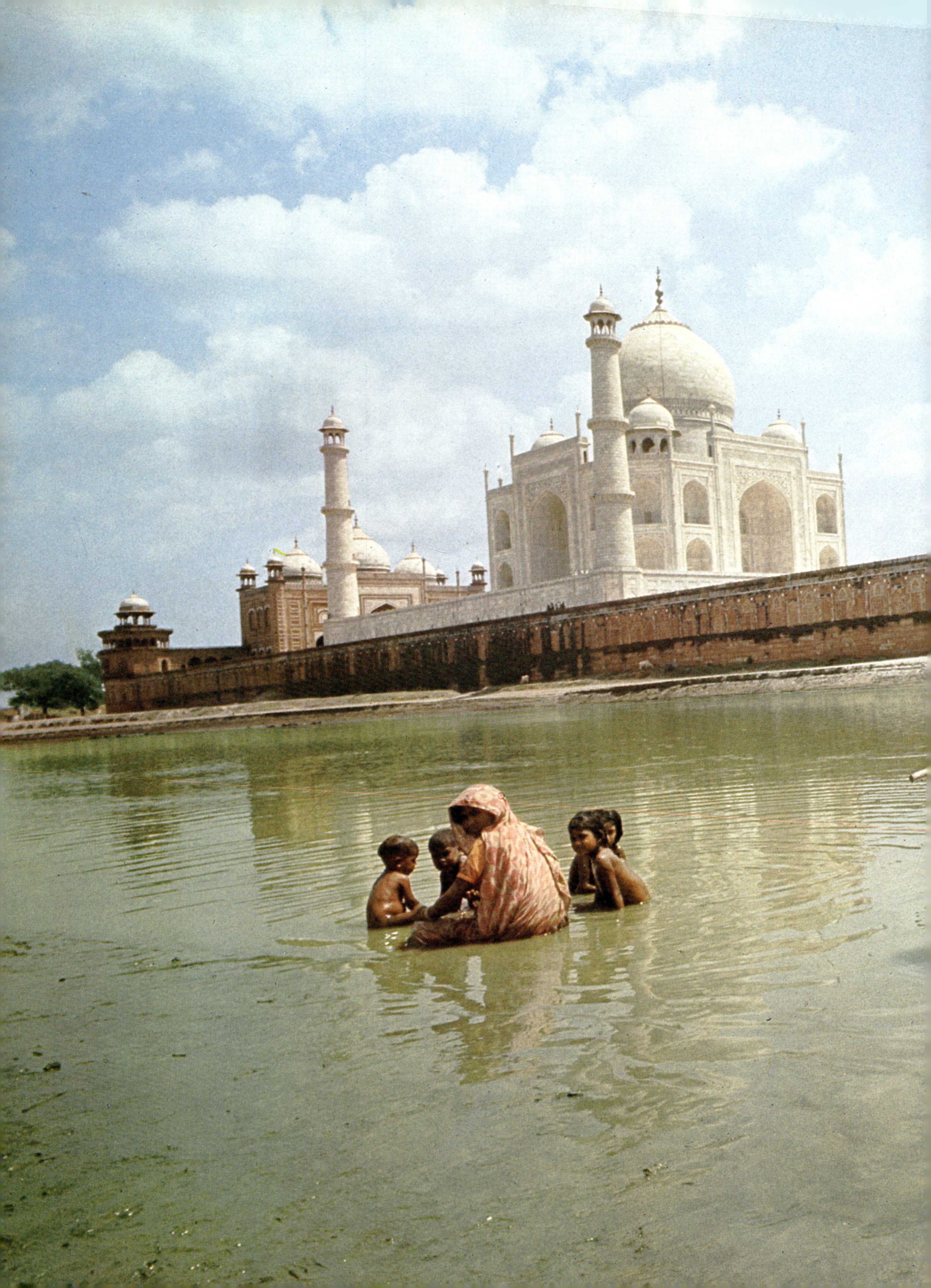

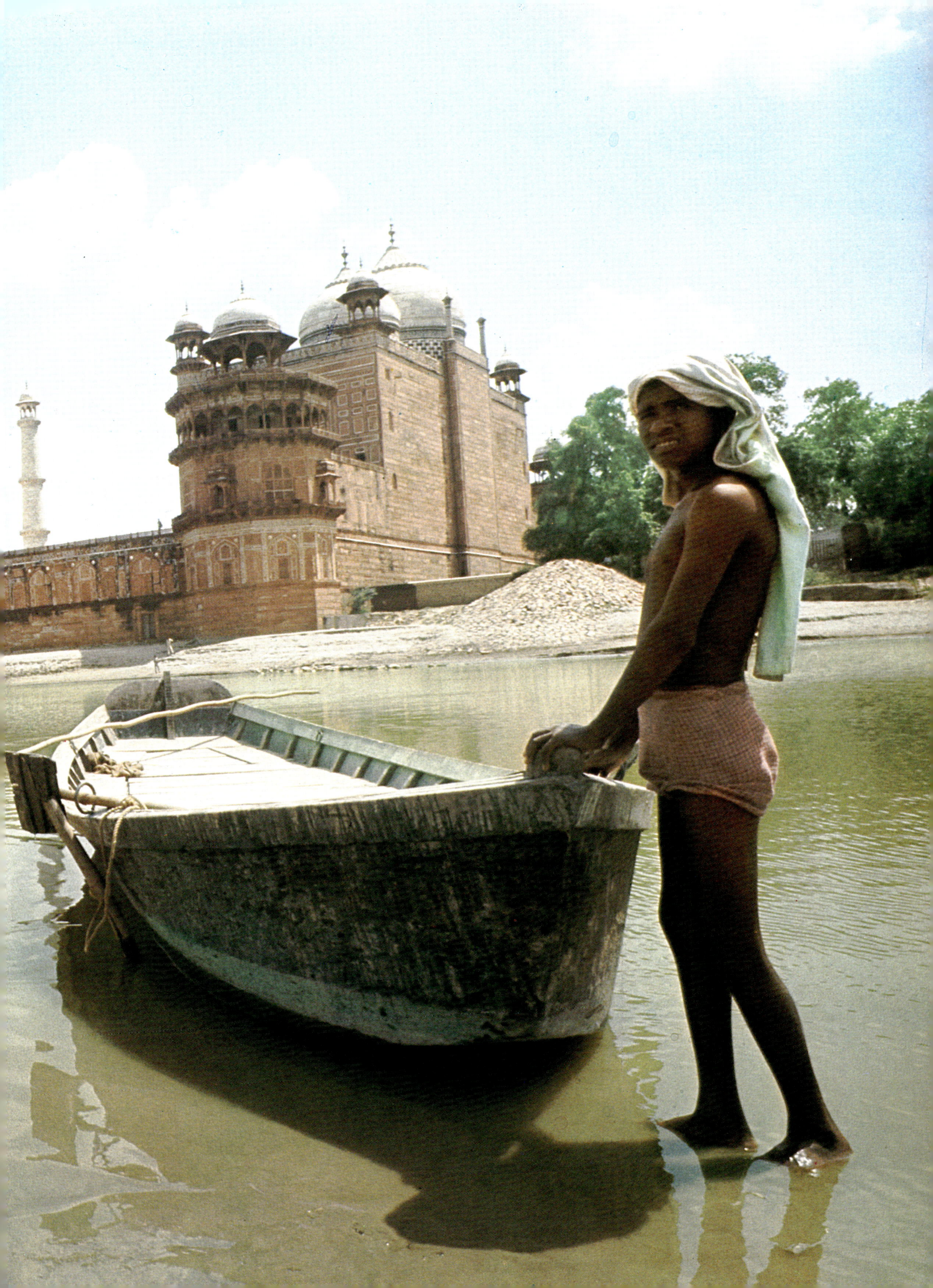

Preceding page, the Taj Mahal complex seen from the banks of the Yamuna River in Agra, India. Left and below, a view from the mausoleum, showing the exquisite Islamic gardens and pools. Above, one of the twin buildings which flank the mausoleum. Facing page, the river side of the tomb and its minarets, or towers, silhouetted against the sky.

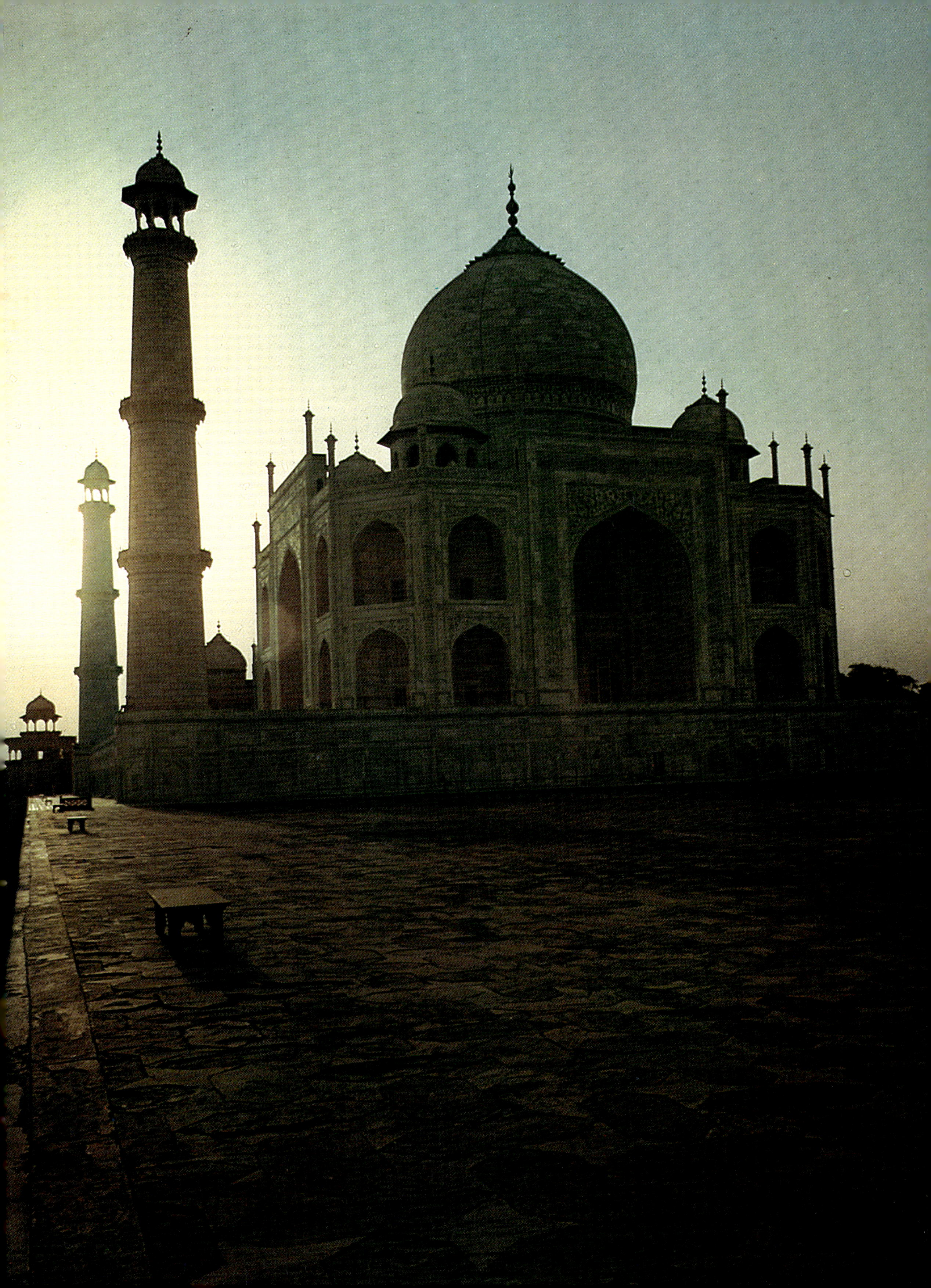

Above, the arched alcove under the great central iwan, or half dome, which is a convention of Persian architecture, adapted here to blend with elements of Mogul design. Above right, a general view of the Taj Mahal and its minarets.

Left and right, details of the mausoleum, showing the intricate inscriptions and stylized designs. Human figures are excluded from the dense ornamentation, as is frequently the case in Islamic art.

Far right, one of the lesser cupolas that flank the central dome.

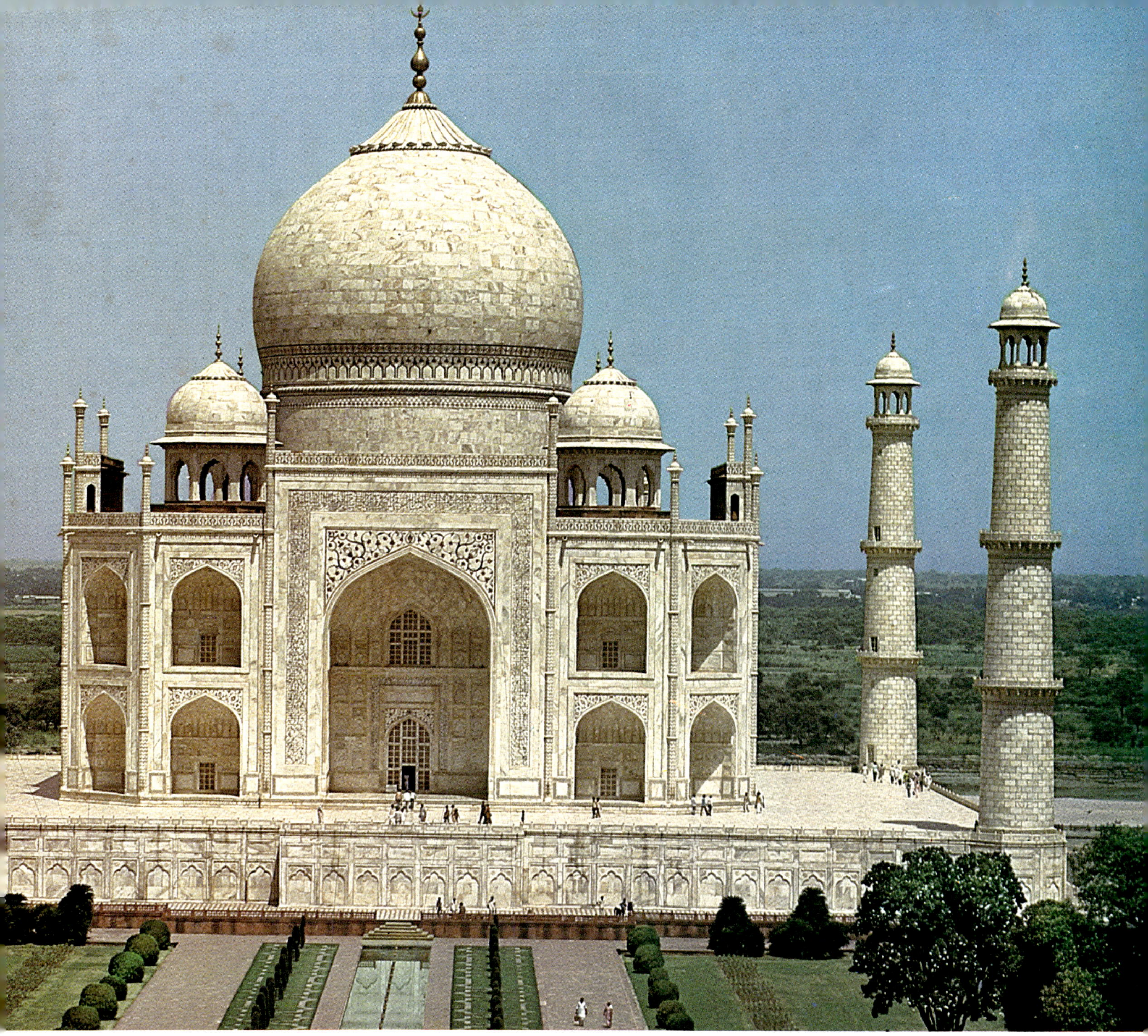

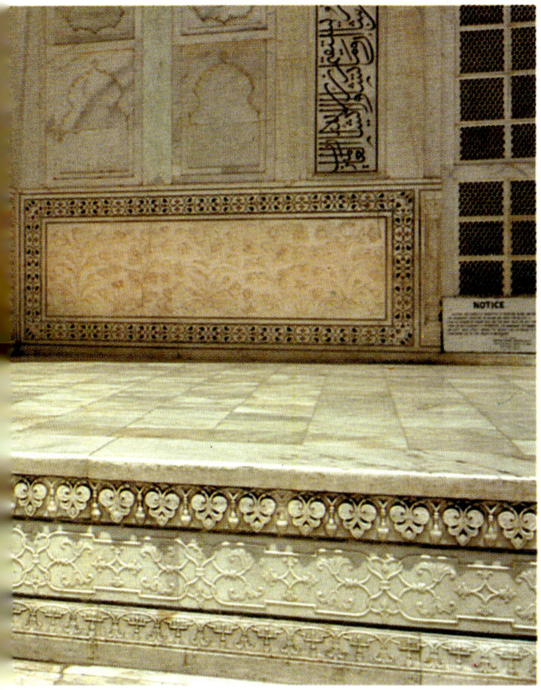
NOTICE

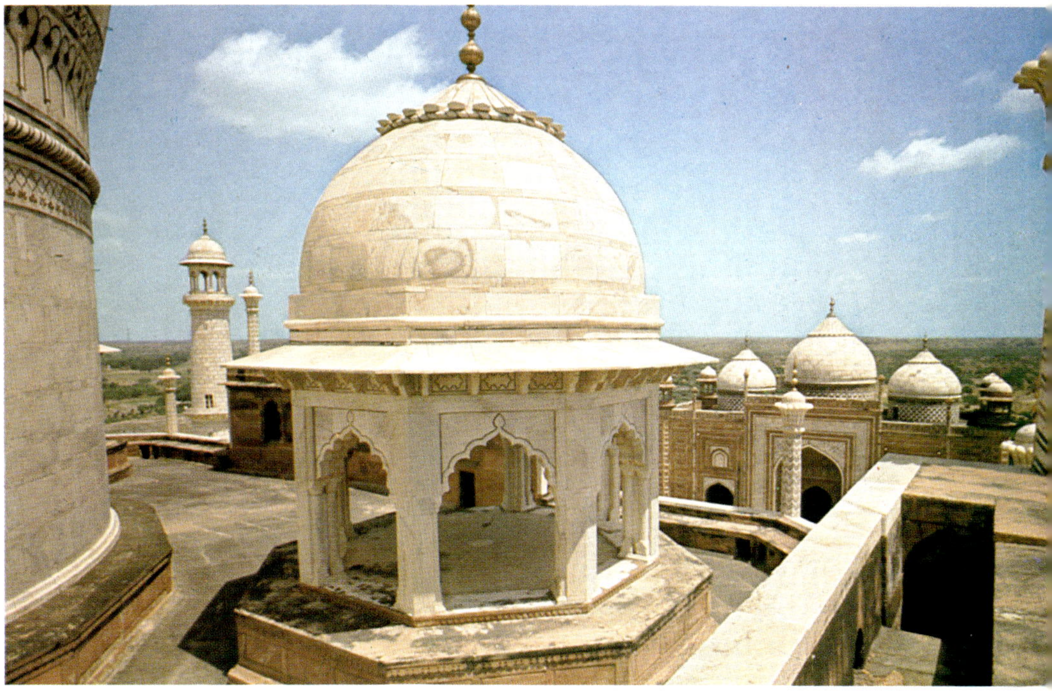

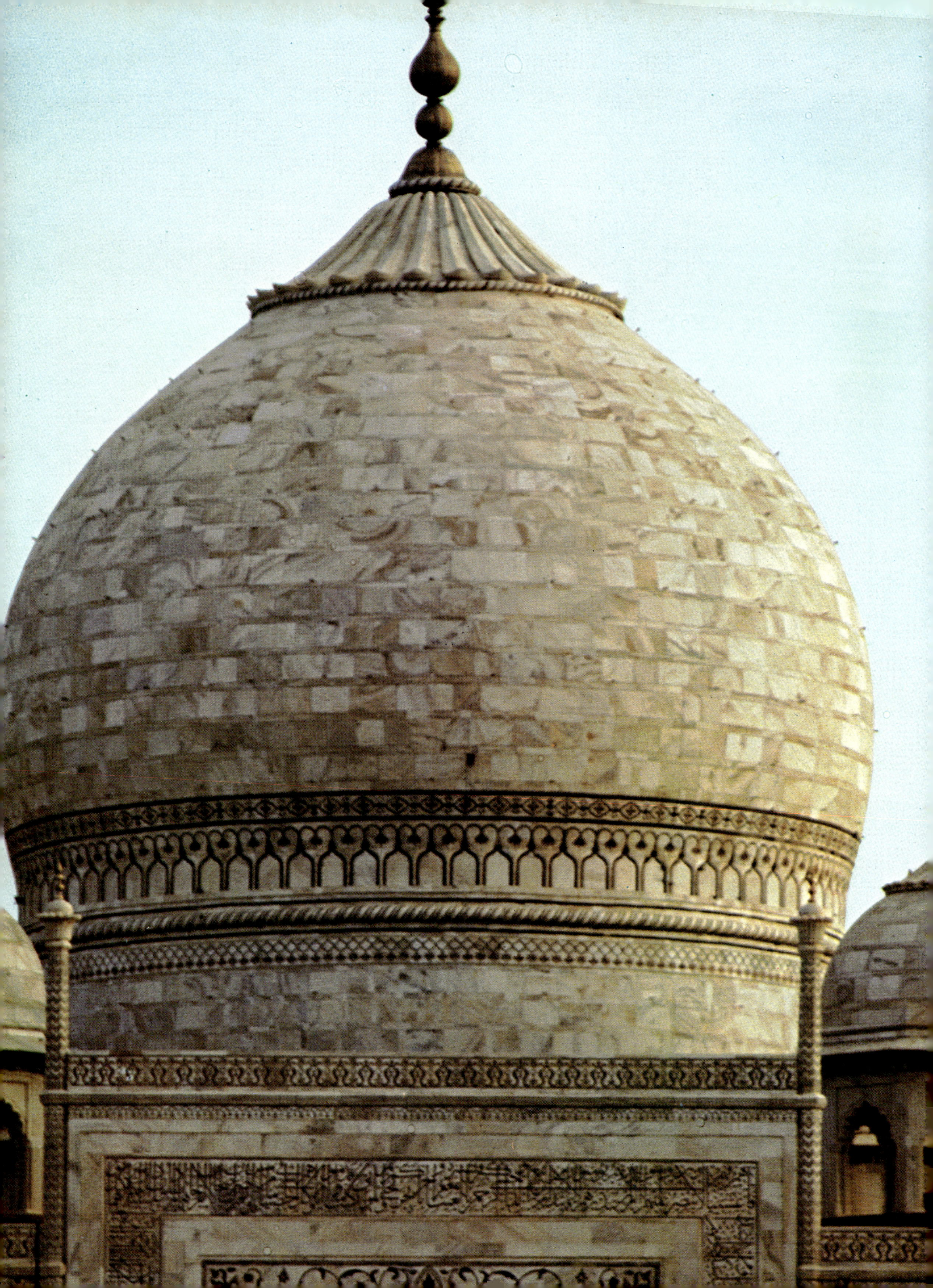

Facing page, the swelling central dome of the Taj Mahal which is the dominant architectural feature of the complex. Above, one of the slender minarets, which rise to a height of 138 feet at the corners of the tomb. The minarets serve to balance the group of buildings, as well as to lighten the effect of the massive dome.

Right, above and below, Indians visiting the tomb of Mumtaz Mahal, one of the most popular shrines in India.

Facing page, the central chamber of the mausoleum showing the two symbolic sarcophagi of Mumtaz Mahal and her devoted husband Shah Jahan side by side. The emperor's sarcophagus is slightly higher than that of his wife and is set to one side, thus becoming the only infraction of the overall symmetry of the mausoleum. However, it was not part of the original design. Shah Jahan had planned to build himself a vast tomb across the river from the Taj Mahal. But when he died, his son Aurangzeb betrayed his father's wish and buried him beside Mumtaz Mahal.

Left, an archway leading through the delicate screens which surround the two sarcophagi. The tombs are opulently inlaid with precious and semiprecious stones and are inscribed with quotations from the Koran.

Above, the filigreed lamp that burns in the chamber, casting an intricate glow upon the two sarcophagi.

Following page, the Taj Mahal, renowned the world over for its serene and timeless beauty.

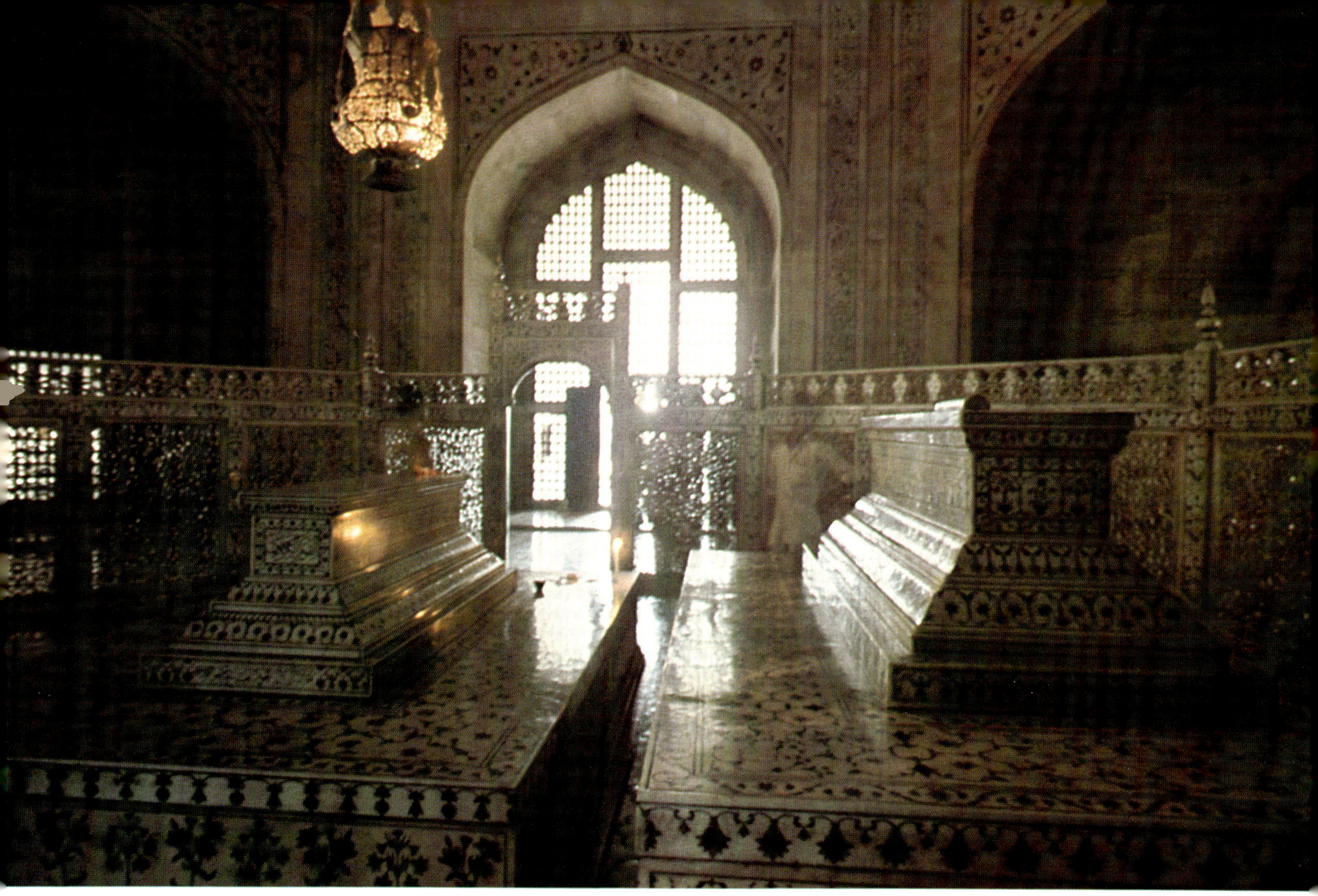

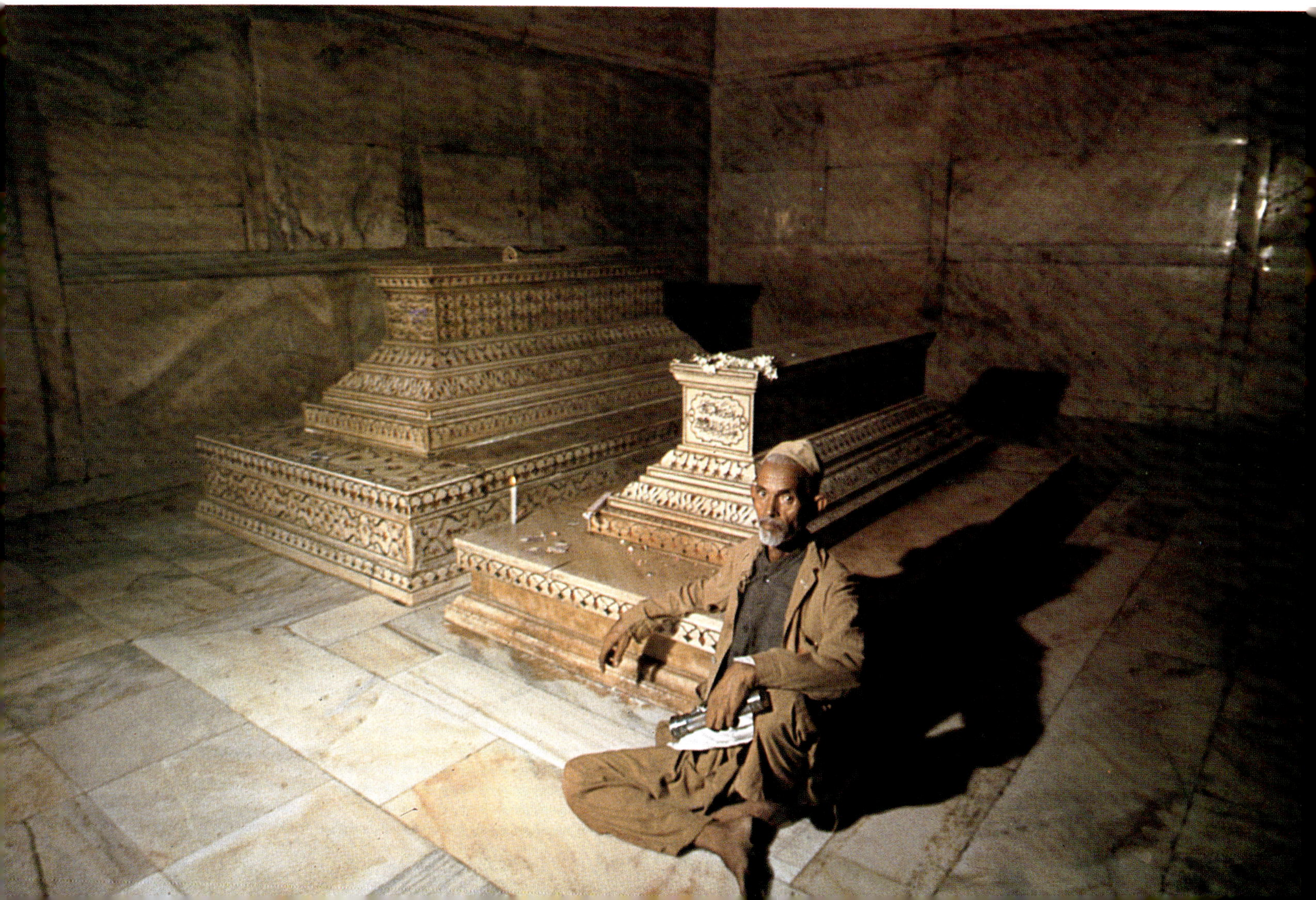

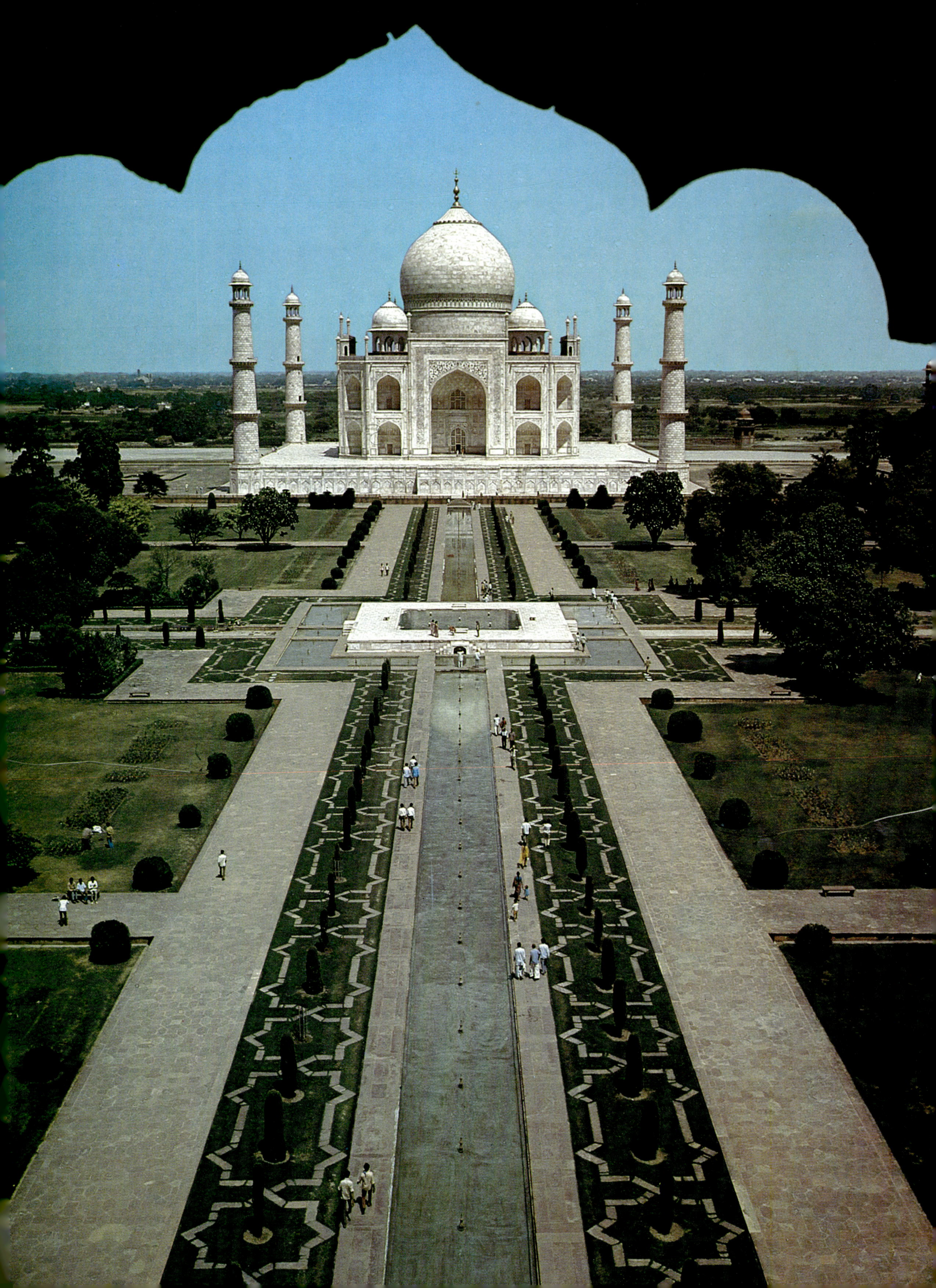

Taj Mahal
India

Love moves mountains, according to the proverb, but rarely does it provide work for the architect. Faith and vanity, throughout the centuries, have more often been the qualities that have inspired men to build. The majestic Taj Mahal, however, is a notable exception. The famous domed building is a memorial to the fervent love of Shah Jahan, the fifth ruler of the Mogul empire, for a cherished wife, who died in childbirth.

According to legend, the queen's last wish was that the shah build a monument so beautiful that whoever saw it could not help but sense the perfection of their love. Indeed, since its construction in the mid-seventeenth century, the shimmering monument of white marble, set among tranquil gardens and pools, has attracted many tourists and pilgrims. Visitors are as moved by the many legends surrounding its creation as they are spellbound by its serene elegance.

The first meeting between the prince and his future wife took place in 1607, in the royal Meena bazaar. This bazaar, which was attached to the royal harem, was a private marketplace where, undisturbed by men, the women of the aristocracy could buy waxes, oils, and other cosmetics. On certain days, however, normal protocol was reversed, and the bazaar became a lively meeting place, open to all classes. Relaxing their reserve for a day,

Above, Shah Jahan, fifth of the Mogul emperors. When he was a young prince, he fell in love with the beautiful Arjumand Banu Begum, the daughter of his father's prime minister, and eventually married her. On the day of her coronation, his bride was given the honorary name of Mumtaz Mahal, the "Chosen One of the Palace." When Mumtaz Mahal died, Shah Jahan built the wonderful Taj Mahal in her memory.

Right, a Mogul illustration of the Taj Mahal. Although the building was strongly influenced by the Persian architecture of the time, it has become the supreme symbol of India.

Left, a drawing of the screen around the two sarcophagi in the mausoleum.

Below, a floor plan of the whole complex, in which the mausoleum is at bottom center, flanked by its mosque and the "reply."

the noblewomen would cast off their veils and peddle their baubles and wares to the milling crowd.

It was on one of these "contrary days" that Shah Jahan, who was then known as Prince Khurram, saw Arjumand Banu Begum, the beguiling daughter of the prime minister. He immediately fell in love with her. According to tradition, when Khurram tried to buy from her the bottom of a bottle cut like a diamond, Arjumand named a price only a prince could afford—ten thousand rupees. Khurram smiled and withdrew the ten thousand rupees from his sleeve. He then went to his father, the emperor Jahangir, to ask permission to marry the trinket seller. Jahangir gave permission, for he, too, had married for love. However, five years passed before the couple was actually married. Shah Jahan was first obliged to make a political marriage with a Persian princess. Eventually, Khurram and Arjumand Banu united, and the bride was honored by her father-in-law with a new name, Mumtaz Mahal, the "Chosen One of the Palace."

Although the name Shah Jahan means "King of the World," the shah could be said to have lived only for his "Chosen One." In their nineteen years together, Mumtaz Mahal was more than a harem wife. She was a close companion, privy to many of his royal deliberations. She bore her husband fourteen children, but the last was fatal to her. She died soon after giving birth to a daughter on the battlefield of Burhanpur, having insisted on following her husband on his campaigns.

After the death of his wife, the shah was stricken with grief. He stayed weeping in his rooms for eight days, refusing to eat or drink. It is said that during this time his beard turned quite gray. Powerless to recall his lost love to his side, he dreamed instead of making her immortal. He would build her a mausoleum so perfect that all who gazed on it would feel the miracle of love and the cruelty of death. He selected the city of Agra, on the banks of the broad slow stream of the Yamuna—the scene of his wife's greatest happiness—as the site of the tomb of the "Chosen One" and named it the Taj Mahal, the "Remembrance of the Palace."

Strangely enough, the architect of the Taj Mahal is unknown, although claimants to the title are legion. Father Sebastian Manrique, a Portuguese missionary who came to Agra in 1642 to ransom a colleague, relates that the architect was a Venetian goldsmith called Geronimo Veroneo. According to the priest, the emperor requested Veroneo to make a large preliminary drawing of his design for a sumptuous tomb for his dead wife. Veroneo complied with the emperor's request, pleasing him with the beauty of his designs. But "in the arrogant manner of a proud barbarian," the emperor flew into a rage at the projected costs, which he considered disgracefully low. It is said that he ordered Veroneo to spend thirty million rupees and "to let him know when this sum had all been spent . . . ."

Two hundred years later, another European visited Agra: a Major Sleeman, who, in his turn, concluded that the Taj Mahal had been built by a Western architect—this time the Frenchman Austin de Bordeaux, also a goldsmith. However, the Indian version of the history of the Taj Mahal credits Ustad Isa, an itinerant from Turkey or Persia, as being the designer. One legend tells that Ustad Isa himself was an inconsolable widower in search of an opportunity to erect a worthy monument to his own wife. Other accounts claim variously that he was from the cities of Isfahan or Samarkand or from Russia and that he was either a Christian, a Jew, or an Arab.

It is probable that the Taj Mahal was not the work of a single master at all but the concerted effort of many artists and craftsmen from all over Asia. Begun in 1631, the mausoleum took some 20,000 workmen twenty-two years to build at a cost of forty million rupees.

In one detail, however, the legends concur. Shah Jahan was apparently so pleased with the elegant mausoleum that he beheaded his chief architect, cut off the hands of the architect's assistants, and blinded the draftsmen, so that they would never be able to create a building to rival it. And the legends are correct on another count: There has never been a tomb to surpass the cool, white beauty of the Taj Mahal.

It is a balanced and symmetric grouping of buildings. A harmonious synthesis of the architecture of Persia, India, and central Asia, it combines, for example, the traditional design of Mogul gardens with the characteristically Indian use of minarets, or towers, and a dominant dome. The placement of a dome over an arched alcove is a characteristic of Persian architecture, successfully adapted in the Taj Mahal to Mogul design.

At the heart of the complex stands the mausoleum itself: a massive eight-sided structure inset with arched *iwans*, or half domes, of a classically Mogul design. It is crowned by an immense, bulbous dome, which is surrounded and set off by four minarets that rise to a height of 138 feet. Flanking the domed structure are a mosque and a second matching building, known as the *jawab*, or "reply." Its sole function is to maintain the symmetry of the entire composition.

An idyllic square garden, divided by oblong pools, is at the front of the mausoleum. These pools, in turn, are divided into fourths by avenues, four being the number sacred to Islam. This planned and calculated reordering of nature and the severe regularity of the lines of trees are characteristic of Persian gardens, which are intended to invite spiritual contemplation. Unlike English and French gardens,

Right, a Mogul miniature depicting the funeral procession of Shah Jahan, taking him to his eternal resting place alongside his beloved wife.

Below, a gold coin from the Shah Jahan's reign. It is Persian in design and style.

the Persian garden is not a setting for recreation and pleasure but rather a retreat or sacred refuge from the disorder of temporal life.

Under the great dome, within an octagonal hall, are the sarcophagi of the two lovers, enclosed by a screen of carved marble. In the exact center is the memorial tomb of Mumtaz Mahal. Next to it, but a little larger and higher, is that of Shah Jahan—the only asymmetrical element of the whole complex. However, both tombs are empty. The actual graves of the royal couple are in a small crypt beneath the burial hall.

The shah's tomb was not part of the original plan. Shah Jahan had planned to build another vast mausoleum for himself across the river from that of his loved one. However, when he died, his son, refusing to incur the expense of another tomb, betrayed his father's last wishes and buried him beside his beloved consort.

Perhaps the single most alluring aspect of the Taj Mahal is the pervasive use of white marble. At different times of the day, the marble surfaces take on varying and delicate casts of color. Some travelers claim that the only way to fully appreciate the Taj Mahal is by moonlight, when its surface takes on an almost incandescent glow. One of the more descriptive—and distinctly Victorian—accounts of the singular effects of light at the Taj Mahal was written by Prince William of Sweden in one of his travel books, after he visited the site in 1832:

The sun shone so intensely on the dead-white marble that one was forced to look with half-closed eyes or to wear smoked glasses to avoid being dazzled. The many delicate details now appeared to great advantage, and the inlaid work, especially with its wealth of stones of different colors, seem to be masterly; otherwise I preferred the lovely moonlight effect of the evening before with its atmosphere of profound feeling, and it is thus that I would choose to remember this costliest gem among all the treasures of India.

The Taj Mahal received such unabashed praise from many other visitors, including such distinguished travelers as the seventeenth-century essayist Jean-Baptiste Tavernier, the English poet Edwin Arnold, and Rudyard Kipling. In the 1830s, Lord William Bentinck, however, who was governor general of Bengal from 1828 to 1833 and who disapproved of the "decadent" Mogul architecture in India, proposed that the building be dismantled and auctioned off in England. During this period, many tombs and citadels were destroyed. Fortunately, the first attempted auction of Taj Mahal relics in England was a dismal failure, and there were no further threats to the building. Nonetheless, throughout the nineteenth century, the British completely disregarded the sanctity of the Taj Mahal. The marble terrace was used for formal dances which were accompanied by brass bands. Picnics and croquet matches were held in the gardens, which eventually became little more than badly maintained parks.

By the beginning of the twentieth century, there was a dramatic revival in Britain's attitude toward precolonial Indian art. Lord Curzon, an Englishman living in India, was active in the efforts to preserve the Taj Mahal. Thanks to his vigilance, the building now appears much the way it did when the great Mogul emperor, Shah Jahan, was alive.

Because of Curzon and other conservationists, the Taj Mahal survives as a magnificent reminder of a unique period of Indian history. The rare beauty of the Taj Mahal and the reasons for its construction have stirred hearts since it was completed in 1664. Edward Lear, the Victorian author and humorist, summed it up with his quip, "Henceforth let the inhabitants of the world be divided into two classes—them as has seen the Taj Mahal and them as hasn't."

Below, a European drawing of the Taj Mahal. The Taj Mahal has long fascinated European visitors including Jean-Baptiste Tavernier, Rudyard Kipling, and Edward Lear.

The Belvedere

Austria

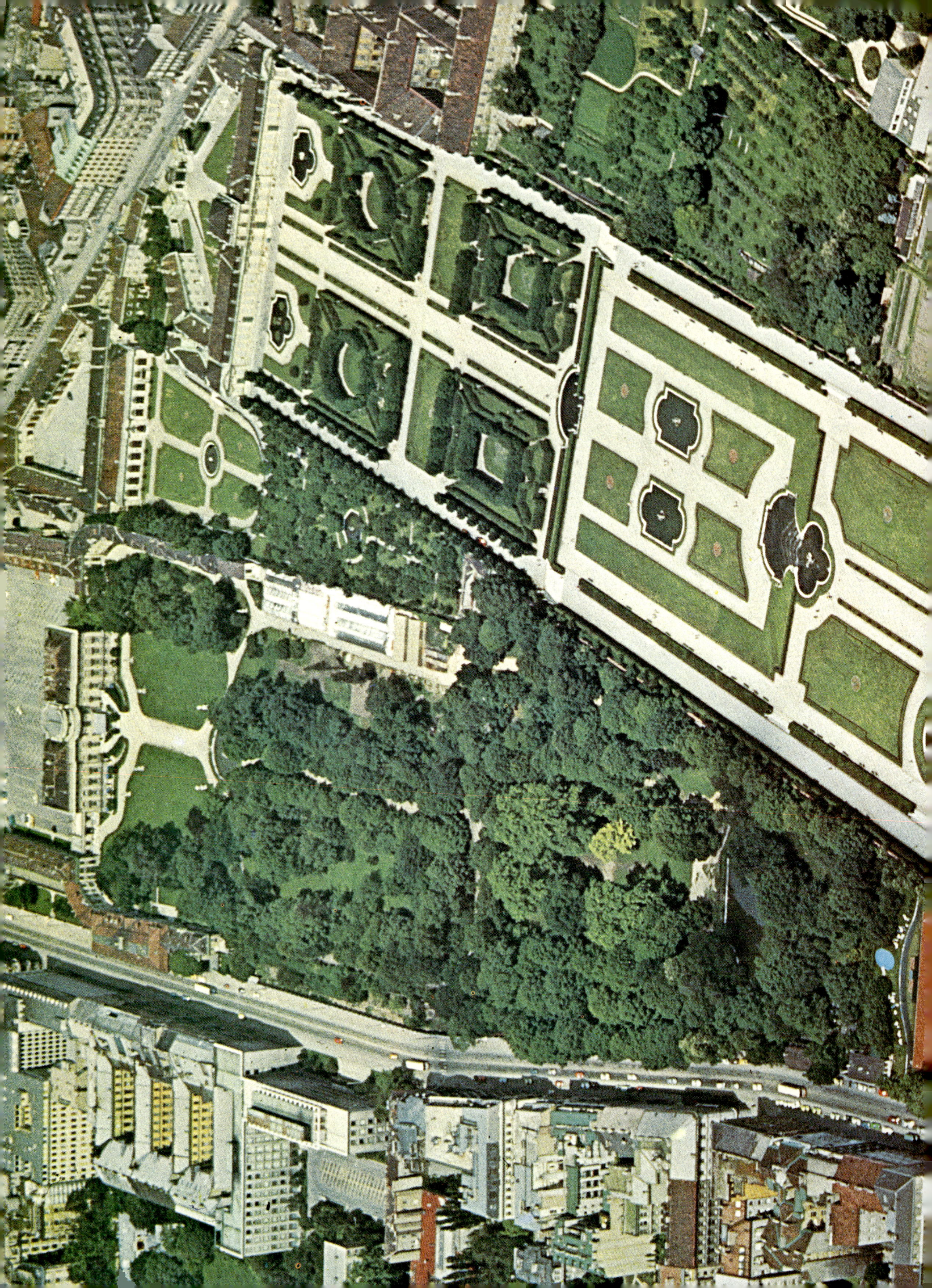

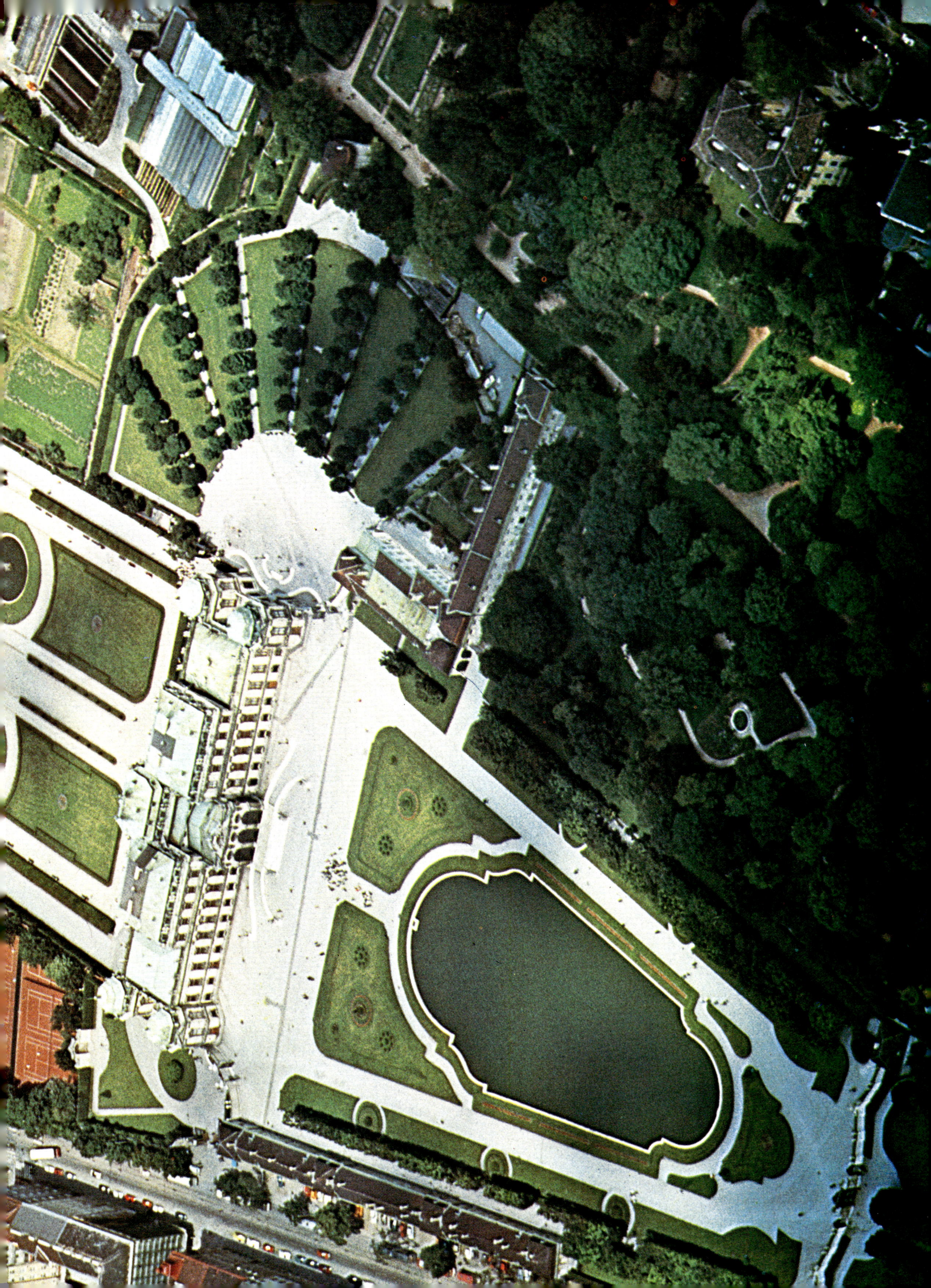

Preceding page, an aerial view of the Belvedere. This Baroque palace in Vienna was the summer residence of Prince Eugene of Savoy (1663–1736), one of history's most brilliant military strategists.

Above, the huge triple wrought-iron gate in front of the Upper Palace.

On either side of the central gateway, gentle-faced lions hold Eugene's escutcheon and coronet, symbols of his title of prince of the Holy Roman Empire (above, and detail far right). This heraldic coronet appears five times on the gate (detail right)—an emphatic reminder of Eugene's nobility. The lions once inspired the epigramist Nikolaus Klauserwitz to pen the following Latin impromptu: "Indomiti Ducis ungue tenent insigne liones, Nam leo magnanimi signa leonis amat" ("Lions bear in their claws the shield of the invincible prince, for the lion loves the insignia of his magnanimous brother"). Left, detail of the gate.

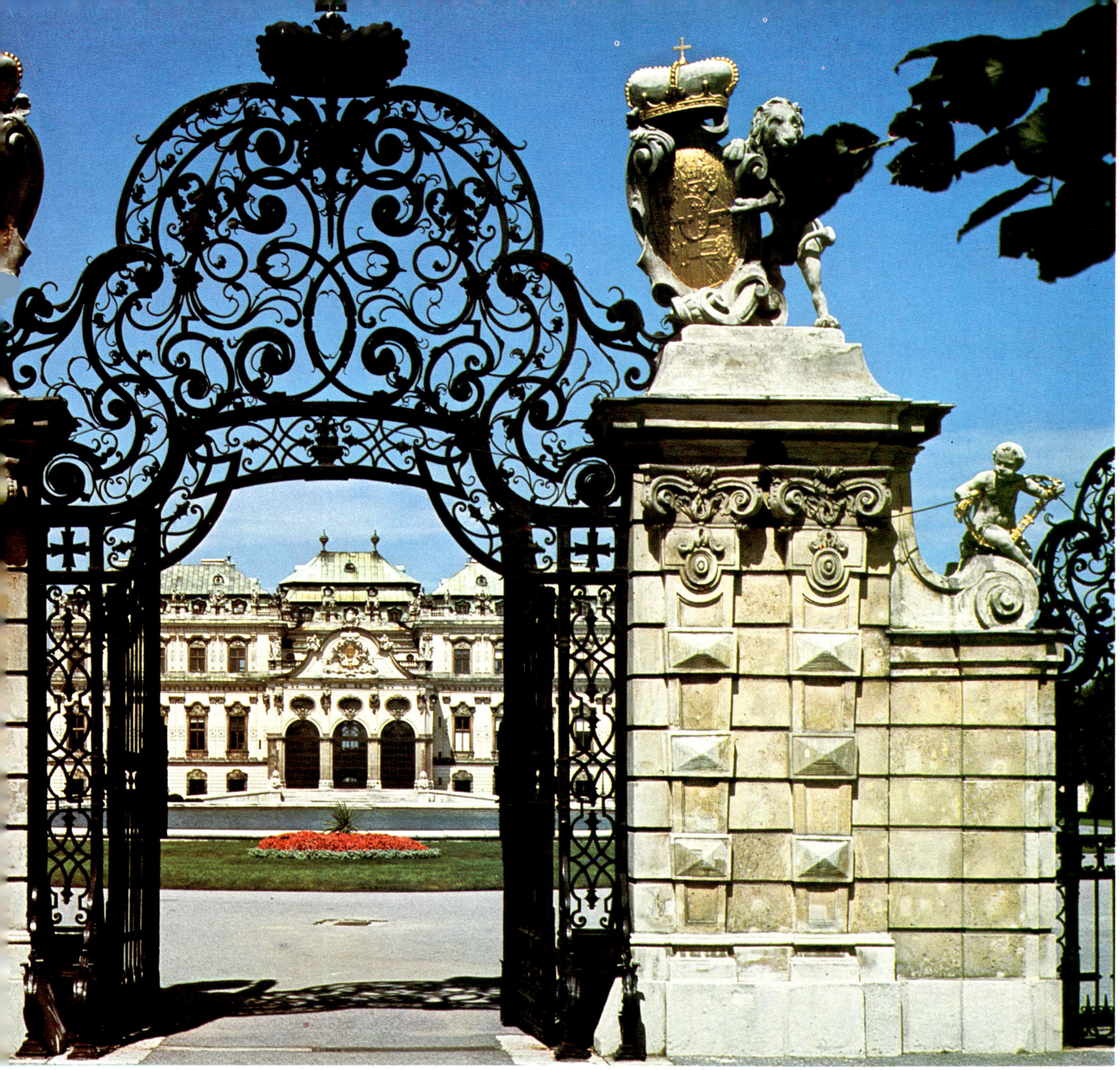

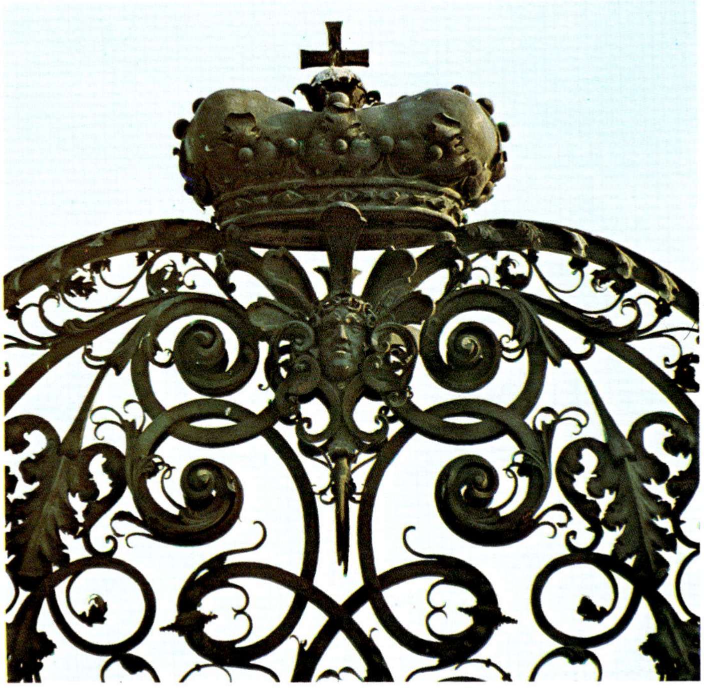

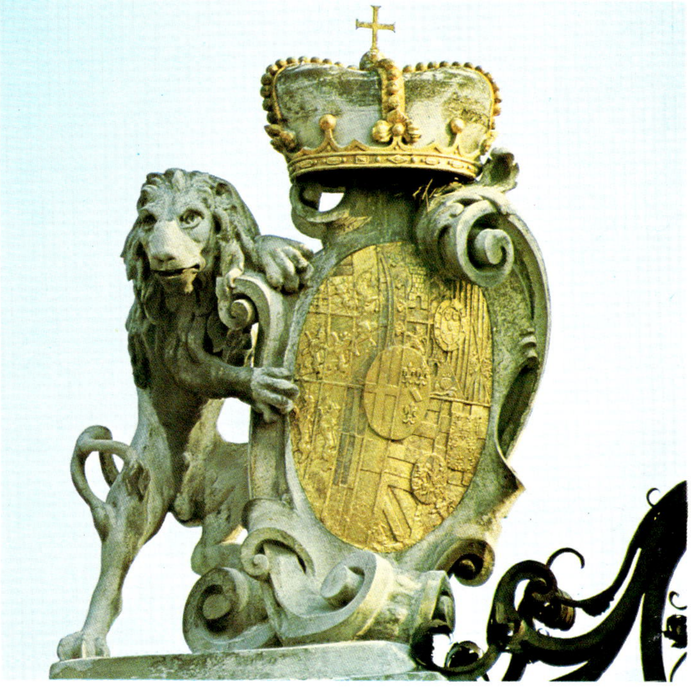

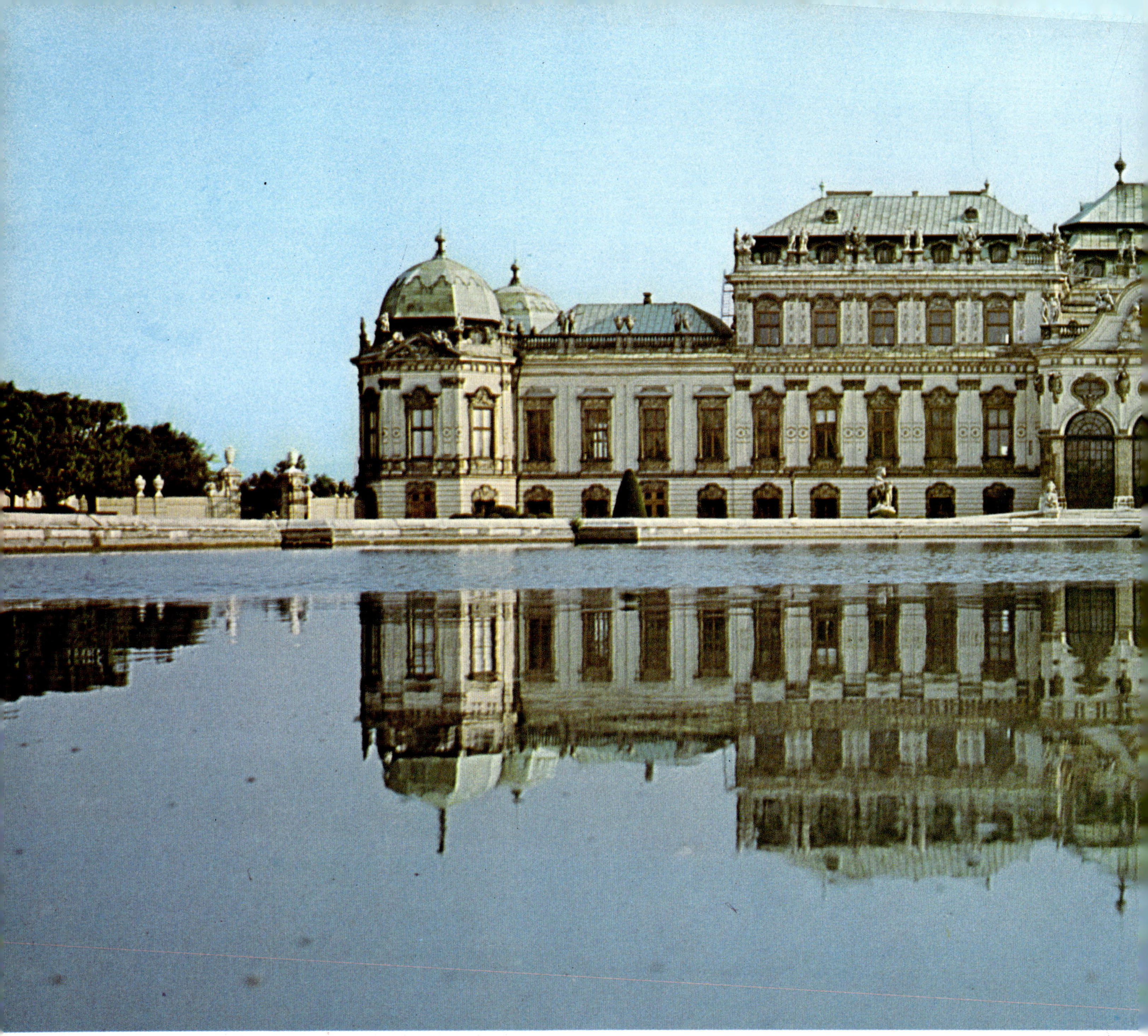

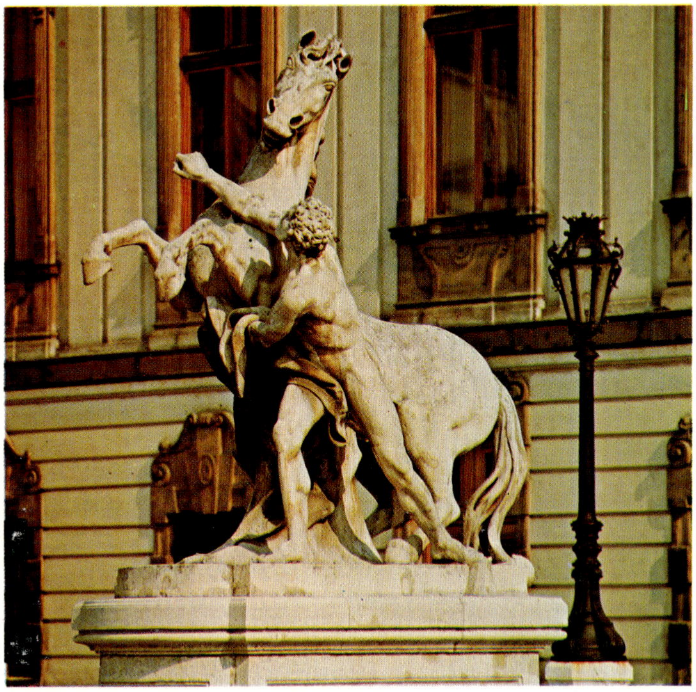

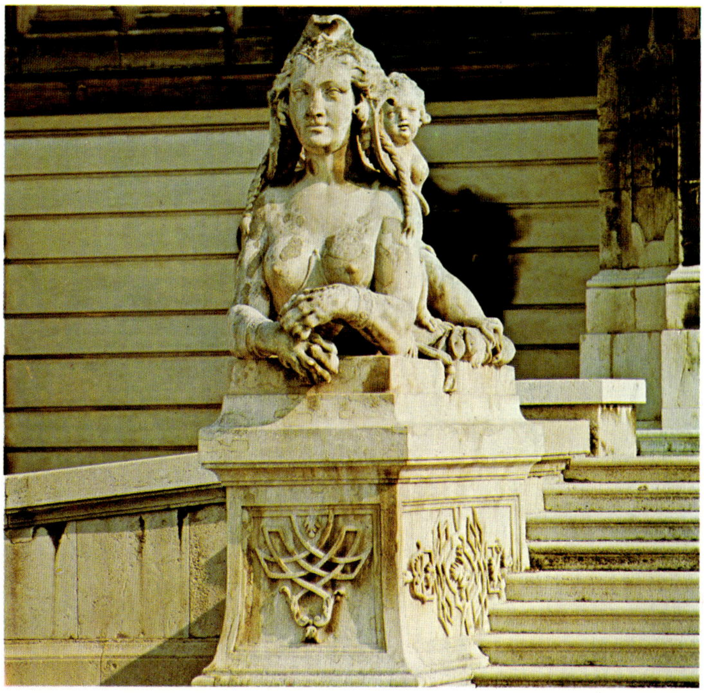

Above, the entrance façade of the Upper Palace, reflected on the smooth surface of the pool. The central entrance portico once provided shelter for the carriages of visitors. The statues in front of the palace include an athlete taming a wild stallion (far left) and a benign sphinx (left). Right, an ornate, wrought-iron lantern, now converted to electricity.

The curves and broken lines of the façade of the Upper Palace are more than matched by its exuberance of detail. Above left, the coat of arms of Eugene of Savoy on the pediment of the central portico. Paired pilasters (left) flank the ornate windows, while copper domes (above), patined with age, crown the four corner pavilions.

Facing page, the entrance portico of the Upper Palace seen across the pool. Dozens of statues, the pagodalike roof, and a wealth of inventive details tend to disguise the fact that the massing of the palace is relatively simple.

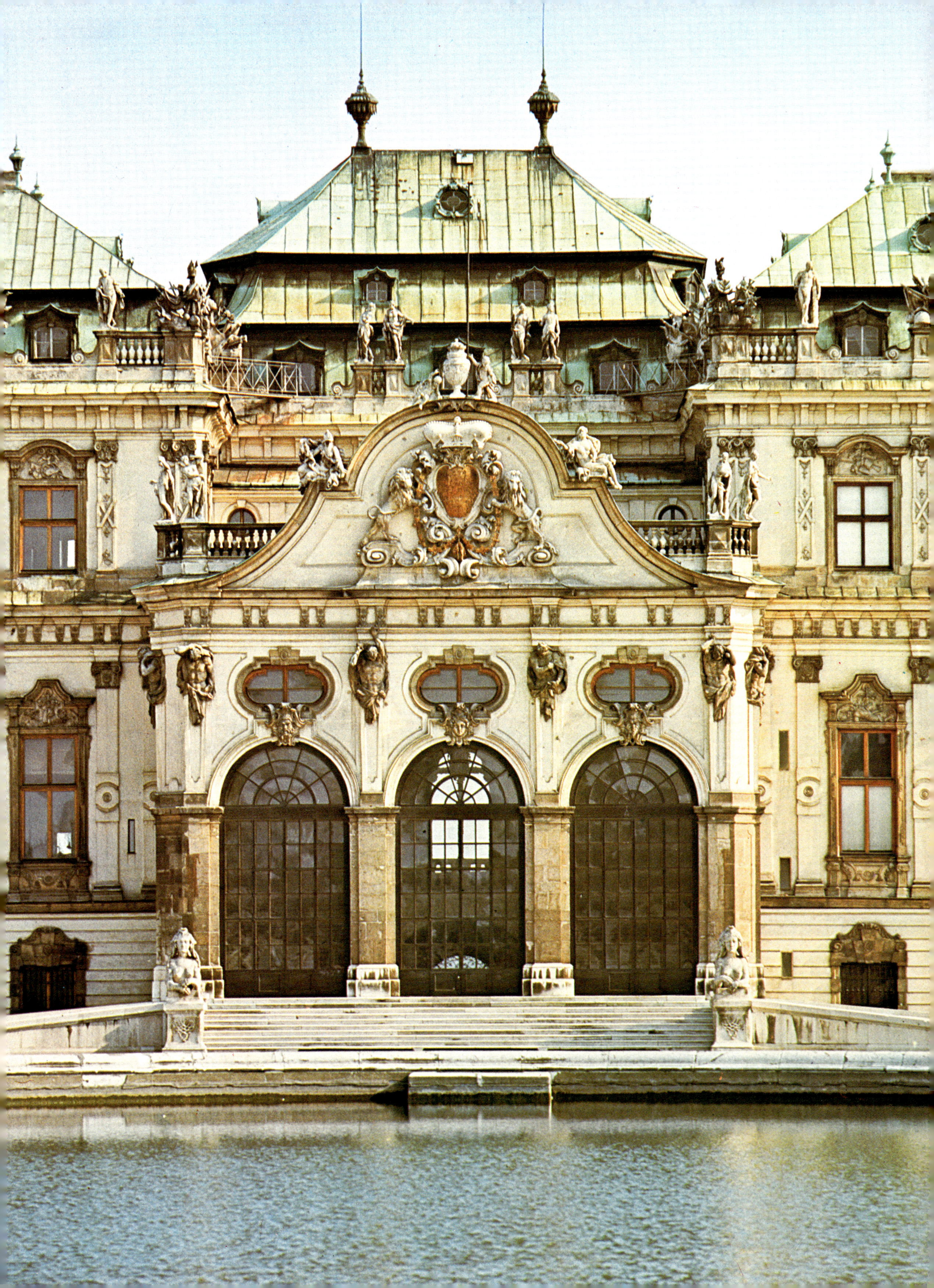

The sloping terraces and geometric gardens contribute an impression of height and elegance to the comparatively simpler garden façade of the Upper Palace (above). Left, detail of Baroque ironwork from one of the palace gates. Right, a sculptural group of putti frolicking with a mermaid, which contrasts with the dignified statues of classical gods and goddesses nearby (far right).

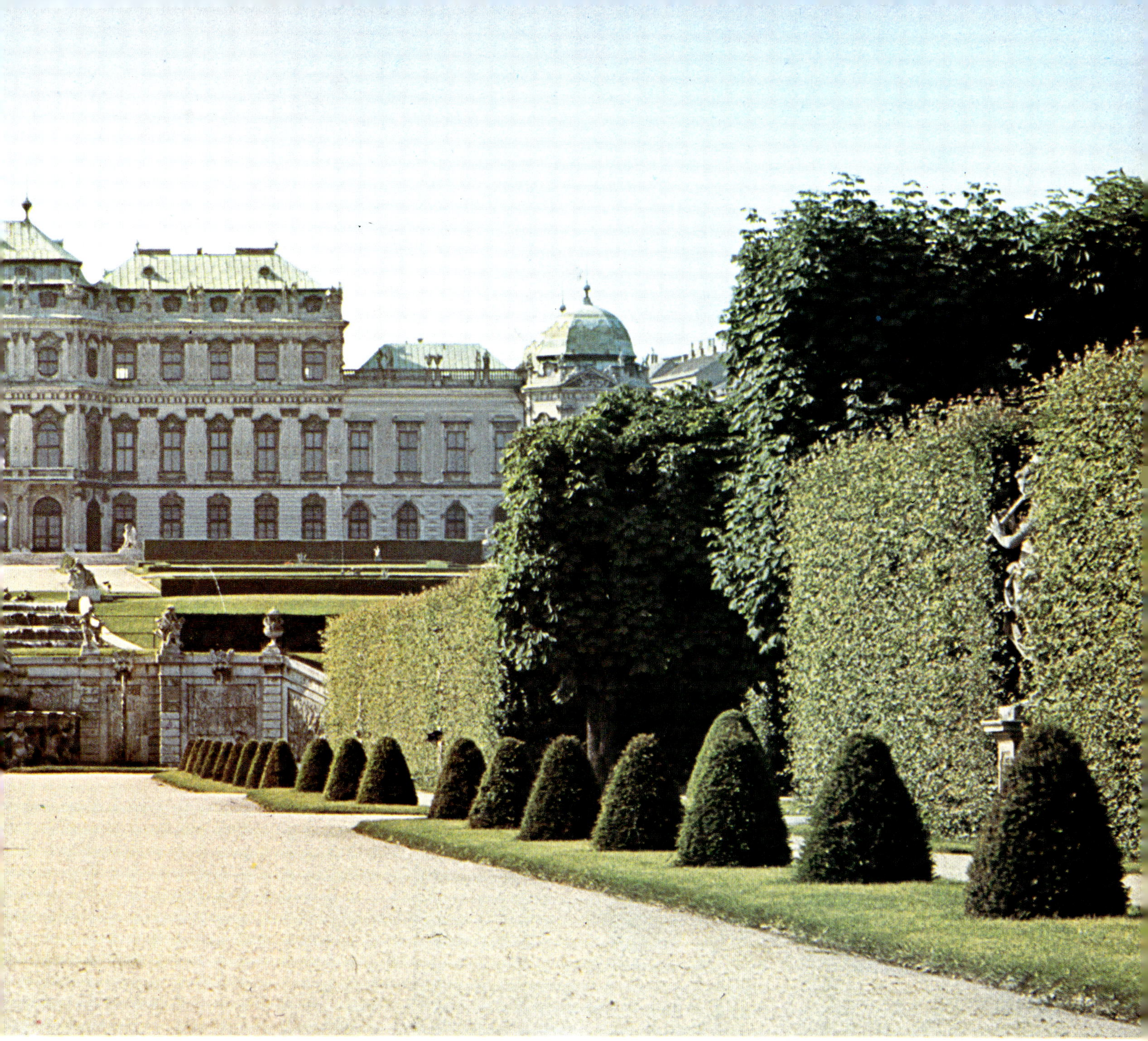

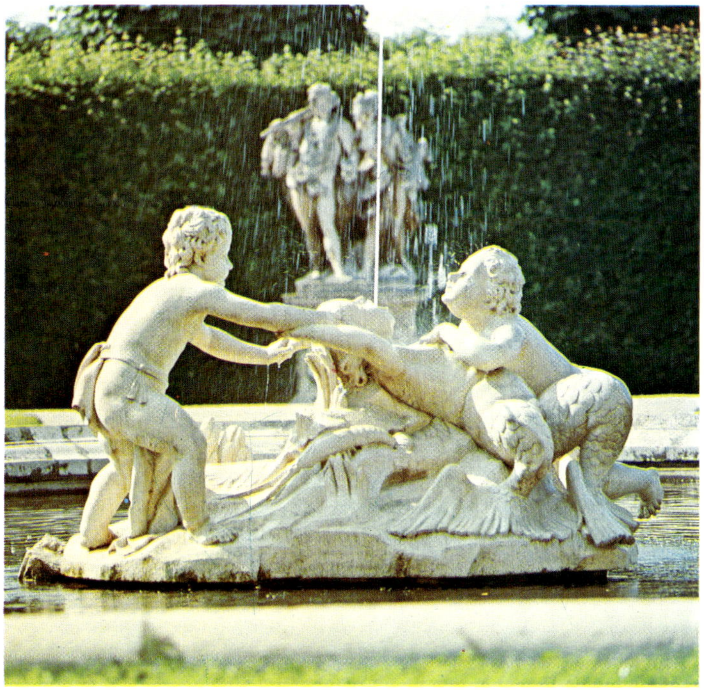

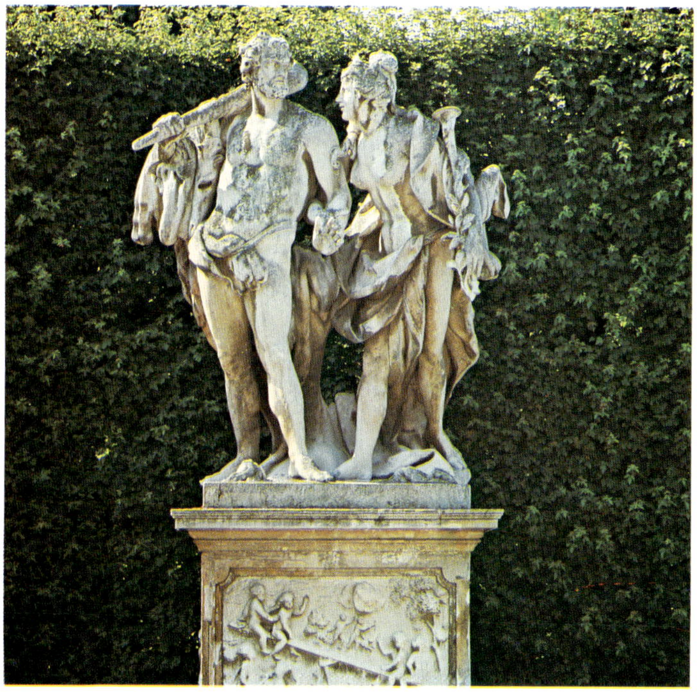

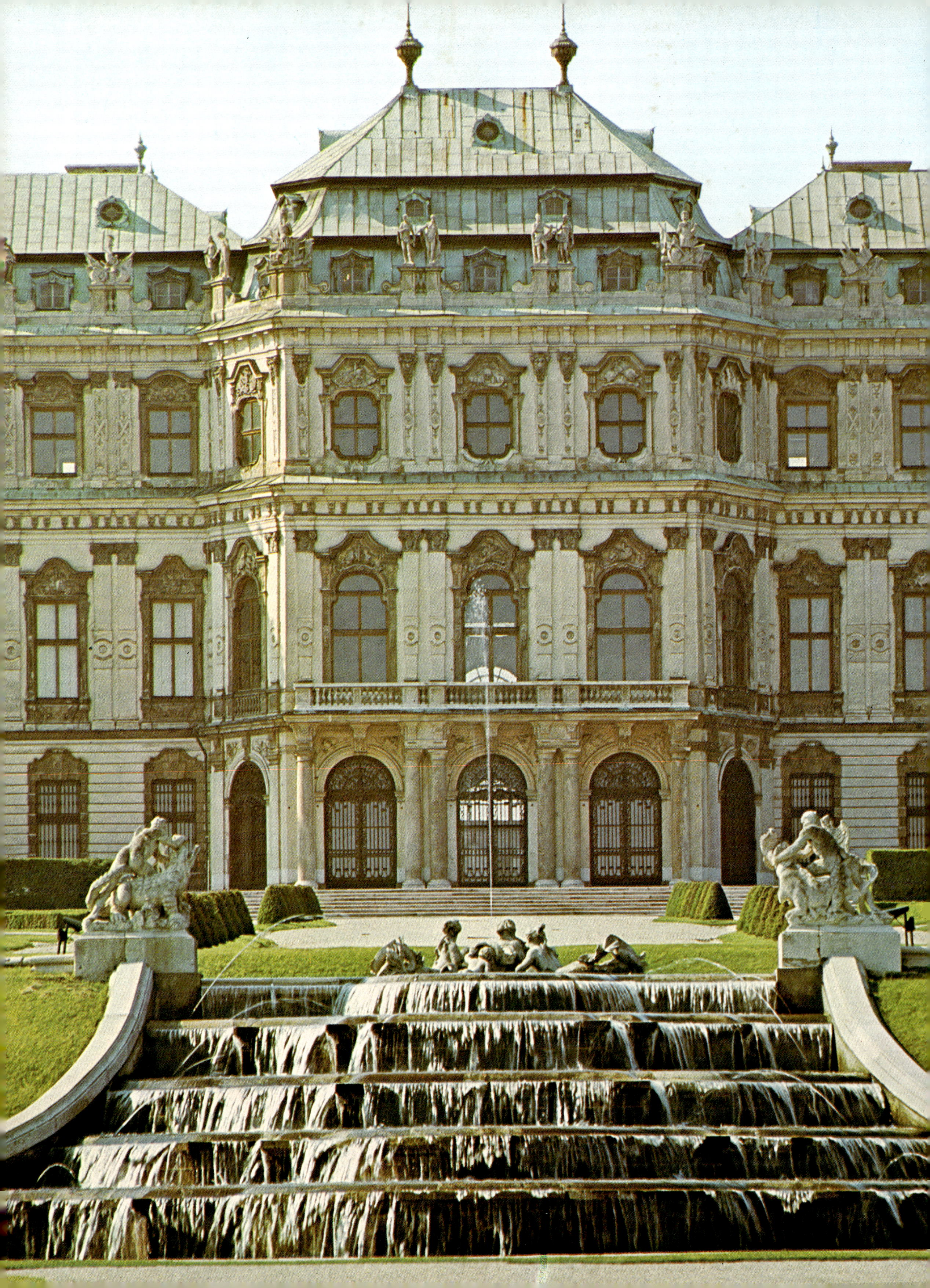

Above, the gardens and Lower Palace as seen from the pool at the top of the cascade.

Right, one of the staircases and ramps connecting the upper and lower levels of the garden. The ramp is decorated with ornamental squares and circles, now barely visible, which are Chinese symbols for the earth and the sky.

Facing page, the central pavilion of the Upper Palace and the cascade. The sculptural groups at either side of the cascade portray heroes subduing primeval monsters. Left, Hercules fighting the dragon of the Hesperides. Right, Apollo conquering the Python.

Following page, a fountain (left, above and below) near the garden façade of the Lower Palace. Right, the Lower Palace with the gardens and Upper Palace beyond.

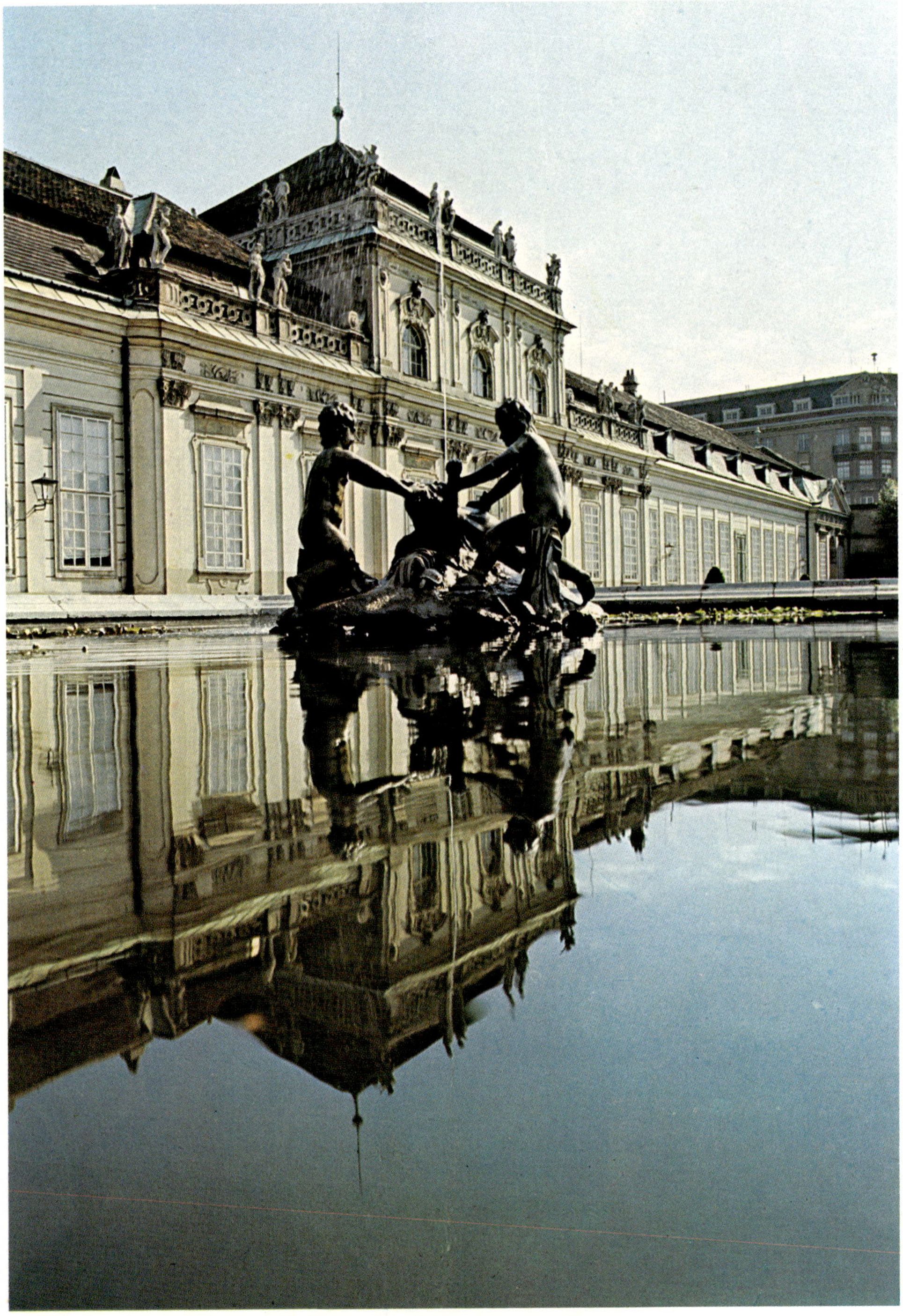

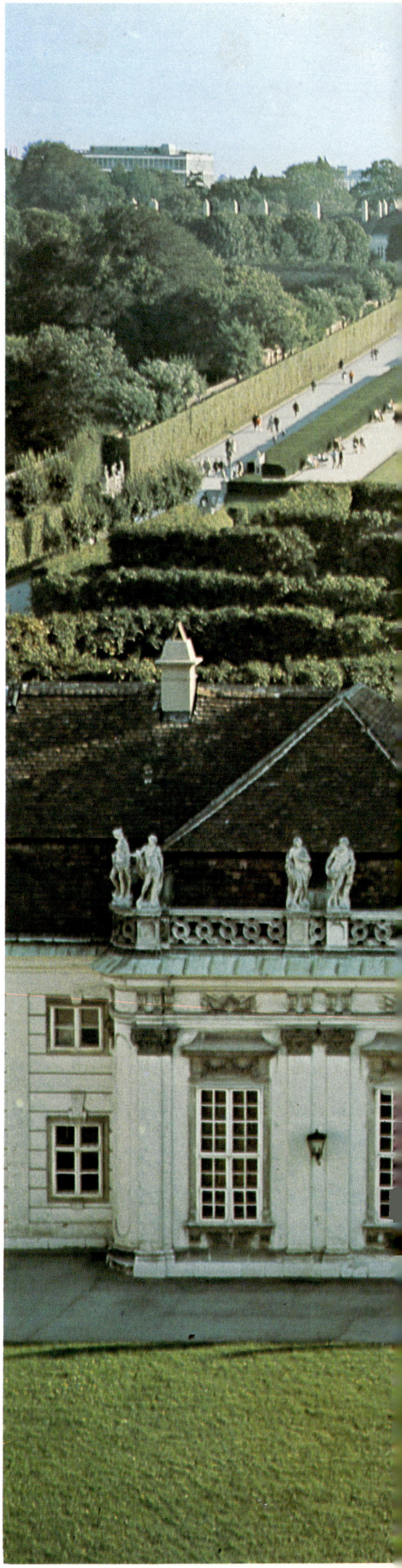

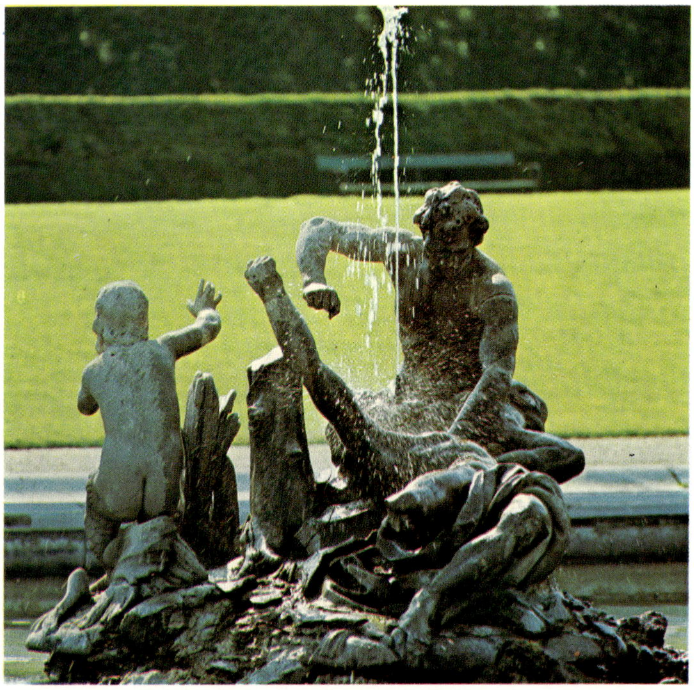

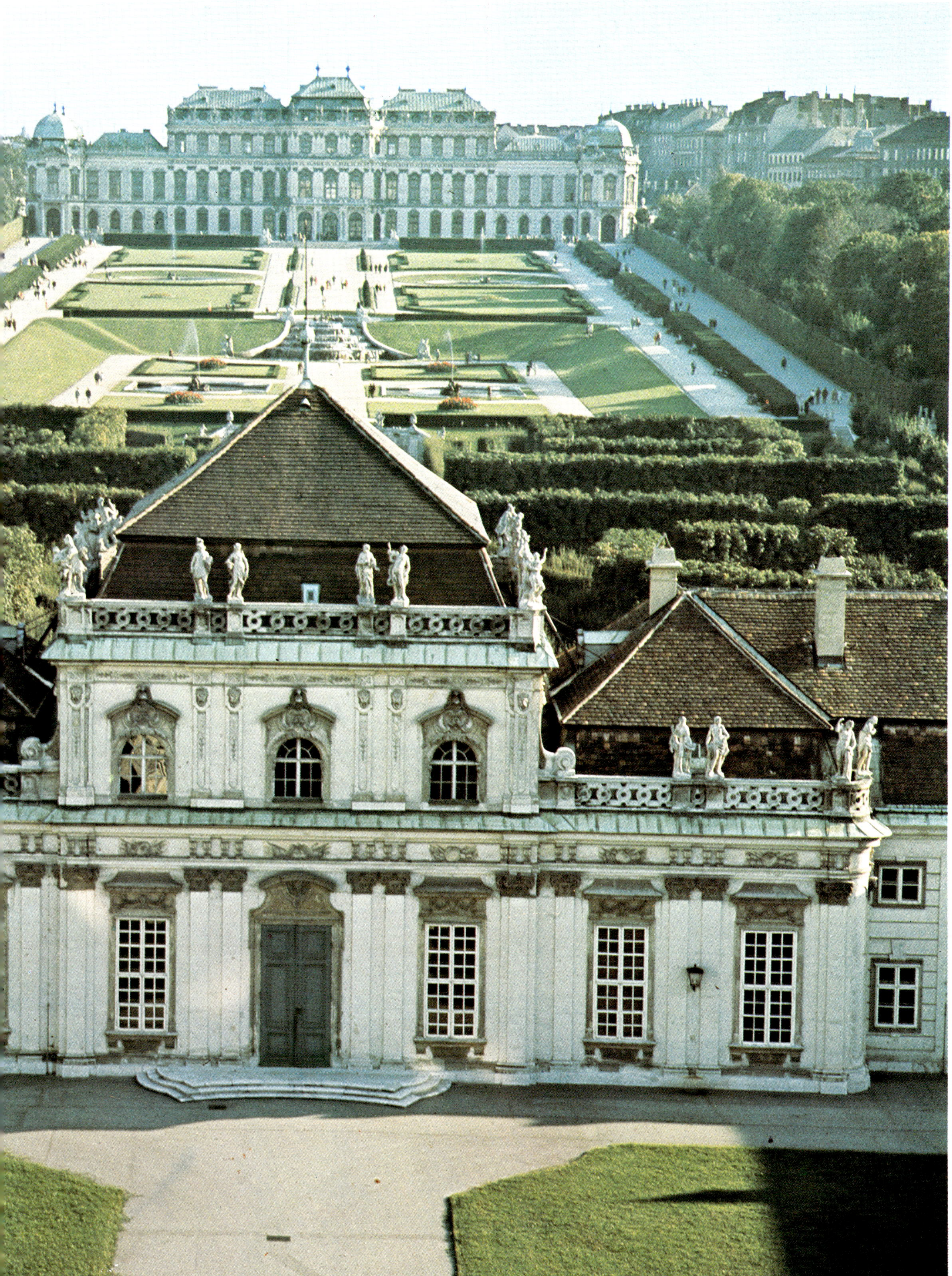

Above left, the vaulted Hall of the Giants in the Upper Palace, which opens directly onto the garden. The staircase in the background leads up to the sala terrena *(facing page). The giants supporting the arches of the vault (detail above) symbolize military strength. The bases of the arches they carry are surrounded by war trophies. Left, one of the stucco cherubs that support the lanterns on the white staircase. Top, detail of the balustrade of the staircase.*

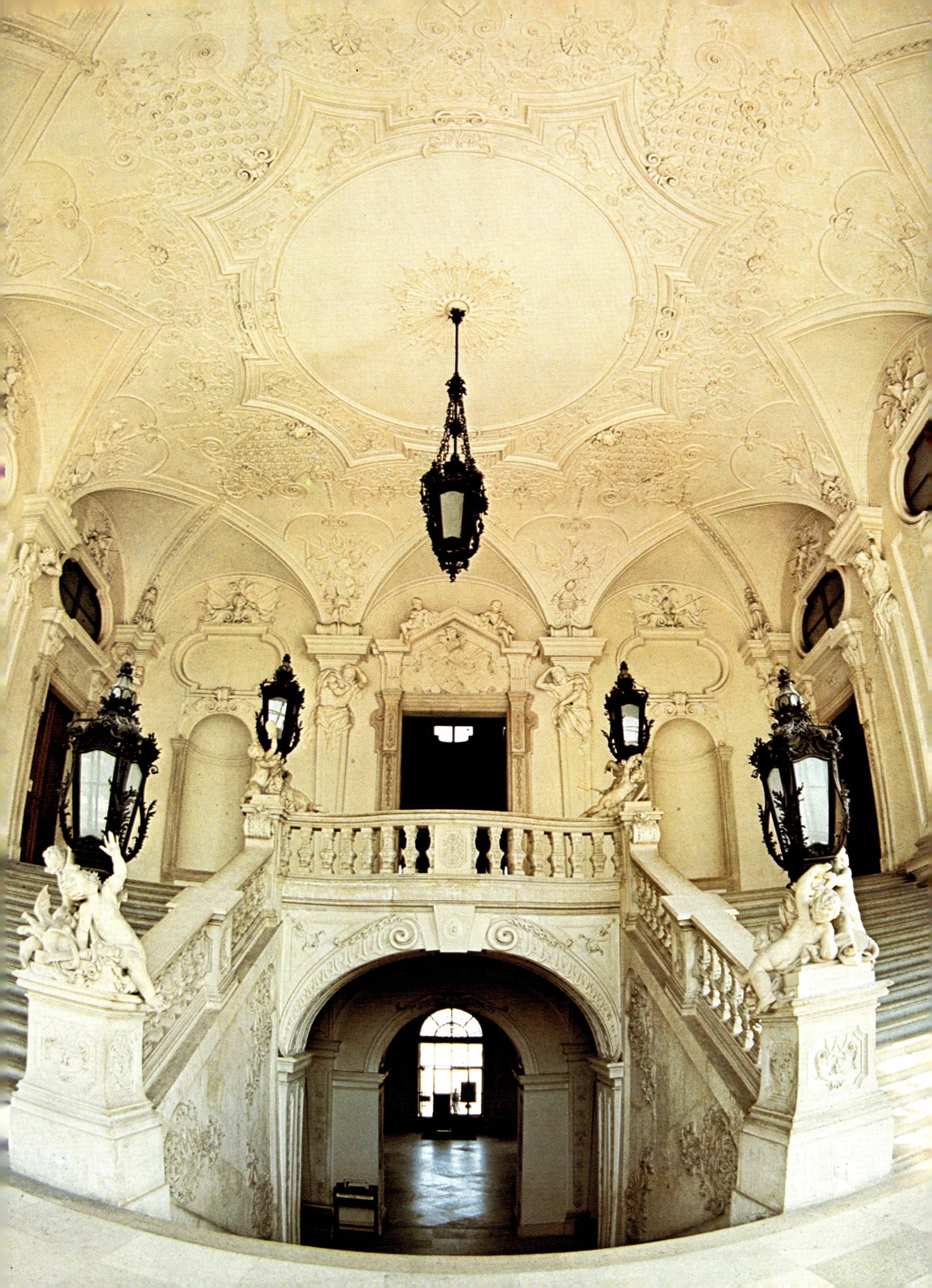

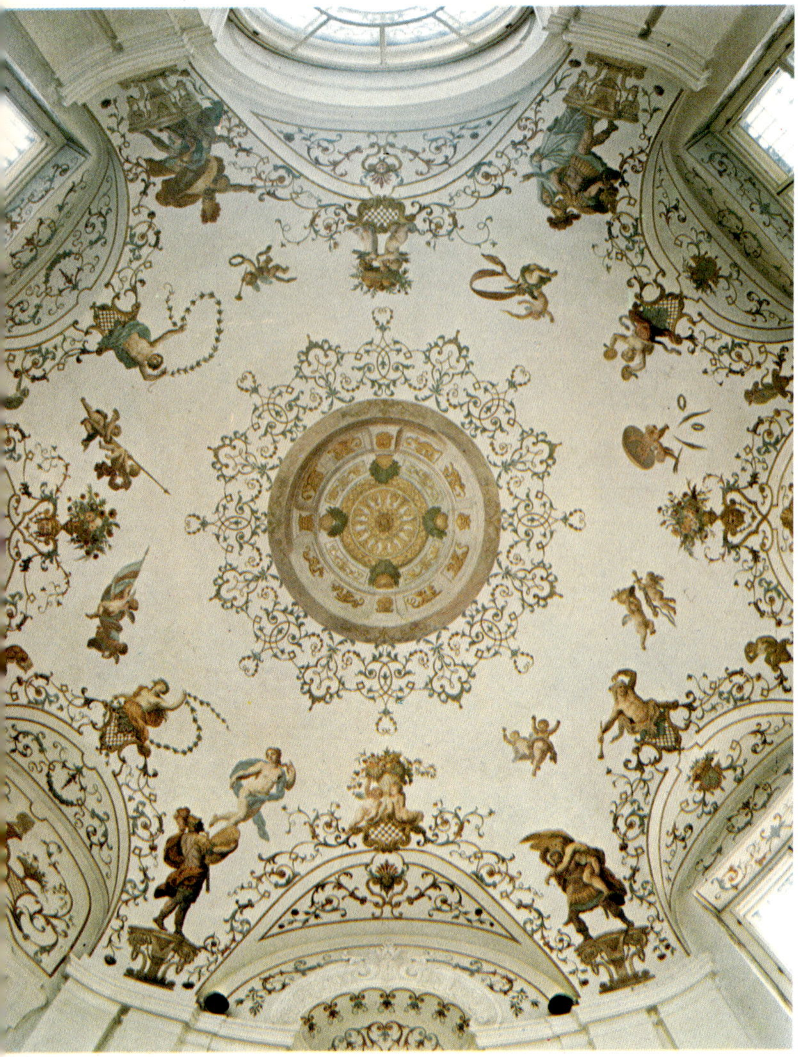
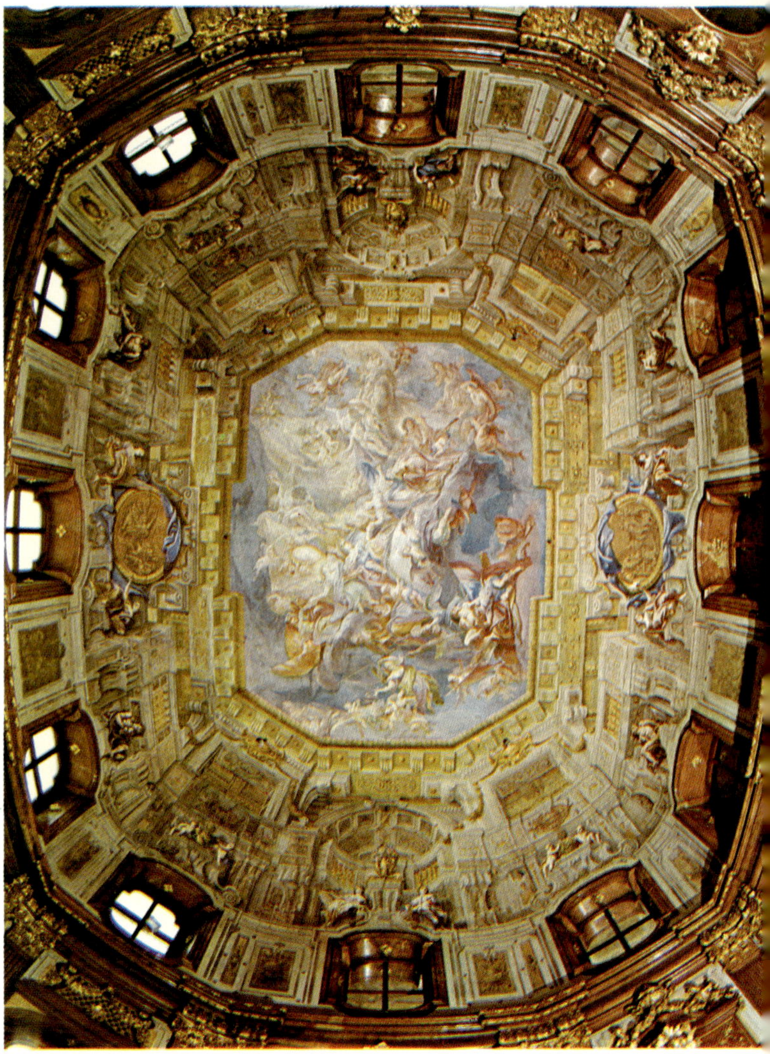
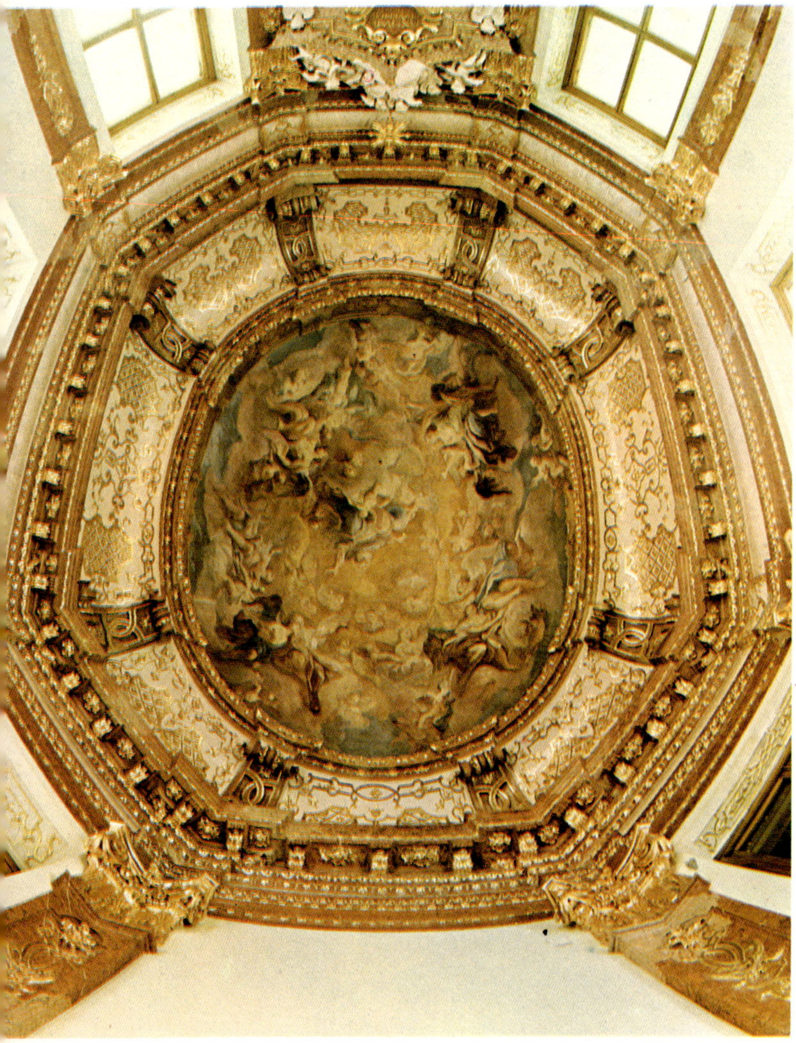
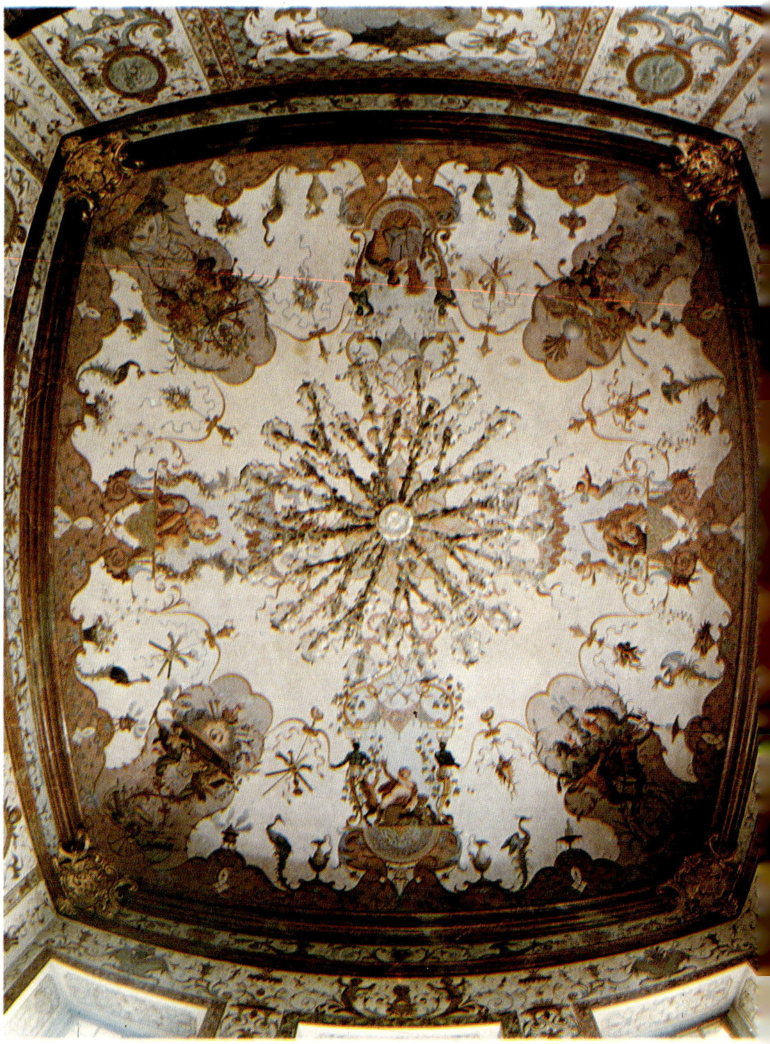

Facing page, four frescoed ceilings at the Belvedere. Clockwise from above left, the ceilings are from: an octagonal ground-floor room in one of the end pavilions on the garden side of the Upper Palace, decorated in a "Roman" style by Jonas Drentwitt; the more Baroque central hall of the Upper Palace, decorated by Carlo Carlone; the Hall of Grotesques in the Lower Palace, executed by Jonas Drentwitt; and the chapel of the Upper Palace, also by Carlo Carlone.

Above, the reception hall of the Upper Palace. The fresco by Carlo Carlone on the ceiling depicts the allegory of Apollo and Diana. Other frescoes in the palace, such as the octagonal room by Jonas Drentwitt (right), are less specific allusions to Eugene's military glories.

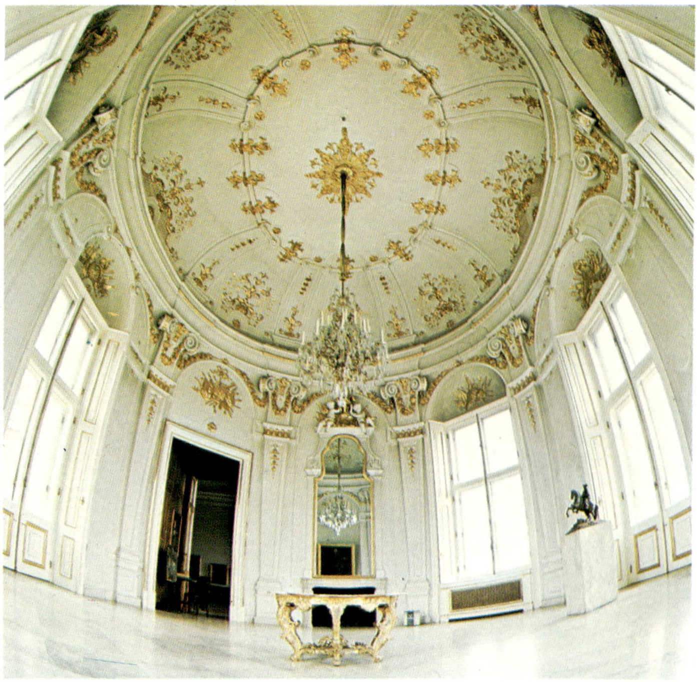

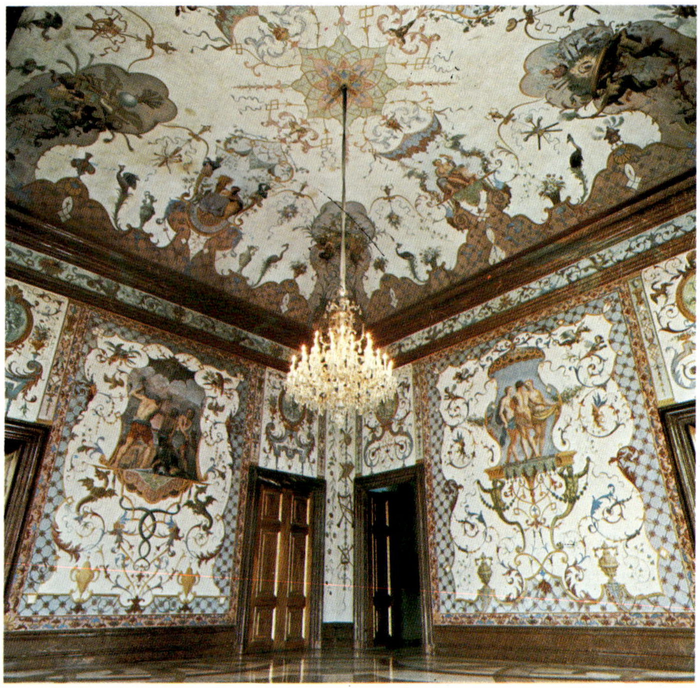

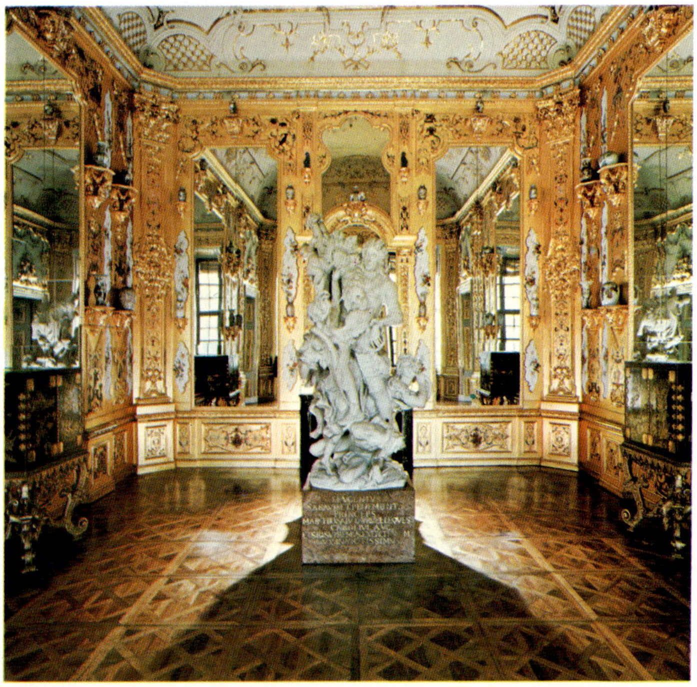

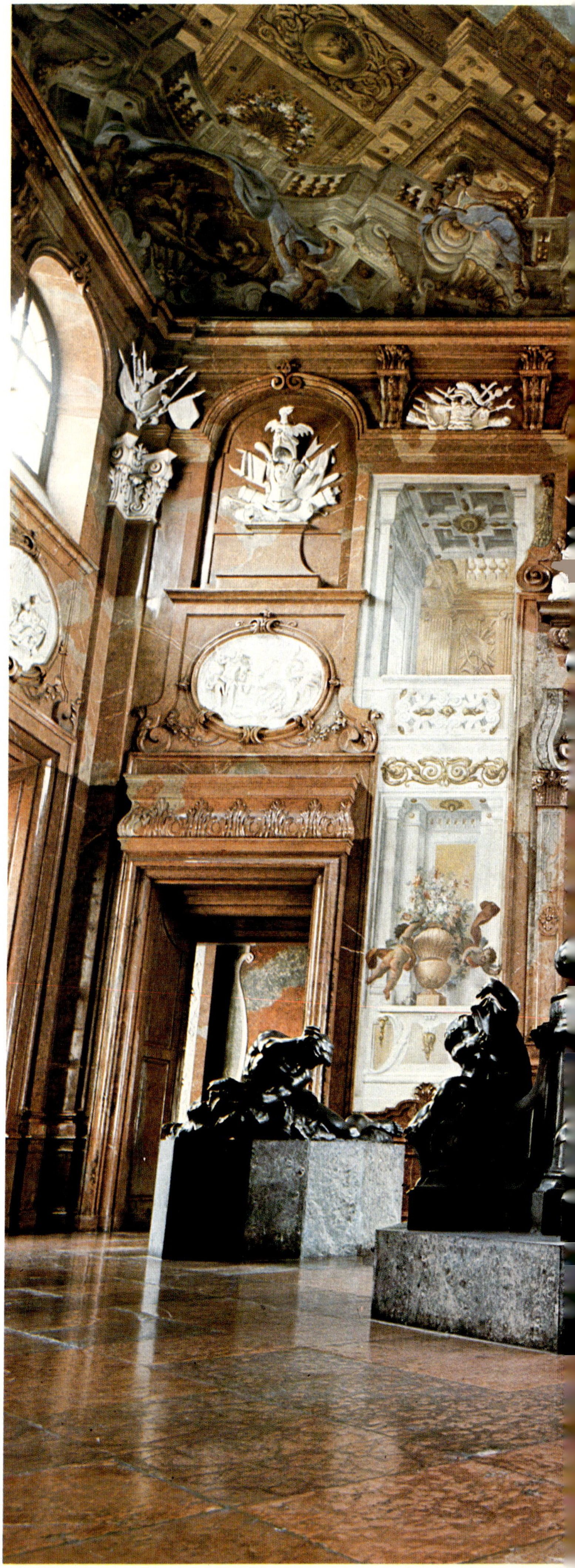

Far left, from top to bottom: the interiors of one of the tower pavilions on the main floor of the Upper Palace facing the garden; the Hall of Grotesques; and the Golden Cabinet of the Lower Palace. The Lower Palace is today the Museum of the Austrian Baroque, and many of its halls are considered exhibits in themselves. The vestibule (left and above) also contains lead statues by Georg Raphael Donner—the originals of the bronzes which still adorn a fountain in Vienna's Neuer Markt.

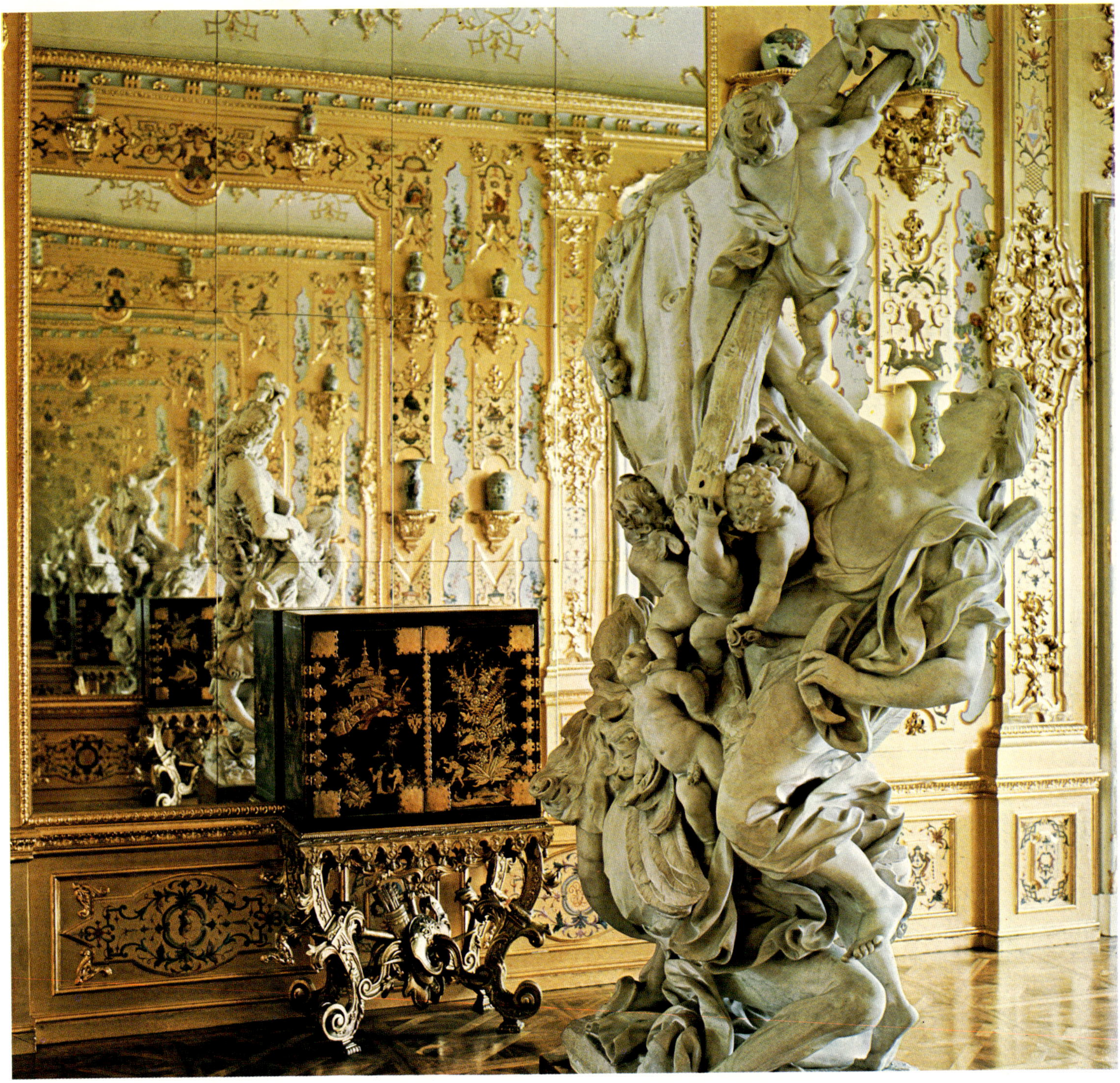

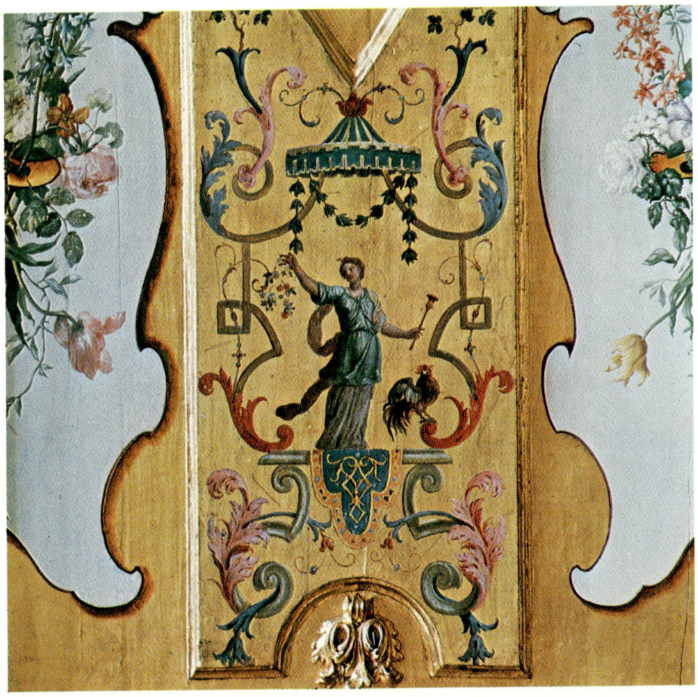

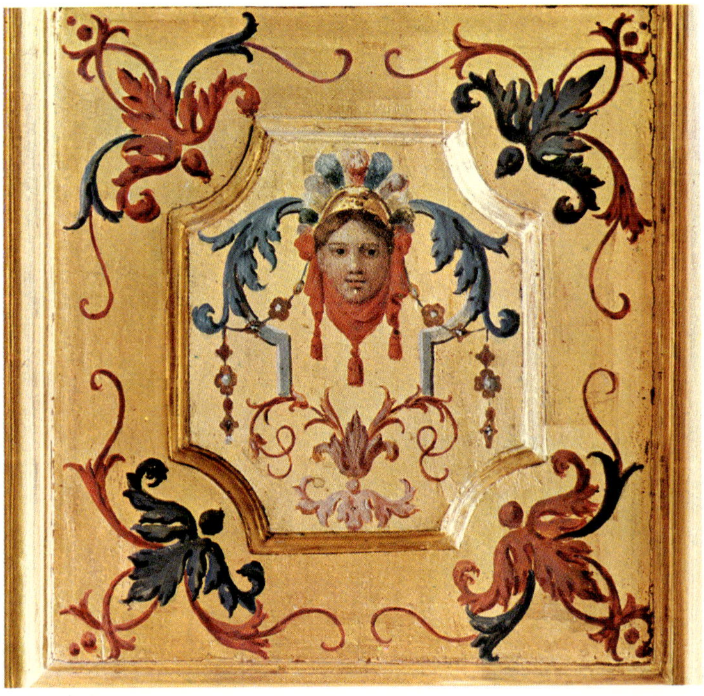

Facing page, the Golden Cabinet. Parallel mirrors create a dizzying regression of gold and glass. The statue represents the apotheosis of Prince Eugene. The decor was further enriched by Maria Theresa. Below, details of the painted gilt walls of the Golden Cabinet.

Right, a statue, completed in 1766, of Empress Maria Theresa, wearing the regalia of queen of Hungary. Maria Theresa purchased the Belvedere some years after Eugene's death. Below left, an equestrian statue of Eugene. Below right, detail of a table in the Golden Cabinet. The table, which dates from the time of Eugene, exhibits the typically Rococo tendency to enliven every surface with decoration.

Following page, the south façade of the Upper Palace, overlooking the reflecting pool. Today, the arcades of the façade are glazed.

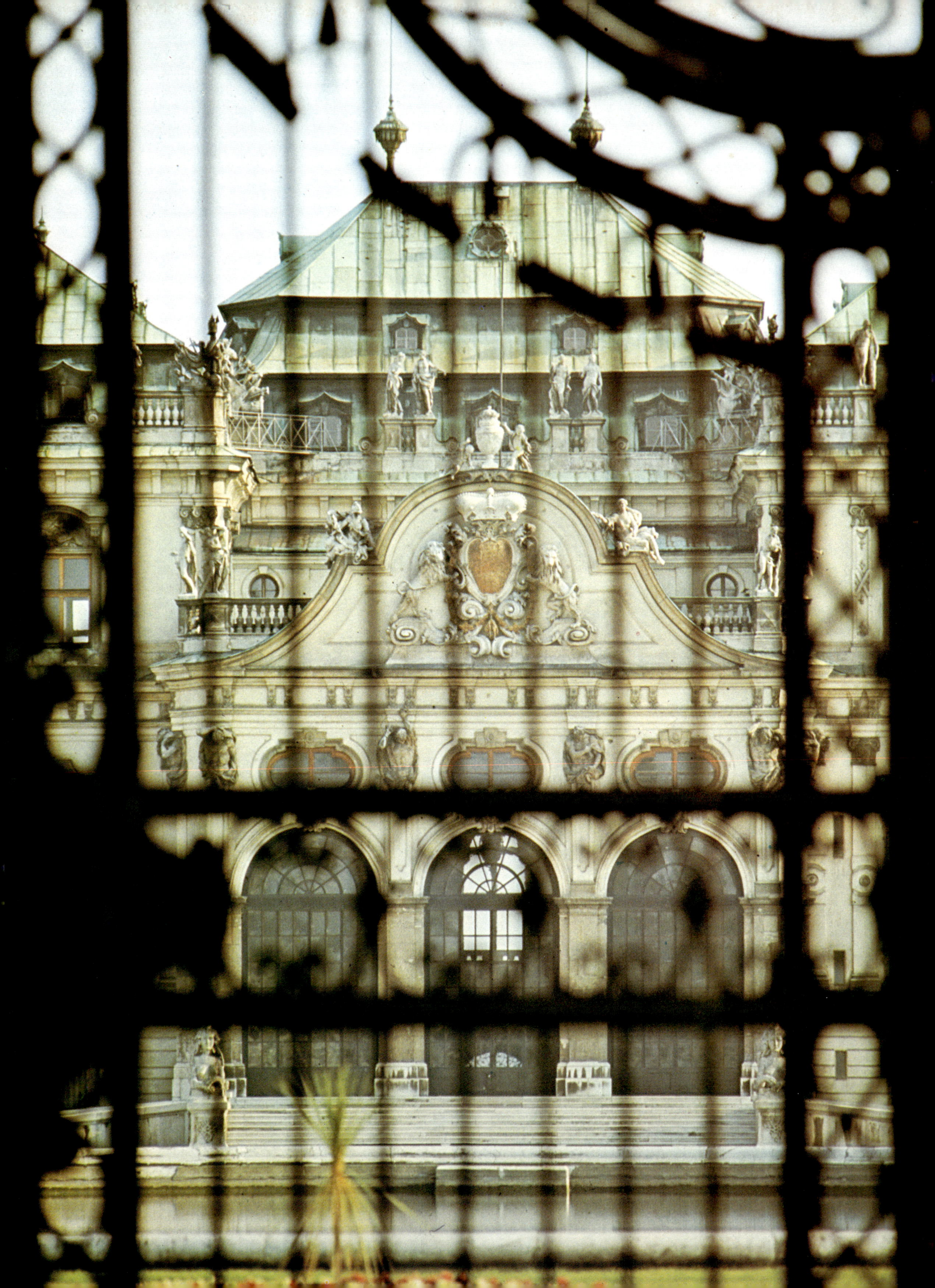

The Belvedere
Austria

One of the most opulent and flamboyant of architectural styles, the Baroque flourished in Europe during the seventeenth and early eighteenth centuries. In Austria, it is characterized by a particular vitality and exuberance.

For more than a century, Austria had struggled fitfully against the threat of domination by the Ottoman Turks, until the enemy was at last repulsed from the gates of Vienna in 1683. The joyful relief that was felt throughout the nation was immediately reflected in an enthusiasm for building and restoration. Where the Turks had wreaked havoc and destruction, the Austrians built churches, royal palaces, and splendid mansions. Thus, the Austrian Baroque spread from the valley of the Danube throughout every province of the Hapsburg dominions. Even in the remotest valleys, the common people followed the example of the elite with enthusiasm. Village bell towers were topped with onion-shaped domes, and scrolled pediments adorned the windows of modest country inns.

Pomp and splendor were the watchwords of the Baroque. The show of wealth and prestige was not only an end in itself but also a symbol of power and prominence. In religious buildings, the Baroque expressed the triumph of the Counter Reformation, the ascendancy of the Church of Rome over Protestantism. In the homes of royalty and the nobility, Baroque architecture was an affirmation of absolute authority, designed to overawe the populace with its display of wealth and brilliance.

The Belvedere Palace in Vienna is the quintessence of this Baroque conception of princely sovereignty. But it is more than an impressive monument to money and power. It also mirrors the personal ideals and preoccupations of its founder, Prince Eugene of Savoy. It illuminates the thoughts and desires of the young soldier who rose to glory despite his physical disadvantages and his unhappy early years spent in the France of Louis XIV.

When Louis XIV became king of France in 1643 at the age of five, the regent, his mother Queen Anne, confirmed the wily Cardinal Mazarin in the office of prime minister and virtually handed him the reins of government. Mazarin, a brilliant statesman, was the center of political intrigue and conspiracies at the court. For reasons of his own, he sent for his sister's three children to join him in Paris. One of them became a favorite playmate and, in time, the amorous consort of the young king. Her name was Olympe Mancini.

Court gossip suspected Mazarin of hoping to marry his niece to the sovereign. However, a politician of his subtlety and vision could not seriously have entertained such a scheme, given the insuperable obstacle of their unequal birth. After Louis had outgrown his youthful—if not so innocent—diversions with Olympe, the girl departed from the royal apartments with impeccable political credentials, to bestow her hand on the Count of Soissons, Prince

The Belvedere was a favorite subject for painters and engravers. Below, one of the innumerable early views of the southern façade of the Upper Palace.

of Savoy. The count was a general in the French army. His frequent absences left Olympe ample freedom to pursue her liaison with the king. However, her political machinations led to her eventual banishment from the kingdom.

Olympe was the mother of eight children. Eugene, the youngest (who was suspected by many to have been a natural son of the king), was born in Paris on October 18, 1663. Eugene of Savoy was a homely child. The Duchess of Orleans wrote of him: "He was small and ugly, with an upturned nose and flaring nostrils, and an upper lip so narrow that he cannot shut his mouth." She added: "He has two large teeth which are visible all the time. He is always dirty and has lanky hair, which he never curls." Possibly as much on account of his unfortunate looks as his mother's intrigues, Eugene was excluded from the French court. When he was just ten years old, Louis decided to have him prepared for a life in the church.

Eugene himself was determined to be a soldier. He engaged in a rigorous program of riding, fencing, and gymnastics to develop his strength and stamina. However, when the young Prince of Savoy requested a commission in the army, Louis refused his petition.

Humiliated, the young prince took a fateful step. In 1683, he left Versailles and offered his services to the Austrian emperor Leopold I. Leopold's domains were severely threatened. The Turkish army was at the gates of Vienna. In the west, Louis XIV had just taken Strasbourg and was hungry for more German territory.

Eugene had much to recommend him to Leopold. As a member of the House of Savoy, he was a prince of the Holy Roman Empire and thus eminently suited to defend the Christian faith against the infidel. Moreover, his brother, Louis Julius, had recently met a hero's death while fighting the Turks in Lower Austria. And Eugene had been spurned by Louis XIV, who was Leopold's adversary. Leopold, therefore, graciously welcomed Eugene to his refuge at Passau in eastern Bavaria. He immediately placed Eugene in charge of a campaign to divert the Turkish siege of Vienna.

Eugene's valor and military genius were soon widely recognized and rewarded. At the age of twenty-one, he was decorated with the Golden Spurs and was given command of the regiment of dragoons of Kufstein. At twenty-two, he was named major general; at twenty-seven, commander in chief of the cavalry; at thirty, an imperial field marshal; and finally, president of the Imperial War Council.

His success was prodigious, even for a prince of a reigning house, but it was well merited. His campaigns against the Turks culminated in the Battle of Tisza. The battle ended Turkish hopes in Europe and won for Eugene the name of savior of Christianity and Western civilization.

These honors and promotions were accompanied by prestige and wealth. The Hapsburgs showered him with titles, money, and land. Having arrived in Austria with only twenty-five guilders to his name, Prince Eugene was by the age of thirty a rich and powerful man. His estate at the time of his death was valued at twenty-five million guilders.

Eugene loved Vienna and made it his

In 1731, Solomon Kleiner published an entire volume of engravings of the Belvedere. This volume was the source of these two views of the Hall of the Giants, the vestibule of the Upper Palace that leads to the gardens. In the upper engraving, the artist has erroneously replaced the real ceiling with one based upon that of the adjacent entrance portico.

Left, an eighteenth-century view of the Belvedere gardens.

home. However, he never used German, relying solely on his French, both in writing and conversation. He built two palaces for himself, one in the center of the city, just steps away from the Hofburg, the imperial court, and a second on the outskirts of town. (It was then customary for members of the aristocracy to spend the summer only a few miles from their winter residences.) But Eugene did not retire to civilian life; on the contrary, he continued to win great military successes. In fact, at the same time as he was planning his new palace, the Belvedere, he was also campaigning victoriously against the armies of Louis XIV in the War of the Spanish Succession (1701–14).

Eugene began to acquire the land for his country estate when he was only thirty. The site he chose for this palace was a sloping pasture. The palace is known as the Belvedere ("beautiful view"). On the crest of the hill, the Upper Palace commanded a sweeping panorama of the woods of Vienna stretching eastward to the plains of the Danube. The location, overlooking the scene of Eugene's earliest victories, may have been a nostalgic choice, though traces of the Turkish encampments had long since disappeared. Moreover, hilltops appealed to the Baroque imagination since they were considered appropriate Olympian sites for those elect spirits who guarded the destinies of entire nations.

The Belvedere reflects Prince Eugene's sensitivity and refinement rather than his enormous fortune—although the palace and gardens can scarcely be called utilitarian. In fact, the Belvedere consists of not one but two palaces, one cresting the slope and the other at its foot, separated by acres of spacious gardens. Yet, Prince Eugene spent little time at the Belvedere. On those rare occasions when he was in residence, he occupied only a few rooms in the Lower Palace. Having little inclination for the rituals of court life, he had no need for vast numbers of reception rooms or assembly and banquet halls. Instead, he continued to be absorbed by military matters and affairs of state until his death and spent his few leisure moments in the company of artists, philosophers, and men of science. The philosopher Leibnitz was among his close friends. In his rare peaceful years between the Peace of Passarowitz in 1718, which finally thwarted the ambi-

Eugene of Savoy served as general to three emperors. In his long career, he suffered defeat only once, at the hands of Vendôme at Cassano. The greatest strategist of his time, he was surpassed as a tactician only by his friend and ally, the Duke of Marlborough. Napoleon ranked him among the seven commanders who had contributed most to the art of warfare. This engraving (above) shows Eugene in armor which, by his time, was more emblematic than functional.

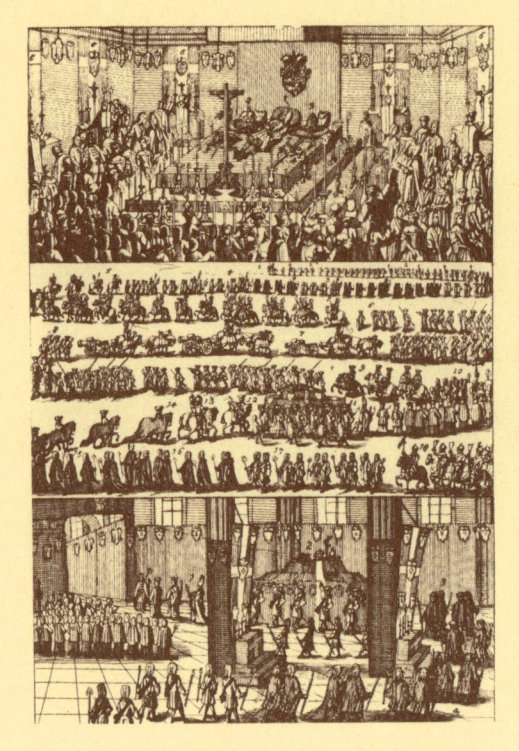

Eugene died in 1736 at the age of 73. His embalmed body, dressed in regimental uniform, lay in state for three days. In accordance with contemporary custom, his heart was sent to Turin to be buried with his Savoy ancestors. The funeral procession (above) took three hours to reach the nearby St. Stephen's Cathedral.

Above right, a broad sheet published by Elias Baeck eulogizing the dead prince.

Eugene established one of the largest zoos of his time, collecting over fifty species of mammals. He was particularly interested in wild birds (below), and he fed his eagles by hand whenever he was at the Belvedere.

tions of the Turks, and the start of the War of the Polish Succession in 1733, Prince Eugene spent his time reorganizing the army and collecting works of art.

But Eugene did not erect the Belvedere as a museum. He wanted above all to build a monument to himself. True to the spirit of the times, he commissioned a palace that both embodied his era's taste for magnificence and celebrated his own glory. Eugene had himself represented as a handsome, fiery Apollo on one of the ceilings of the palace—just as Louis XIV was depicted at Versailles.

The palace gardens also reflect the power and status of the prince. The vagaries of nature are dominated and controlled. All is measure and proportion. The gardens are laid out geometrically to echo and complement the adjoining buildings. In their formality and integration with the palace complex as a whole, they follow the vogue for the French gardens popularized by the work of Louis XIV's landscape architect André Le Nôtre at Versailles.

The parterres—formal planting beds—closest to the Upper Palace, although once more elaborate, have always been open and mostly treeless. Statues and decorative urns accent the clear and spare design, divided by neat symmetrical paths. Still pools mirror its vast spaces, and an artificial waterfall exemplifies the Baroque fascination with flowing, swirling water. Near the Lower Palace, the parterres of hedges and squarely pruned shrubs, aligned in perfect order, underline the geometry of the design. Formal but not portentous, and festive but not frivolous, the palace and its gardens were conceived as a harmonious unity, displaying an idealized, refined, and perfected nature.

The arrangement of the Belvedere, with its two facing palaces, is unique in all Europe. The huge Upper Palace commands the hill. The Lower Palace below is smaller and more intimate—by princely standards. Architecturally balanced, the palaces are linked by the central axis of the sloping garden, the "spine" that also unifies the design of the garden. Any undue emphasis or oddity of detail is lost in the overall impression of order and harmony.

The design of the Belvedere resulted from a fertile collaboration between

Prince Eugene and his architect Johann Lucas von Hildebrandt. Hildebrandt had served under the prince as field architect in the imperial army in the Piedmontese campaigns of 1695 to 1696. Of Italian extraction, he had studied firsthand the works of the great Italian Baroque and Mannerist architects in northern Italy and Rome. In 1700, he was appointed court engineer. He later became a leading court architect and was employed by many noble Austrian families. Moreover, the talented and superior craftsmen employed by Eugene and Hildebrandt worked with exceptional skill and inventiveness. Most of these artists were Italian, including Martino Altomonte, Carlo Carlone, Gaetano Fanti, Santino de Bussi, Francesco Solimena, and Giacomo del Po.

The Lower Palace was built between 1714 and 1716. Typically Baroque in conception, it is, however, less flamboyant than the Upper Palace. Primarily a single story in height, the building has a distinctive horizontal emphasis, which is enlivened by its interesting roof line. The only truly dramatic element is the grand en-

Above, below, and center, three eighteenth-century views of the Upper Palace. The Upper Belvedere, with its shimmering reflecting pool and geometric garden, was conceived as a magnificent architectural gesture, reflecting the Baroque fascination with stunning effects.

102 • Individual Creations

From top to bottom: the entrance façade of the Upper Palace; the garden façade; the plan of the upper floor; the plan of the main floor (left); and the plan of the ground floor (right).

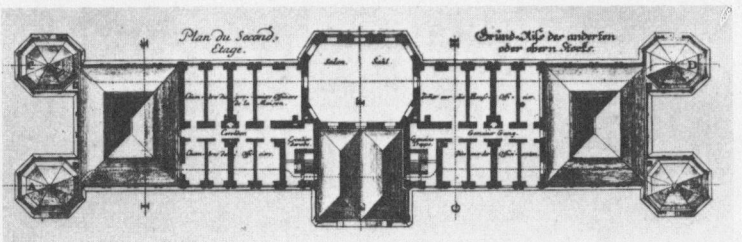

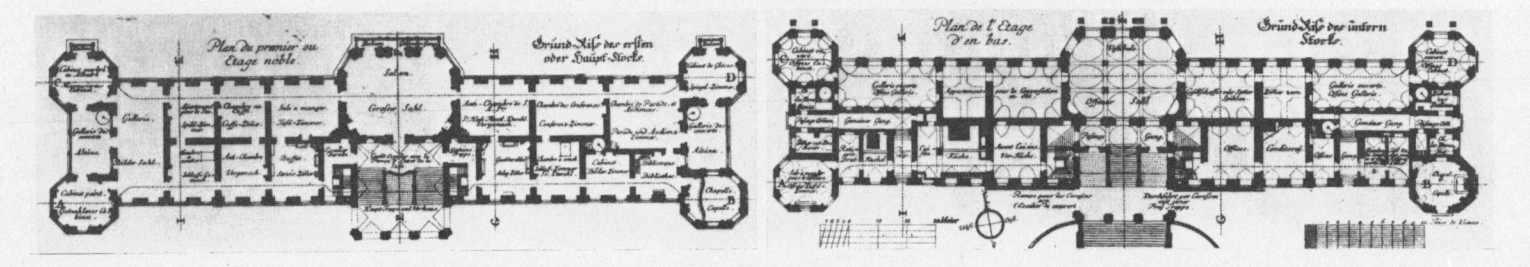

trance salon, which projects out slightly from the quietly elegant façade into the spacious courtyard. Despite the urns, military trophies, cherubs, and allegorical figures representing the prince's wisdom and strength, the predominant effect is one of simplicity.

Neither the gardens nor the exterior of the palace hints at the splendor within. In the vaulted entrance hall, the dusky rose sheen of the marble floor and walls contrasts with the glow of the ivory-colored plaster work and gilded moldings that rise in tiers to the frescoed ceiling. To the right and left stretch suites of halls which, with their doors arranged on a central axis, create a magnificent effect of spaciousness.

Today, the Lower Palace houses the Museum of the Austrian Baroque. The rooms have been preserved as Eugene knew them: the Hall of Grotesques; the Hall of Mirrors, with its outstanding collection of Chinese vases; the dining room, decorated in red and white (the colors of the House of Savoy, whose family coat of arms was a white cross on a red field); and the study, with its doors, columns, and walls shining with gold leaf.

The bold stroke of crowning the garden with the Upper Palace did not figure in the original plan for the Belvedere. The idea only matured in 1715, and the Upper Palace was actually completed in 1724.

For this palace, Eugene merely indicated a general idea. He left the chief responsibility to Hildebrandt, and the architect surpassed himself. A single glance reveals its distinctive grace. Supremely confident of the lasting value of his masterly creation, Hildebrandt did not hesitate to repeat motifs from the Belvedere in later commissions. Lantern-bearing cherubs, for example, are also to be seen in the main staircase of his Palais Kinsky, scarcely a mile away.

The three-story central section of the festive Upper Palace is flanked by wings of two stories. The outer corners of each of these wings end in domed octagonal pavilions, which evoke the military image of

From top to bottom: two longitudinal sections of the Upper Palace cut through the entrance vestibule and through the Great Hall, and two transverse sections cut through the central axis (left) and through one of the wings (right). The main entrances from the forecourt and the garden are linked by a stairway, which also leads to the Great Hall overlooking the garden.

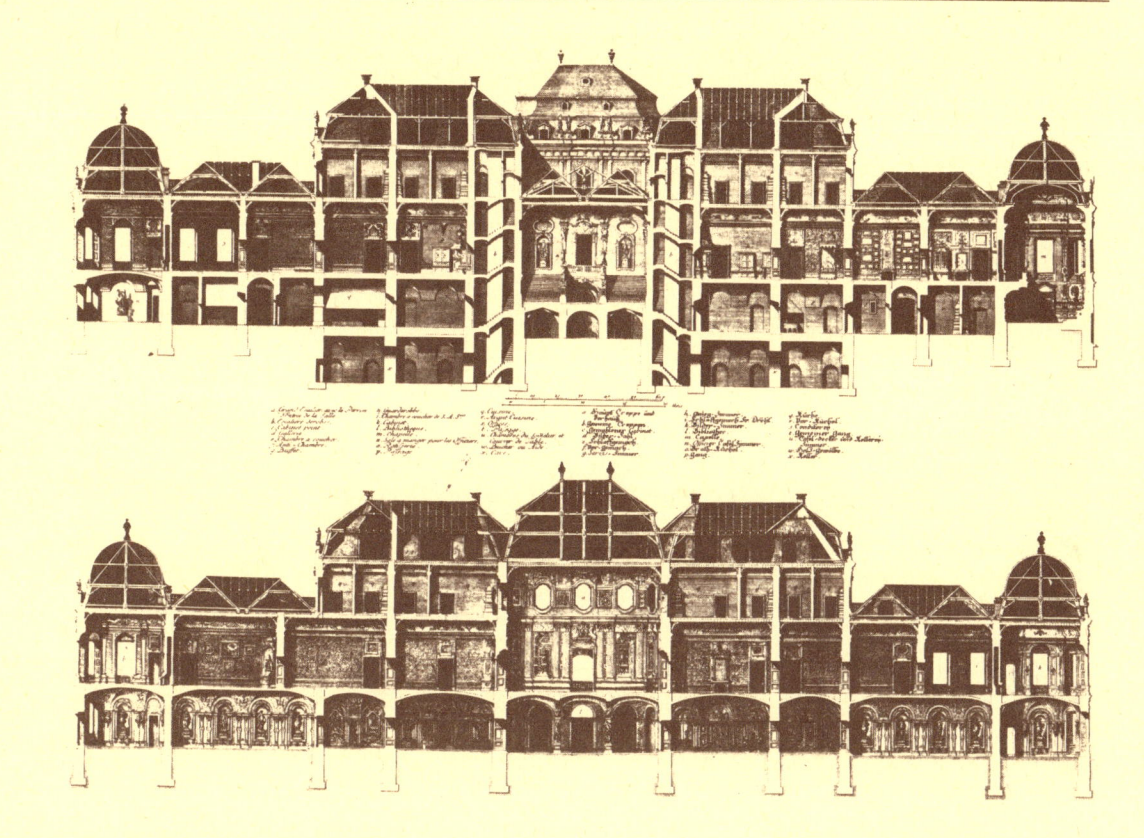

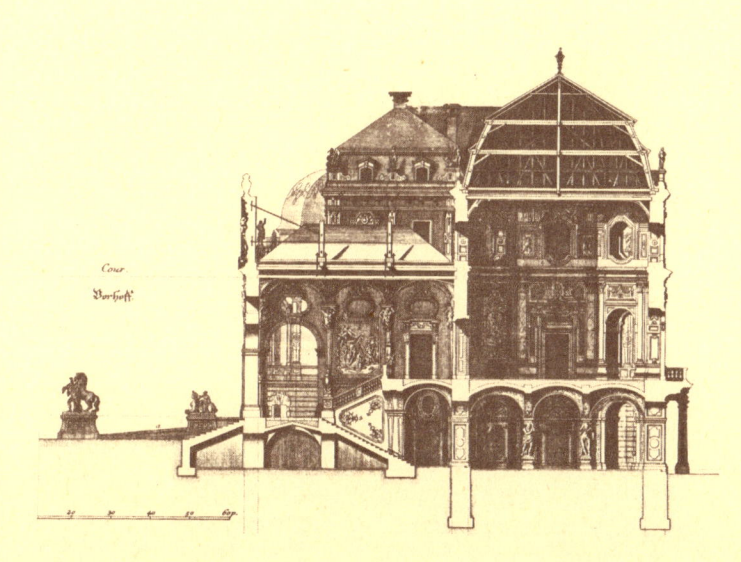

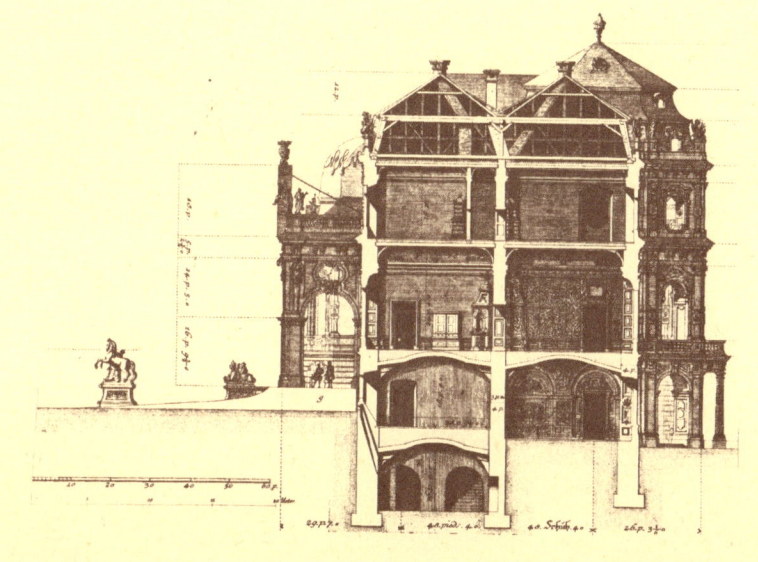

the corner towers of a castle. In the center, above the entrance hall, the patined copper roof rises like a pagoda. Decorative details—expanses of cunningly wrought stucco balustrades in stately progression, a profusion of marble statuary, and military "trophies"—suffuse the façade with a mellow autumnal richness.

At the entrance to the palace stands a colossal wrought-iron gate, decorated with lions and cherubs displaying princely arms and coronets. The awesome mass of the palace rises beyond. Its reflection in the huge pool lends it a distant and ethereal air. The path to the palace follows the perimeter of the wide stretch of water, so that as one approaches the palace, the constantly changing angle of vision gradually transforms the fantasy of the shimmering image into the solid reality of the giant piers, pilasters, and entablatures.

The interior of the Upper Palace matches the magnificence of the façade. The theme of the building—the exaltation of the grand and enormous—is echoed in the four colossi by Lorenzo Mattielli that carry the vault of the once-open portico overlooking the garden.

The ceaseless insistence upon dazzling and stunning effects is also reflected in the central double staircase. Plump cherubs holding outsize lanterns light the way to the splendid Hall of Marble on the main floor. Here, in the light that floods through two lofty rows of windows, white medallions and gilt moldings gleam against the red marble of the columns and cornices. The trompe l'oeil perspectives of the painted wall panels and the frescoed cupola, with its Olympian vistas of seated deities, have the effect of further increasing the vastness of the hall. Scorning intimacy, the hall reflects the Baroque love for the grand gesture and public spectacle. The vistas glimpsed through the doorways into receding suites of richly decorated rooms invite the visitor to embark on voyages of discovery.

Today, the Upper Palace houses a collection of modern Austrian paintings, including many by Gustav Klimt, whose gilded and rapturous compositions blend well with the Baroque spirit of the palace as a whole.

Modern visitors are amazed at such sumptuous expansiveness in a bachelor's residence, a "second" summer home. The ubiquitous allegories of strength and power at the Belvedere—the festoons of chains, the giants in the atrium, banners, arms, and military trophies—have been seen as the prince's attempt to compensate for his poor physique and homely appearance: the Baroque penchant for mythologizing cannot fully explain the deceptive flattery of his deifying portraits.

Prince Eugene died in 1736—not at the Belvedere but at his city residence in Vienna. He left no direct descendants. His entire fortune, including the Belvedere, fell to his niece, Princess Anna Victoria of Savoy. Within a few years, the princess had sold whatever she could. Eugene's patiently collected treasures were scattered to the ends of the earth. In 1752, however, the empress Maria Theresa put an end to the depredations by purchasing the palace.

The Hapsburgs used the palace for official receptions and, on occasion, as a residence for members of the imperial family. And it was at the Belvedere, in 1770, that a splendid farewell ball marked the departure from Vienna of one of the empress's sixteen children, Marie Antoinette.

In the following century, the Belvedere served as the imperial picture gallery until Archduke Ferdinand adopted it as his residence. From there, he and his wife set out in 1914 on an official tour of the Slovenian, Serbian, and Croatian territories of the Austro-Hungarian Empire. They never returned. Their assassination at Sarajevo triggered the carnage of World War I, which put an end to the Hapsburg monarchy. Since the war, the Belvedere has been a state museum.

But the Belvedere's days of pomp and circumstance have endured beyond the end of the empire. Its imposing halls have witnessed several events of enormous consequence in the modern age. On November 20, 1940, according to Hitler's express wish, Germany, Hungary, and Italy signed their tripartite pact in the central hall of the Upper Palace. And in May 1955, another treaty was signed there restoring the independence of the Republic of Austria after seventeen years of foreign occupation. On that occasion, a huge crowd of Viennese celebrated their regained freedom in the gardens of the Belvedere—gardens which owed their very existence to the liberation of their city nearly three centuries earlier.

The Belvedere's garden was opened to the public in 1800. It almost immediately became a popular place for leisurely promenades (above).

Below, Vienna as seen from the Belvedere. Just right of center is the spire of St. Stephen's Cathedral, where Eugene's body lies in a private burial chapel.

Sagrada Familia

Spain

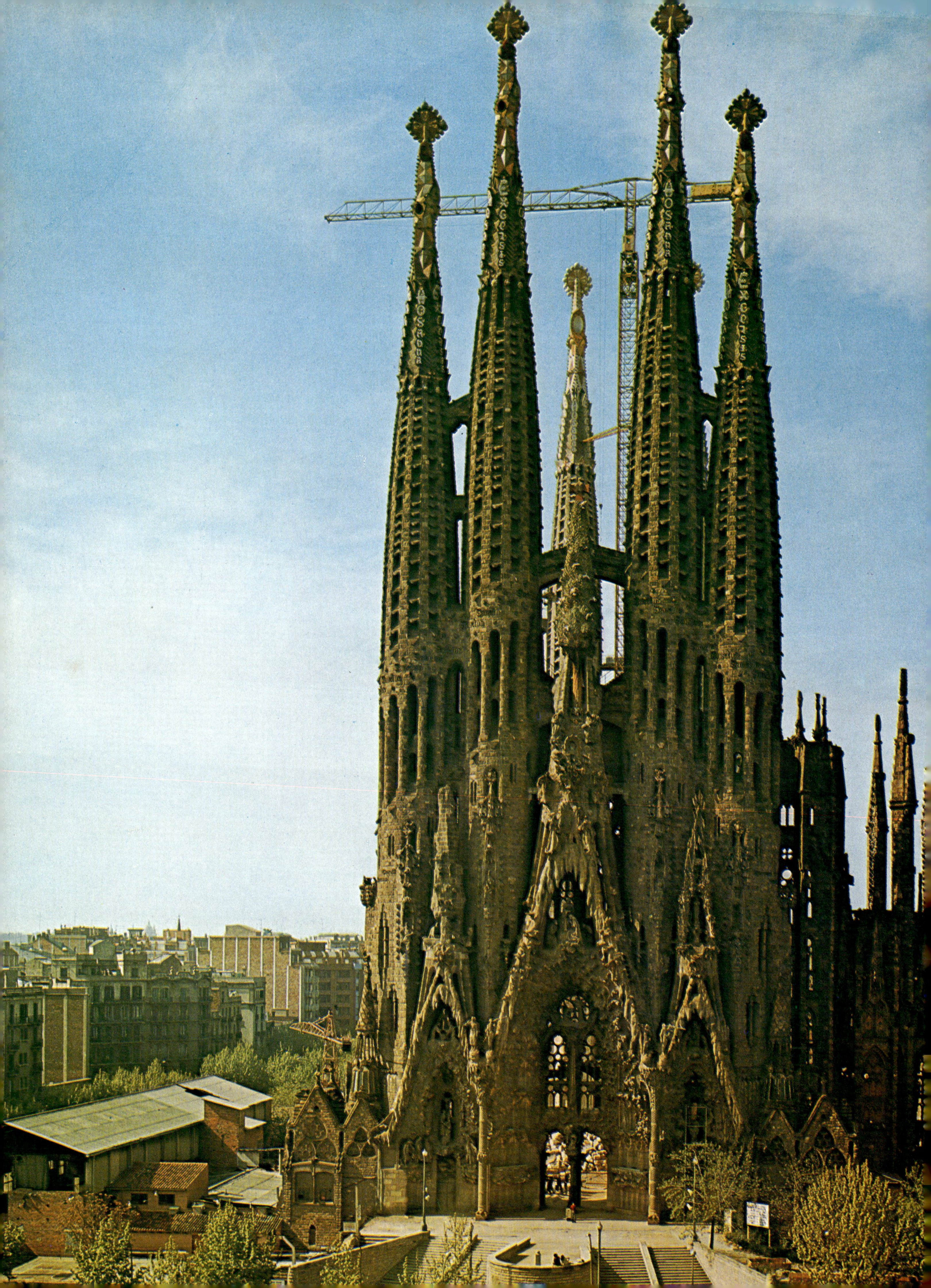

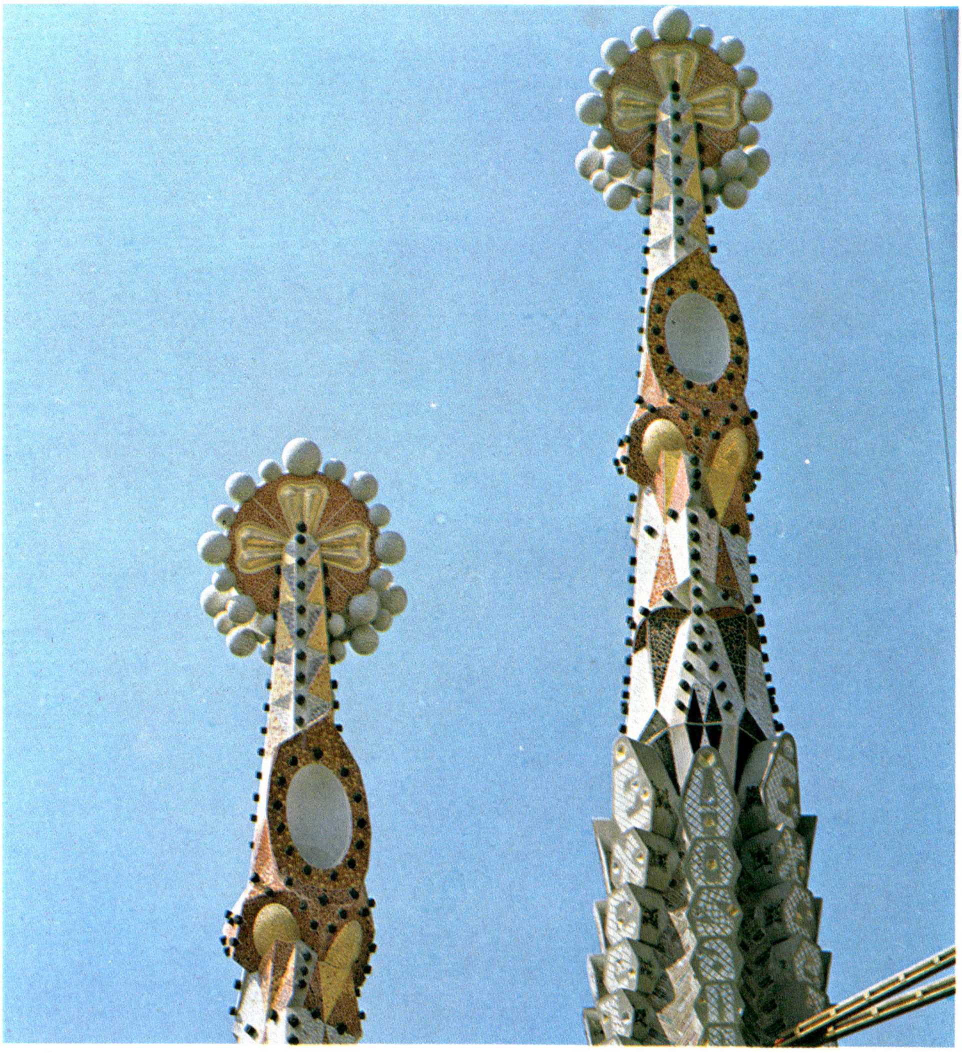

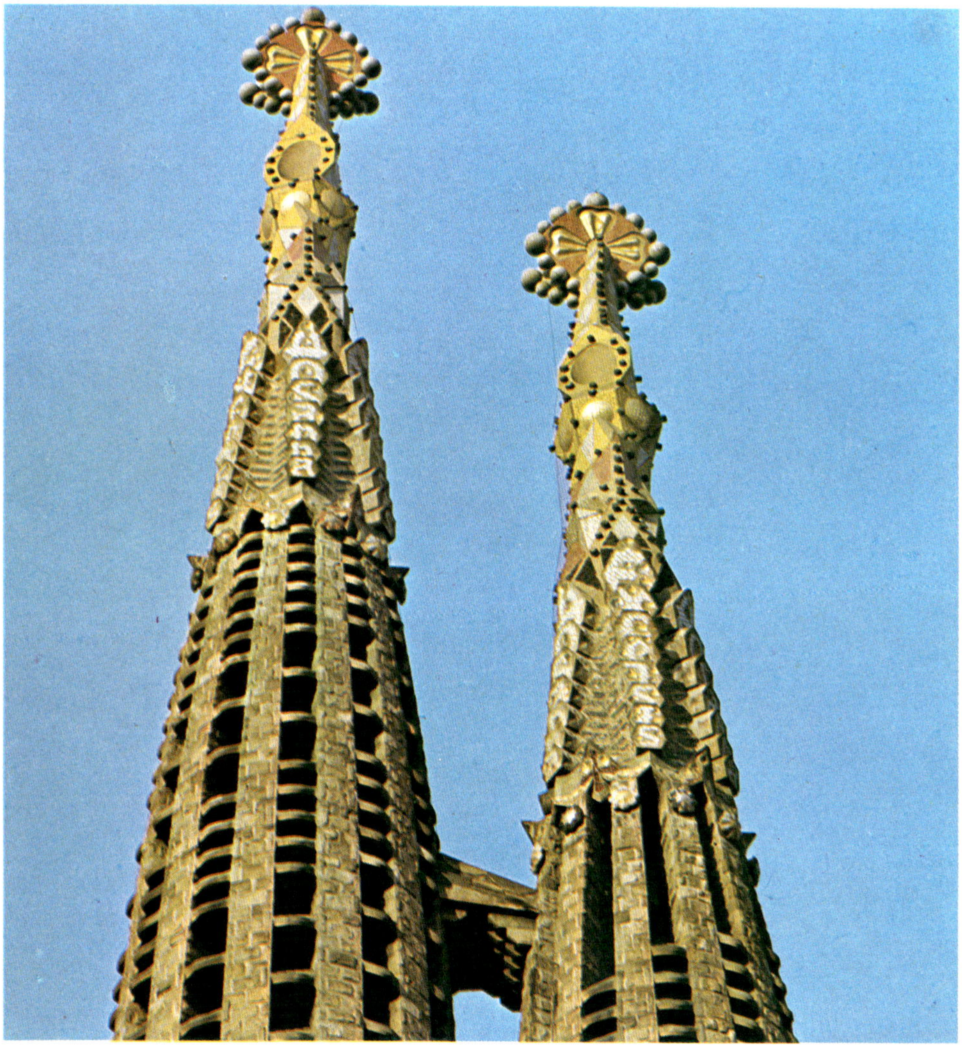

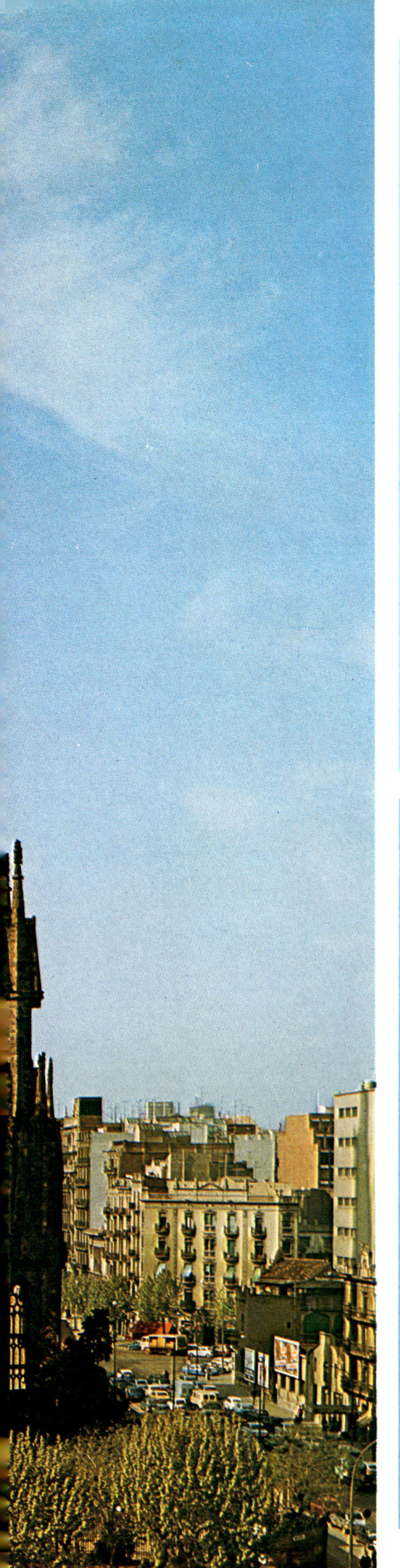

Preceding page, the northeastern façade of the Sagrada Familia, dedicated to the Nativity, with its slender mosaicked spires. The unfinished church transcends stylistic classification and has been termed "a ruin of the future." At present, the church consists of this façade, the crypt, and the exterior wall of the apse—all begun by Gaudí or his predecessor—as well as the façade of the Passion, which was begun after World War II.

Left, the delicate towers of the Sagrada Familia soaring above the Barcelona skyline. Gaudí's plan called for twelve such towers, arranged in groups of four, symbolizing the Apostles.

Facing page, the Nativity portal, with details (below). Sculptural scenes of the birth of Jesus are framed by sinuous arrangements of vines and plants which recall the Catalan Modernista style.

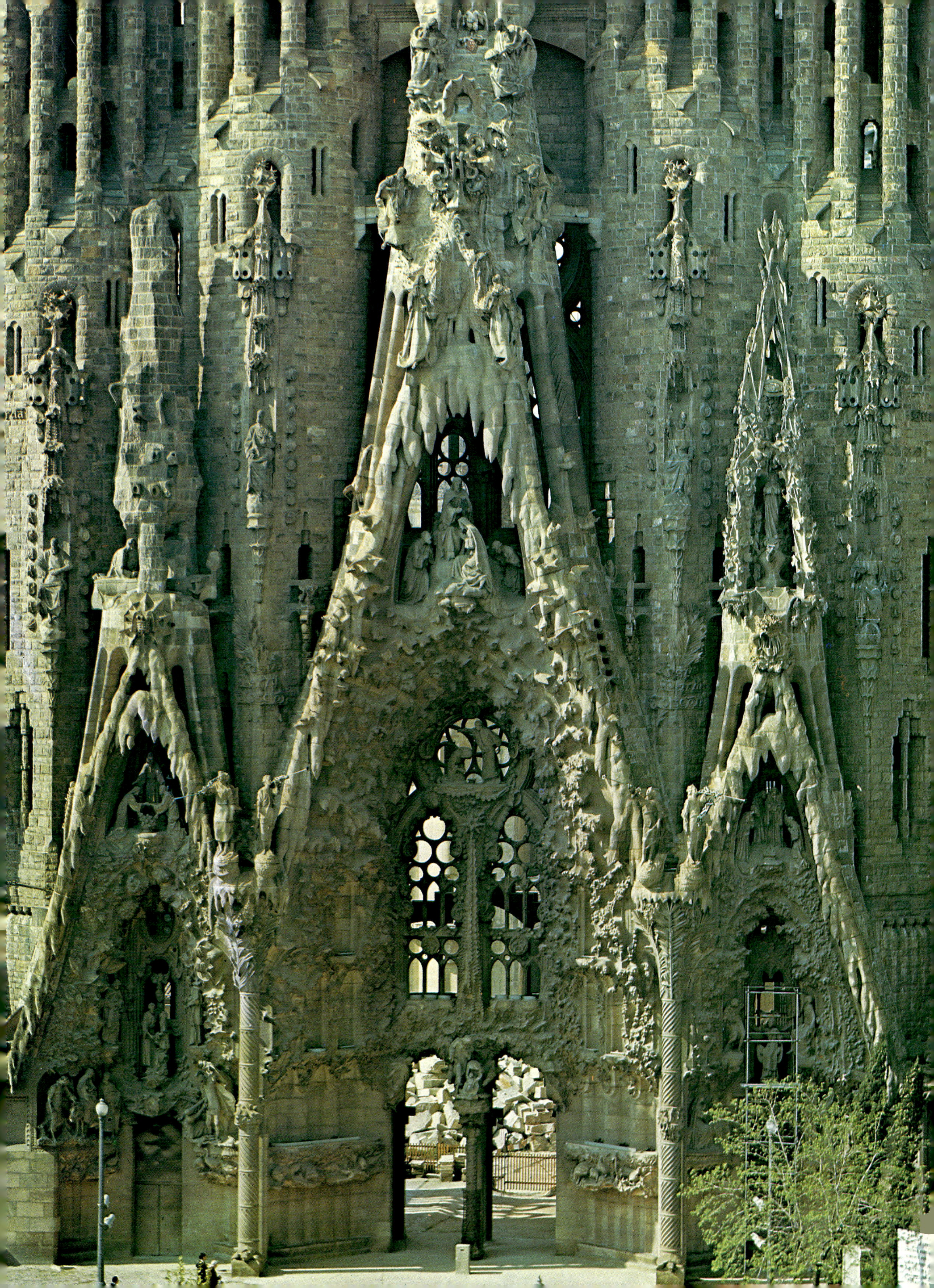

The elaborate decorativeness of the Nativity portal takes many forms. Many of the sculptures illustrate scenes from the New Testament, such as the birth of Jesus (right) and the killing of the first-born (below), and are framed by exquisite and intricate carvings of leaves and tendrils (above). Further examples of the wealth of ornamental inventiveness are to be seen in the shaft of a column (far right, center), from which the name "Maria" projects gracefully, and, in contrast, the prickly top of one of the lesser pinnacles (far right, below).

Far right, above, the Nativity rose window tracery, held in place by temporary supports.

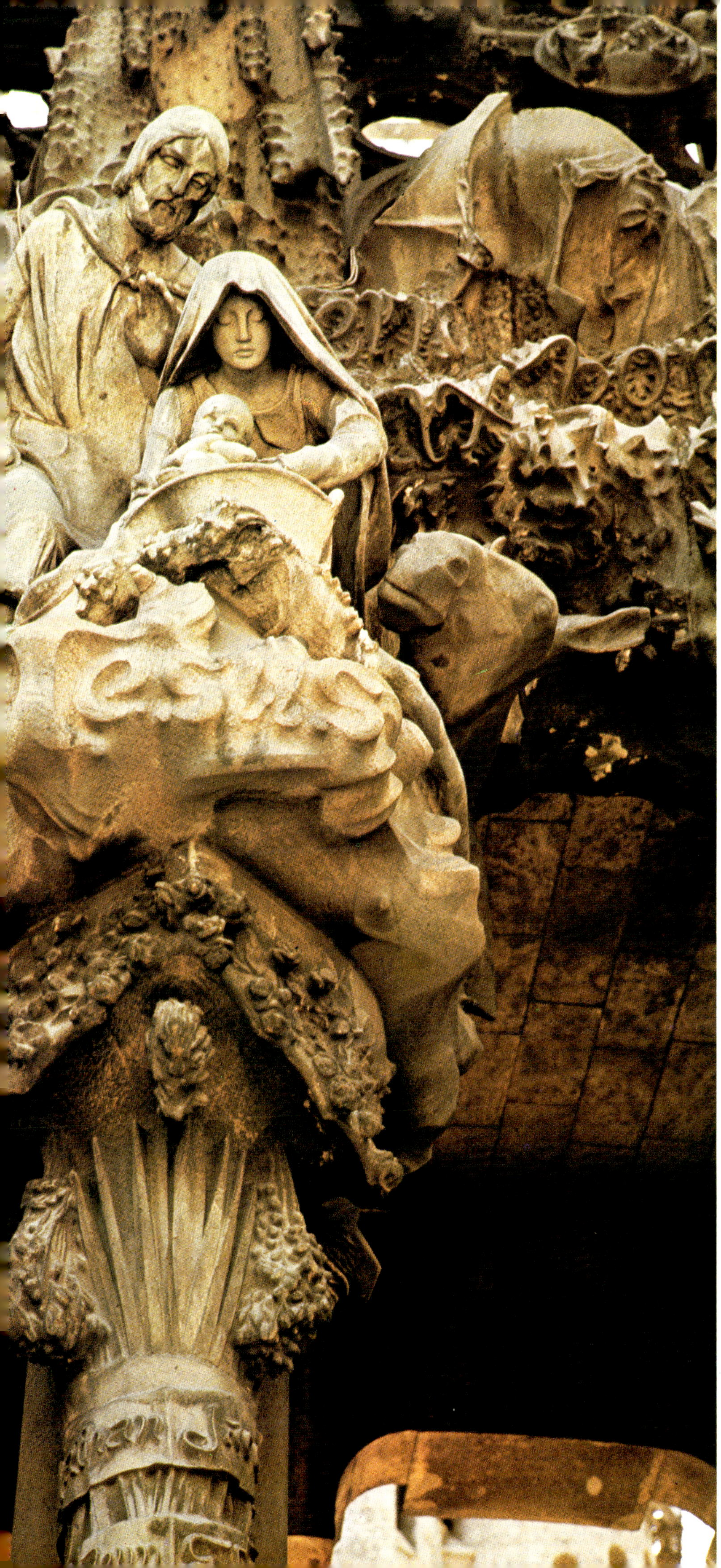

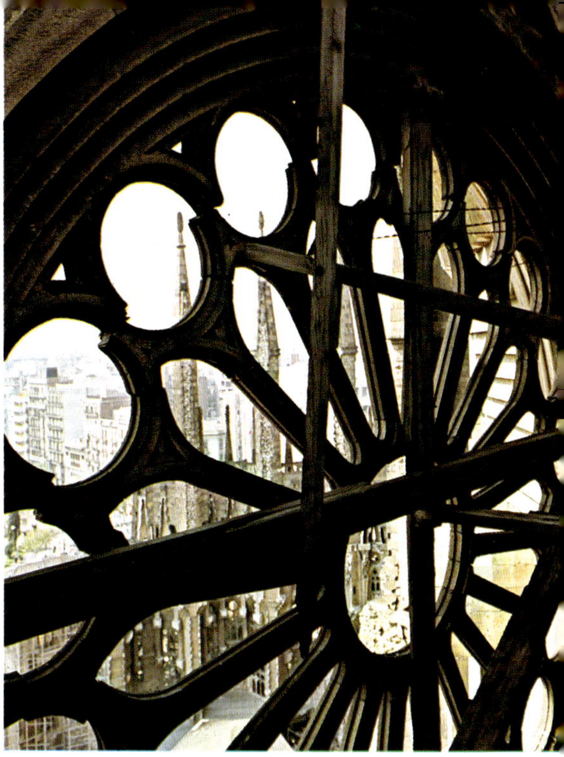

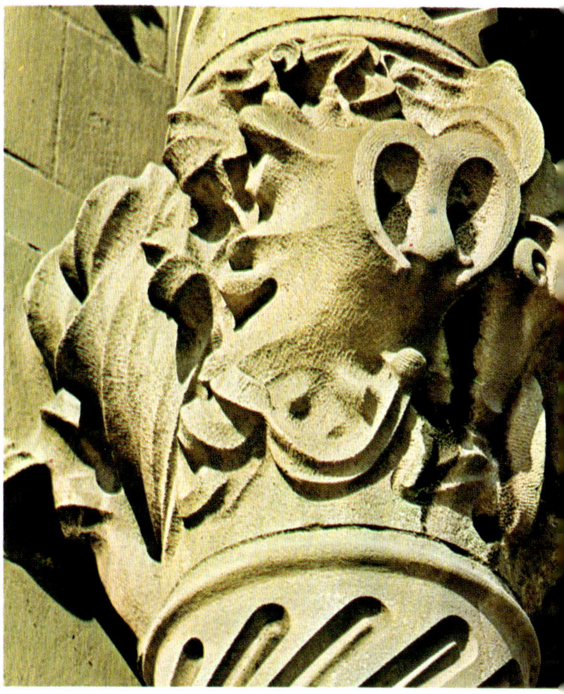

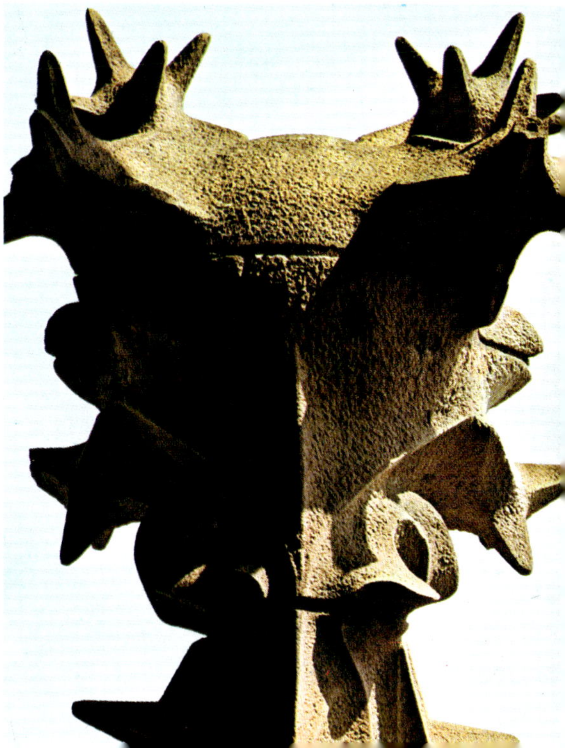

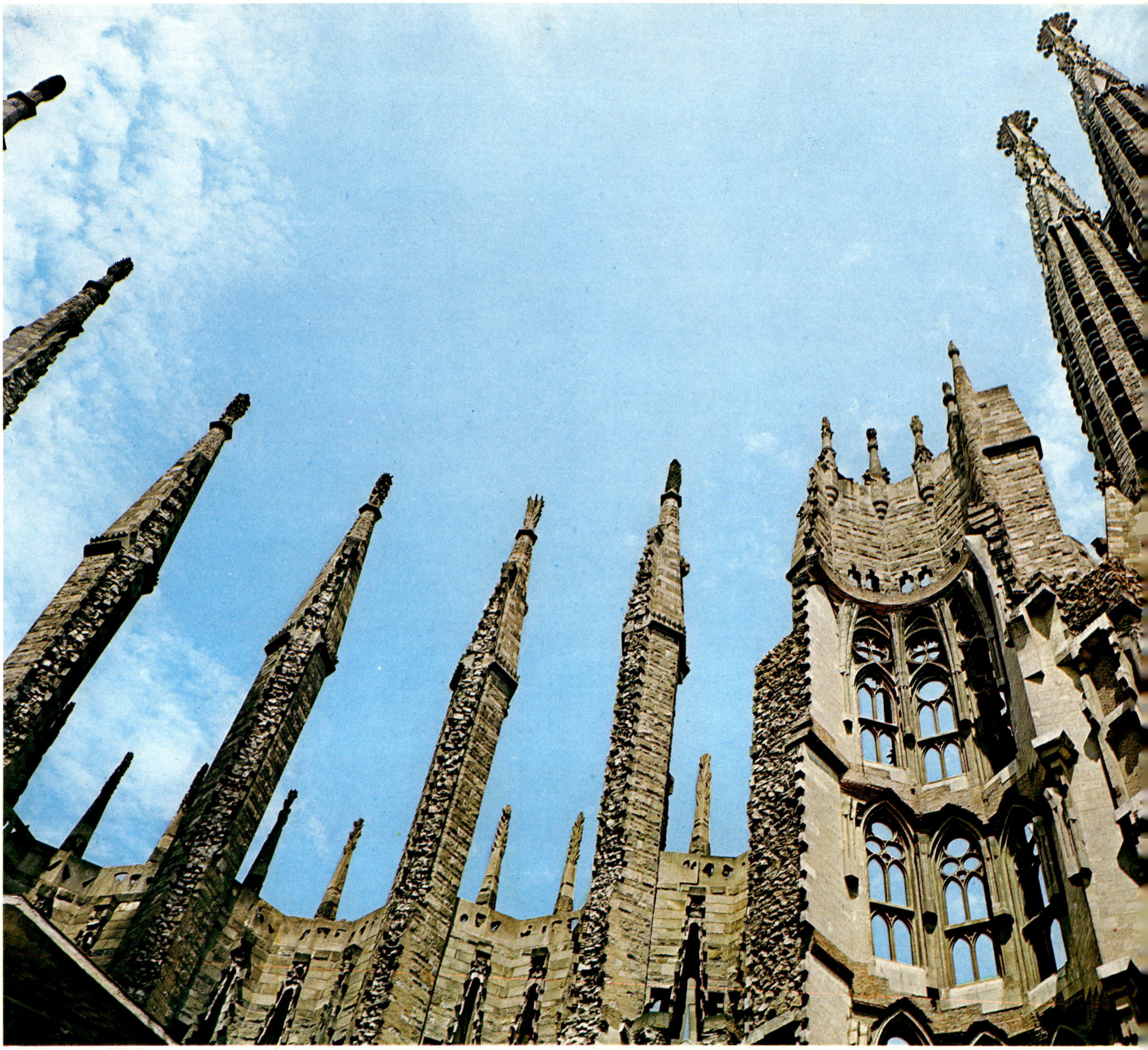

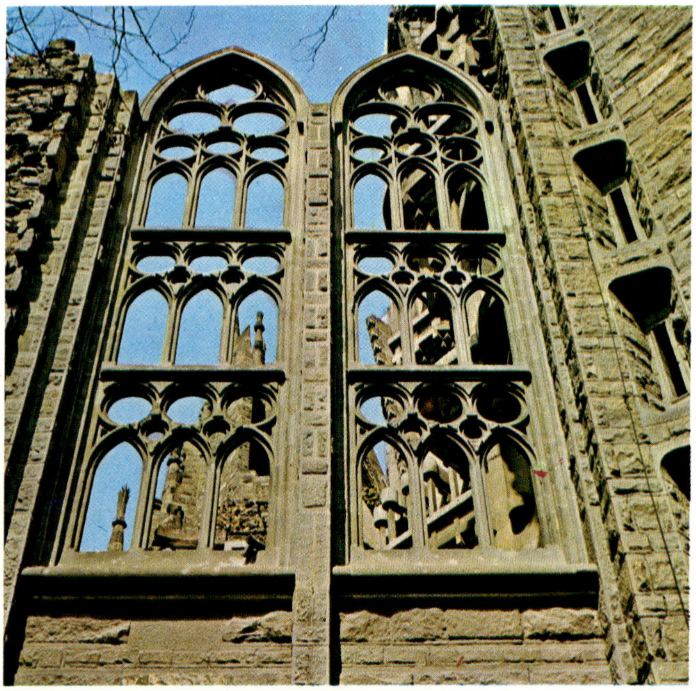

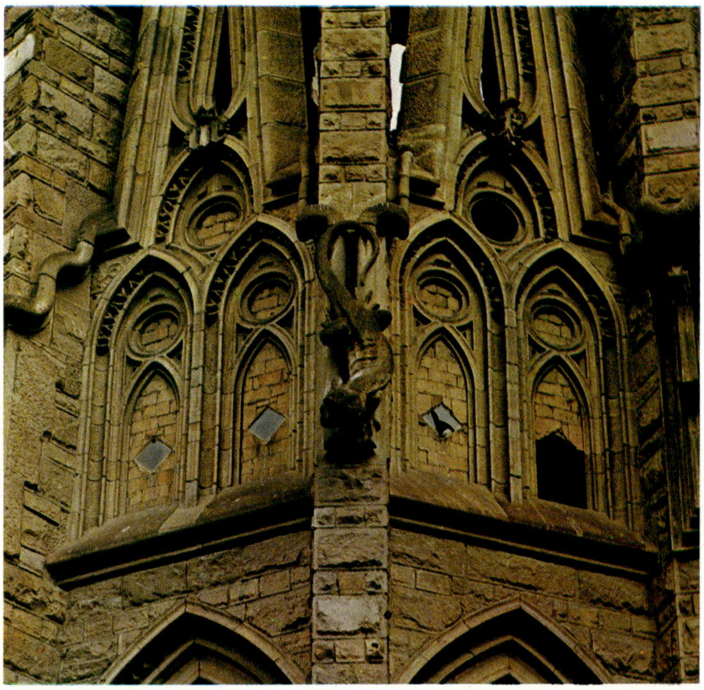

Gaudí has often been labeled a Gothic architect, but his Gothicism is as much spiritual as stylistic. Gaudí's own religious fervor and his dedication to his work on the Sagrada Familia recall the tradition of medieval masons who devoted their lives to the building of the great cathedrals.

Above left and left, views of the apse.

Far left, the "west" window in the "south" transept. (The Sagrada Familia is not oriented on an east-west axis in the traditional way.)

Right, a view over Barcelona from behind the sculpture in the Nativity portal.

Left, the interior of the façade of the Nativity, which has a completely different spirit from the exterior. The Sagrada Familia appears to incorporate elements from countless themes and influences. Yet, in the eyes of his admirers, Gaudí has fashioned from this potpourri a unified and coherent masterpiece. The stones in the foreground which will be re-used in the Sagrada Familia come from demolished buildings of Barcelona. Today, this recycling of materials is an economic necessity, particularly as the stone which was originally used for the church is now ground up at the quarry for concrete.

Far right, center and below, details of the interior elevations of the Nativity façade.

Far right, top, detail of a recently constructed tower on the opposite transept.

Right, above and below, spiral staircases within the Sagrada Familia. They recall those of the great cathedrals, although they are made all the more daring by the omission of the centerposts of their medieval models.

Following page, the Sagrada Familia by night. Today, floodlights beam upward onto the church from across the street, but it was apparently Gaudí's intention to illuminate the church by lights set into the towers themselves.

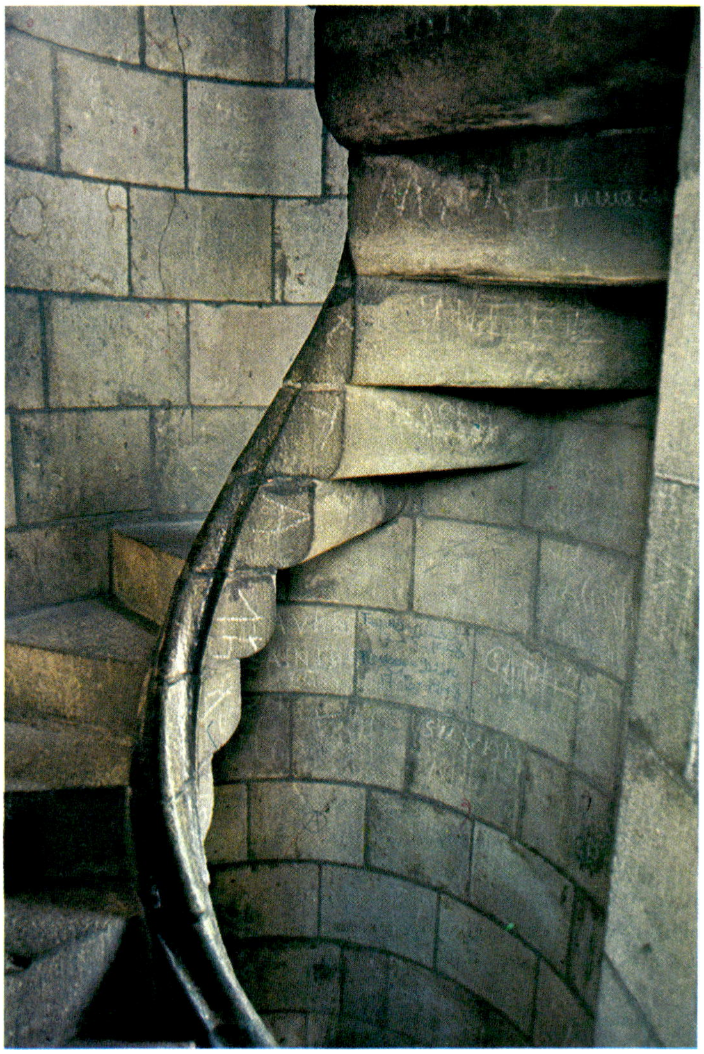

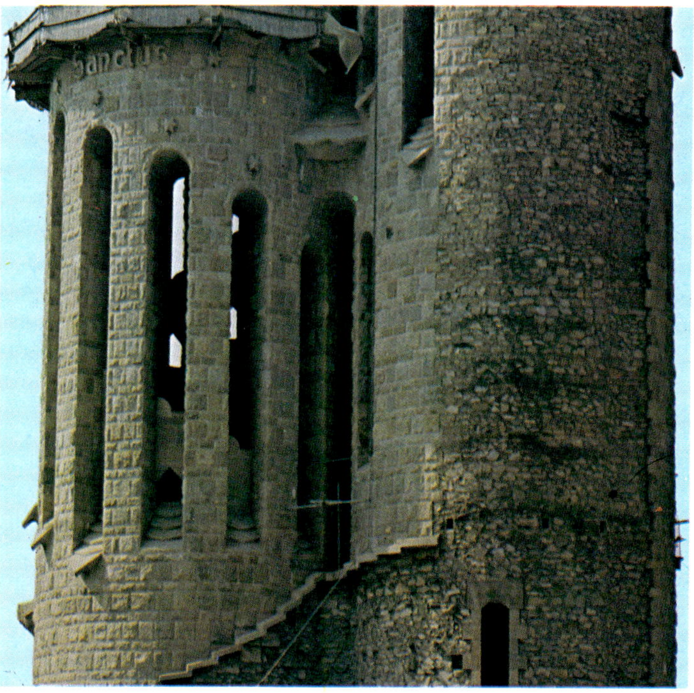
Sanctus

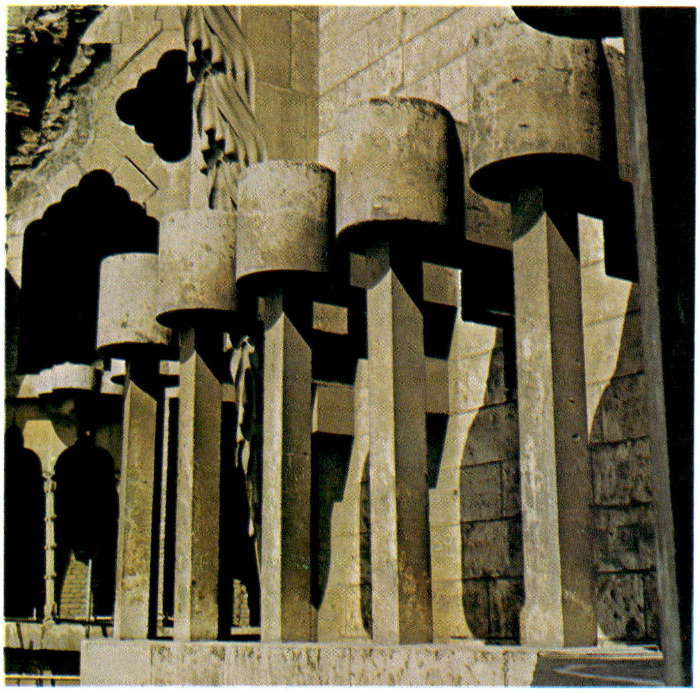

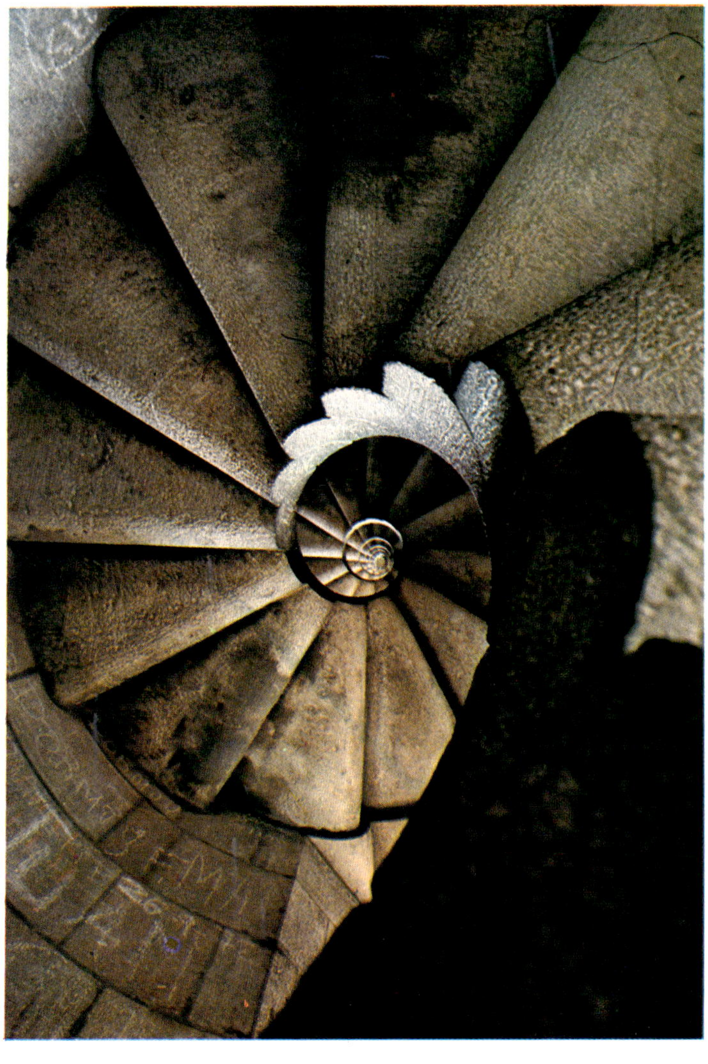

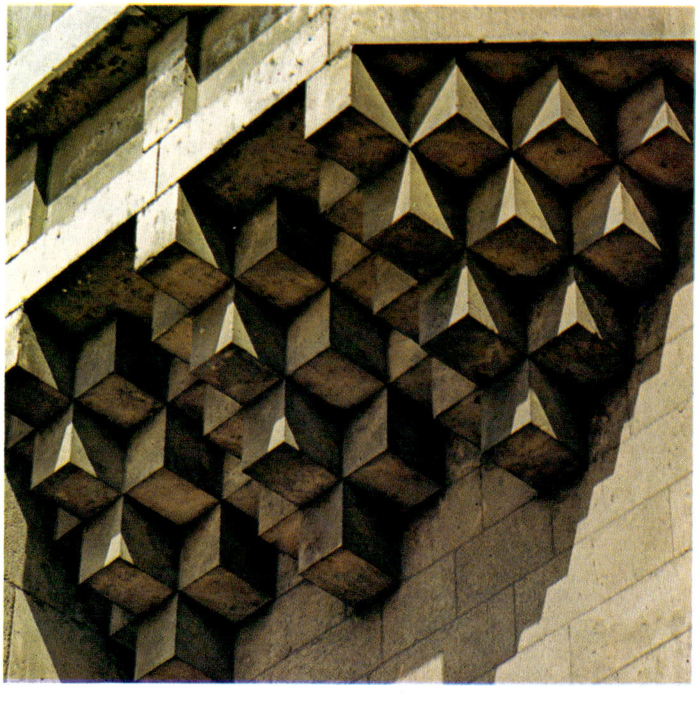

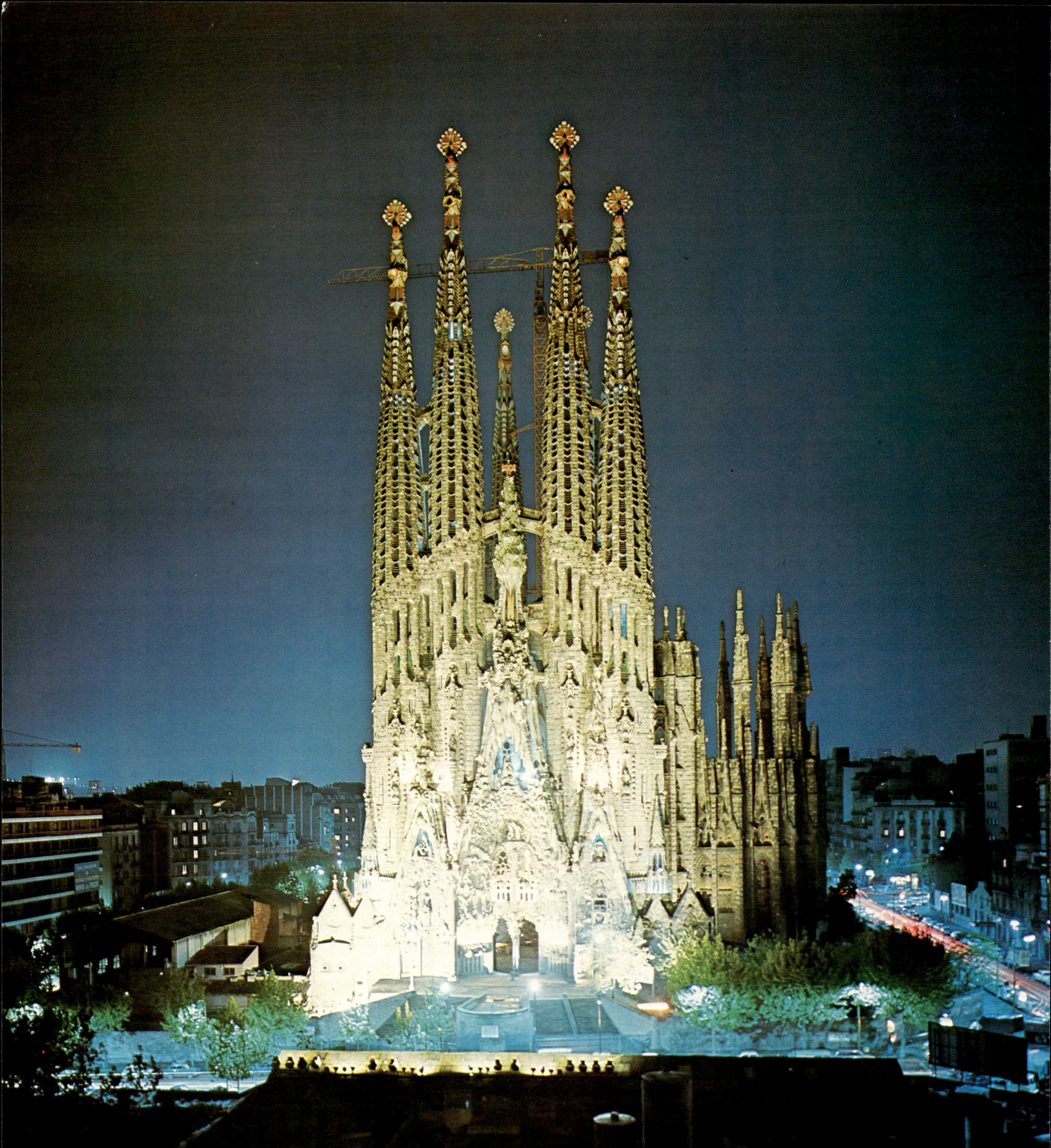

Sagrada Familia
Spain

One day, more than half a century ago, an elegant young woman was visiting the site in Barcelona where the Sagrada Familia was under construction when she came upon an old man. Noting his threadbare suit and unkempt beard, she took him for an indigent and offered him a few coins. The man smiled and accepted her alms, which he then placed in a collection box for work on the church.

Unknowingly, the woman had crossed paths with none other than Antoni Gaudì. And this was by no means the first occasion on which Gaudì, one of the most imaginative architects of the modern age, was mistaken for a beggar. When his friends asked him why he always accepted such alms, he replied quietly that he had no desire to discourage charity. But aside from this, Gaudì desperately needed funds for his work on the Sagrada Familia, the great votive church to which he dedicated much of the last forty-three years of his life, from 1883 until his death in 1926.

The story of the Expiatory Temple of the Holy Family, or the Sagrada Familia, is very much the story of its architect. Gaudì, the son of a coppersmith, was born in 1852 in the provincial town of Reus in Tarragona. Here he received a rigorous Catholic education, and these early years of schooling may have instilled in Gaudì the piety and faith that sustained and inspired him throughout his life.

At the age of sixteen, Gaudì went to Barcelona to study architecture and, soon after, adopted the city as his home. Aside from a few short excursions, he spent the rest of his life there. Gaudì was apparently an undistinguished student, perhaps more interested in the artistic than the more prosaic aspects of his field. After he qualified as an architect, he lived for a while like a dandy, indulging a taste for expensive clothes and foppish mannerisms. It was his habit during this period to ride to building sites in a carriage, from which he would issue commands to the workers. But after taking on the Sagrada Familia, he abandoned these pretensions. He became more religious and eventually quite ascetic. Taciturn and withdrawn, he refused most social invitations, though he did enjoy the company of such distinguished visitors as Albert Schweitzer and the Catalan poet Maragall, who was, like Gaudì, a fervent supporter of Catalan independence.

Gaudì never married. After his father died, he lived alone, tended by two Carmelite nuns from a nearby convent. Dur-

Above, Gaudì, aged seventy, attending a Corpus Christi procession in Barcelona.

Right, a drawing for the Sagrada Familia, which was Gaudì's passionate concern from 1883 until his death in 1926.

Above left, an early study by Gaudì for the portal of the Passion. Left, a portrait of Gaudì by his friend Opisso, made in 1900. Above, Gaudì's only drawing of the projected cathedral in its entirety (1906). Many of his sketches are based on the lines of stress within the structure. Right, a late study by Gaudì of the nave.

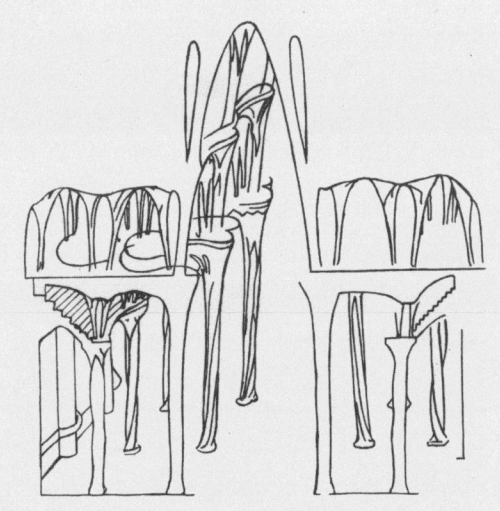

ing the last nine months of his life, he even slept in the office at the building site.

After work on June 7, 1926, Gaudì was walking to church, as he always did, when he was struck by a streetcar. Because of his shabby appearance, passers-by were slow to come to his aid. He was eventually taken to a hospital, where he died three days later. Appropriately, he was buried in the crypt of his great unfinished church.

The idea for a church dedicated to the Holy Family had originated with a wealthy bookseller named José Maria Bocabella. A deeply religious man, Bocabella regularly went on retreats—occasionally accompanied by the young Gaudì—to a shrine at Montserrat. In 1881, Bocabella purchased an entire city block with the intent of erecting a church. A strict traditionalist, he was dismayed at the city planners who had laid out the new extensions of Barcelona as a checkerboard of large square blocks, catering to traffic rather than to the city residents. He wanted to stem what he saw as a trend toward a material and overly rational urbanization by building a church that would rest on the solid foundations of the Gothic tradition.

Bocabella chose Francisco del Villar, the official architect of the diocese, to build the church. In 1882, work was begun on the crypt. But a few months later, Villar resigned and Gaudì, then thirty-one, was recommended to replace him.

Thus in 1883, Gaudì began the project which he eventually came to regard as his life's work:

I have no family, no obligations; I have left my clients, I have refused commissions; I do not wish to work for other than the Sagrada Familia, I wish for nothing but that.

In his deep religious faith, his devotion to architecture, and his enduring commitment to the Sagrada Familia, Gaudì himself recalled the tradition of the medieval builders who devoted their lives to the great cathedrals.

Gaudì's method of designing was a process of ceaseless research and discovery, a continual exploration of formal and stylistic possibilities. His innumerable sketches for the church, made over many years, reveal a constant evolution and refinement of his ideas, which were only gradually committed to concrete form. As a result, Gaudí repeatedly broke his work schedules. He was both unwilling and unable to keep within estimates.

Gaudí inherited from Villar's design only the crypt, which he transformed by raising the height of its vault to over thirty feet. This preliminary gesture was an early indication of the soaring Gothic spirit which was to shape the whole project. Gothic art, in the words of William Blake, is aspiring art. The Sagrada Familia embodies the imaginative impulse of its architect in much the same way as the cathedrals of the Gothic period reflected the aspiring spirit of the masons and artisans who built them.

The choice of the Gothic (specifically Catalan Gothic) style for the church thus reflected Gaudí's personal religious fervor. But the choice was also undeniably a political gesture. It symbolized the Catalan nationalism which had come into its own during the latter half of the nineteenth century. This nationalism brought with it a renewed interest in the Catalan language and history and a revival of Catalan art and literature. Catalonia, with its capital of Barcelona, was a commercially and industrially prosperous region. The citizens of Catalonia felt that they were carrying the economic burdens of a bankrupt medieval Spain, and they resented being governed from Madrid. Gaudí himself was a passionate supporter of the nationalist movement. He refused to speak anything but Catalan—his name "Antoni" is a Catalan variation of "Antonio."

If the Sagrada Familia was to be a worthy symbol of Catalan aspirations, Gaudí wanted it to be not the last of the great medieval churches but the first of the new—a church such as the Gothic architects would have built, had they lived in the nineteenth century. "The Gothic is sublime but incomplete," he stated. "It is only a beginning stopped short by the deplorable Renaissance." While holding true to many of the principles of Gothic design, Gaudí developed and refined some of its elements. He replaced the pointed arch with a parabolic one. And instead of the flying buttresses (which he scornfully called *muletas*, or "crutches") typical of the High Gothic style, he introduced pillars set at angles according to the stresses they had to bear.

As he worked on the project, Gaudí's design coalesced into a kind of "mystery play" or sacred pageant of incredible complexity and vastness. He envisioned his church as a union of architecture and sacred scripture, infused throughout with traditional Christian symbolism. The design was to be completed by hundreds of statues and reliefs, as well as by frescoes, enamels, majolica, and wrought iron.

Rejecting Villar's plans, Gaudí increased the dimensions of the church, so that they stood to each other in a ratio of three to one—a basic piece of Christian symbolism. The Latin-cross plan was to consist of a single nave and four aisles. Twelve towers representing the twelve Apostles were to surround a cupola, symbolizing the glory of Christ. The cupola was to reach a height of over 500 feet—taller than the dome of St. Peter's in Rome.

The four great columns which would support the dome were to symbolize the four Evangelists. There were to be three entrance façades, each with three doors representing Faith, Hope, and Charity. The northeastern façade—the first to be touched by the rays of the sun—was to be dedicated to the birth and infancy of Jesus. The southwestern façade would depict his Passion and death, and the southeastern and principal entrance would represent the Last Judgment. And in a mingling of Christian symbolism and Catalan and Iberian pride, the eight forward columns of the central nave were to represent the Spanish cities of Valencia, Granada, Toledo, Saragossa, Burgos, Valladolid, Santiago, and Seville—with the conspicuous absence of Madrid.

Like the great cathedrals of the Middle

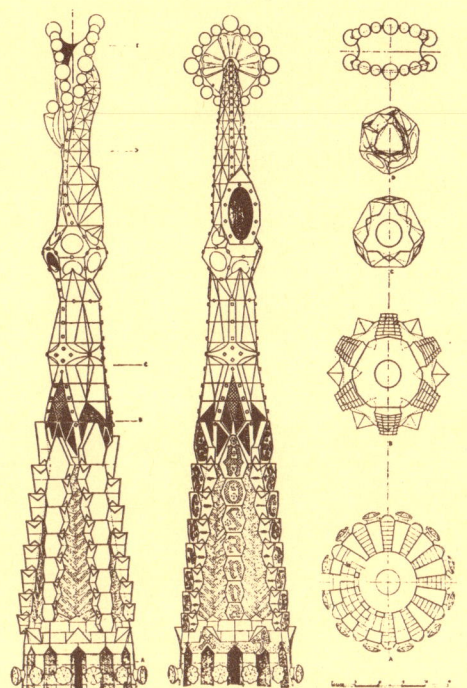

Above, views and sections of a bell tower.

The longitudinal section of the church (right) may suggest the richness of surface ornamentation which Gaudí had once envisioned for the interior. Note that the projected forecourt of the church spans a busy city street.

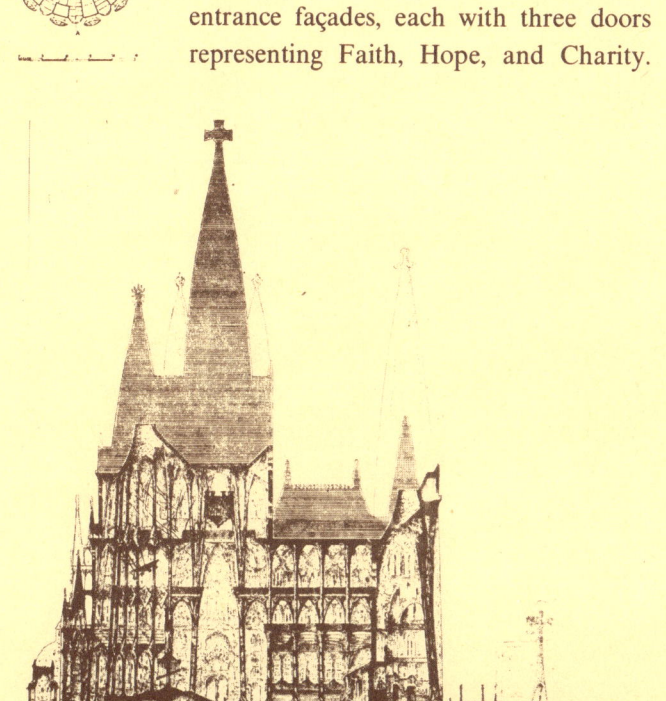

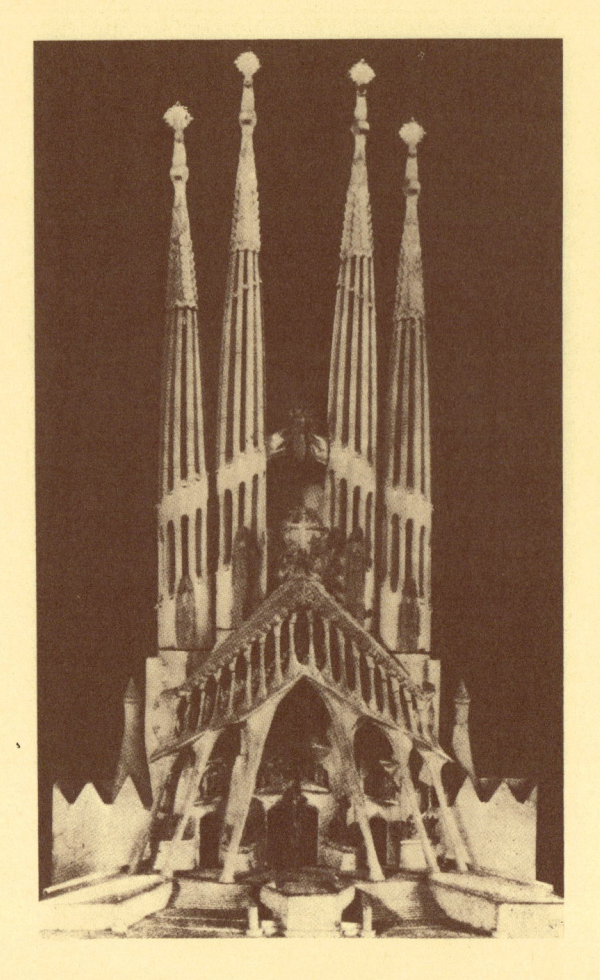

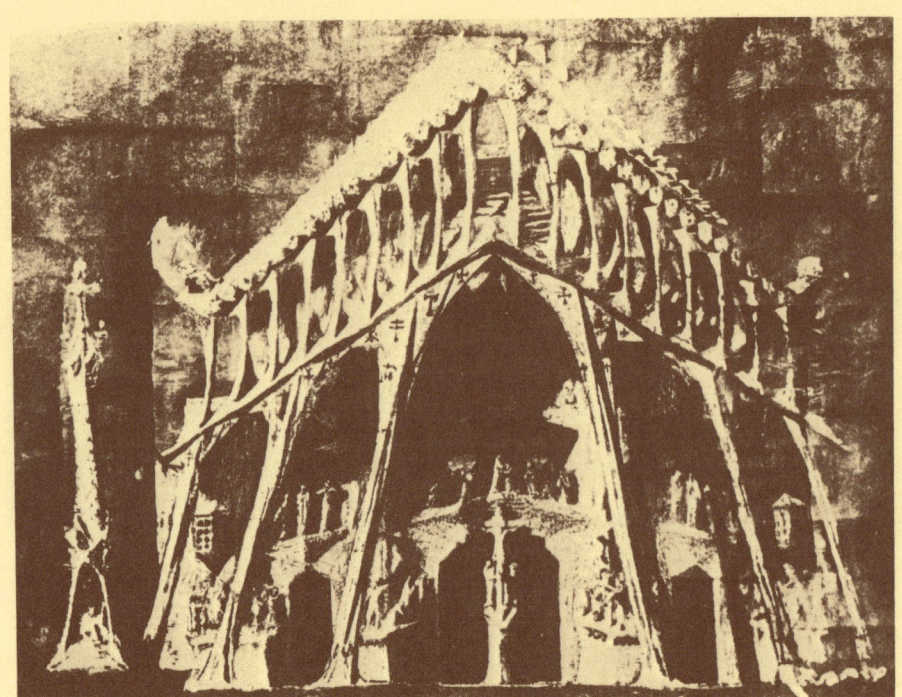

Two studies—a model (left) and a drawing (above)—of the final version of the recently completed portal of the Passion.

Ages, the Sagrada Familia was not completed during the lifetime of the architect. Gaudì was only able to build a small part of his ambitious design. At the time of his death, the Sagrada Familia consisted only of the crypt, the northeastern façade, and the apse. Today, however, the towers of the façade as well as the southwestern façade of the Passion have been completed, according to the original designs of the architect.

Gaudì might have attracted more support for the church by first building the façade which faced the city. However, he believed that the more severe Passion would be more difficult than the Nativity for the citizens of Barcelona to understand. Therefore, he began with the northeastern façade in 1891. In 1903 the basic structure and doorways were finished. Soon after the façade was begun, a donation of over seven hundred thousand pesetas was received for the church. Fearing that the bishop of Barcelona might decide to allocate the money elsewhere, the church administrators encouraged Gaudì to press ahead with the northeastern façade, using as much money as he needed.

Accordingly, the Nativity façade is richly ornate. Intricate stone sculptures above the portals depict scenes of the Nativity and are framed by arrangements of carved vines and leaves. These sinuous lines and plantlike forms are reminiscent of the Modernista style, a peculiarly Catalan form of Art Nouveau. The center portal is crowned by a huge stone fir tree, a symbol of the birth of Christ.

Gaudì lived to see the completion of two of the striking Nativity towers, and all four were completed by 1930. These slender, parabolic towers, encrusted with delicate, fairylike detail, soar above the skyline of Barcelona. Capped with exuberant geometric forms of brilliant mosaics, the towers were apparently designed to hold spotlights which would beam down upon the church and the city at night.

The words "Sanctus Sanctus Sanctus" are carved midway up each tower. Gaudì planned that these words should be yellow, red, and orange, symbolizing the three members of the Holy Trinity. Indeed, Gaudì intended color to play an integral symbolic role throughout the church. The Nativity façade was to be decorated with bright colors. On the west side, the solemn mood of the Passion would be echoed in somber tones that would reflect the colors of the sunset. Within the church, the walls and sections of the vaulting were to be colored according to the various ritual uses of each section of the church.

The Sagrada Familia, still far from completion, has been called a "ruin of the future." But Gaudì's inexhaustible religious imagination lives on in his sketches and notes for the church, and in recent years, the façade of the Passion has been constructed. Of course, had Gaudì lived long enough to supervise the construction, he would doubtless have made further modifications and refinements.

Gaudì has sometimes been called a "baroque" architect. But the Sagrada Familia ultimately transcends classification. It is both a universal statement of Christian doctrine and a symbol of the Catalan people. But the church is, above all, a highly personal expression of faith. As Gaudì said of his work for the Sagrada Familia: "What I am doing is my duty, nothing more; and I must do it."

Chapel at Ronchamp

France

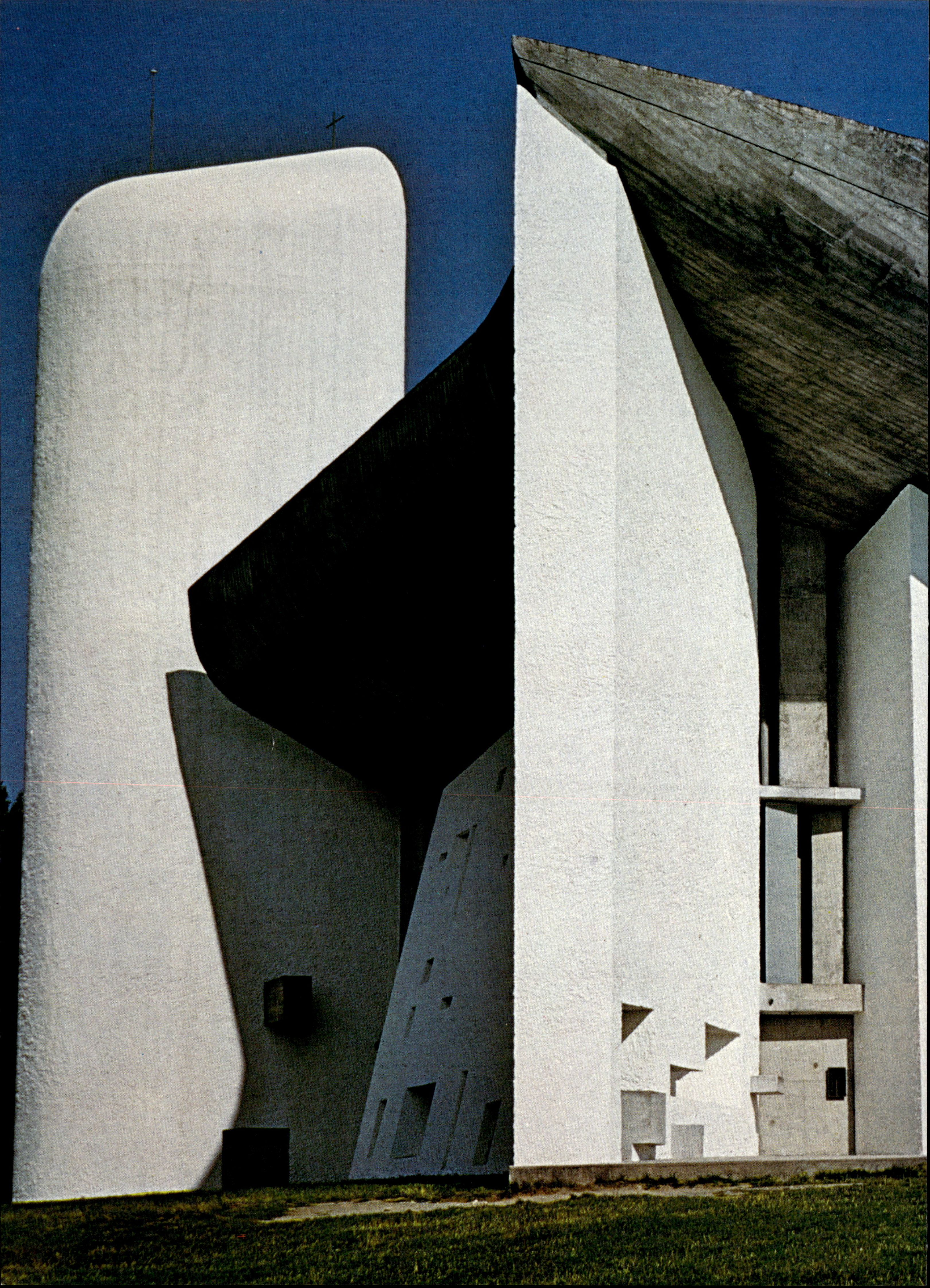

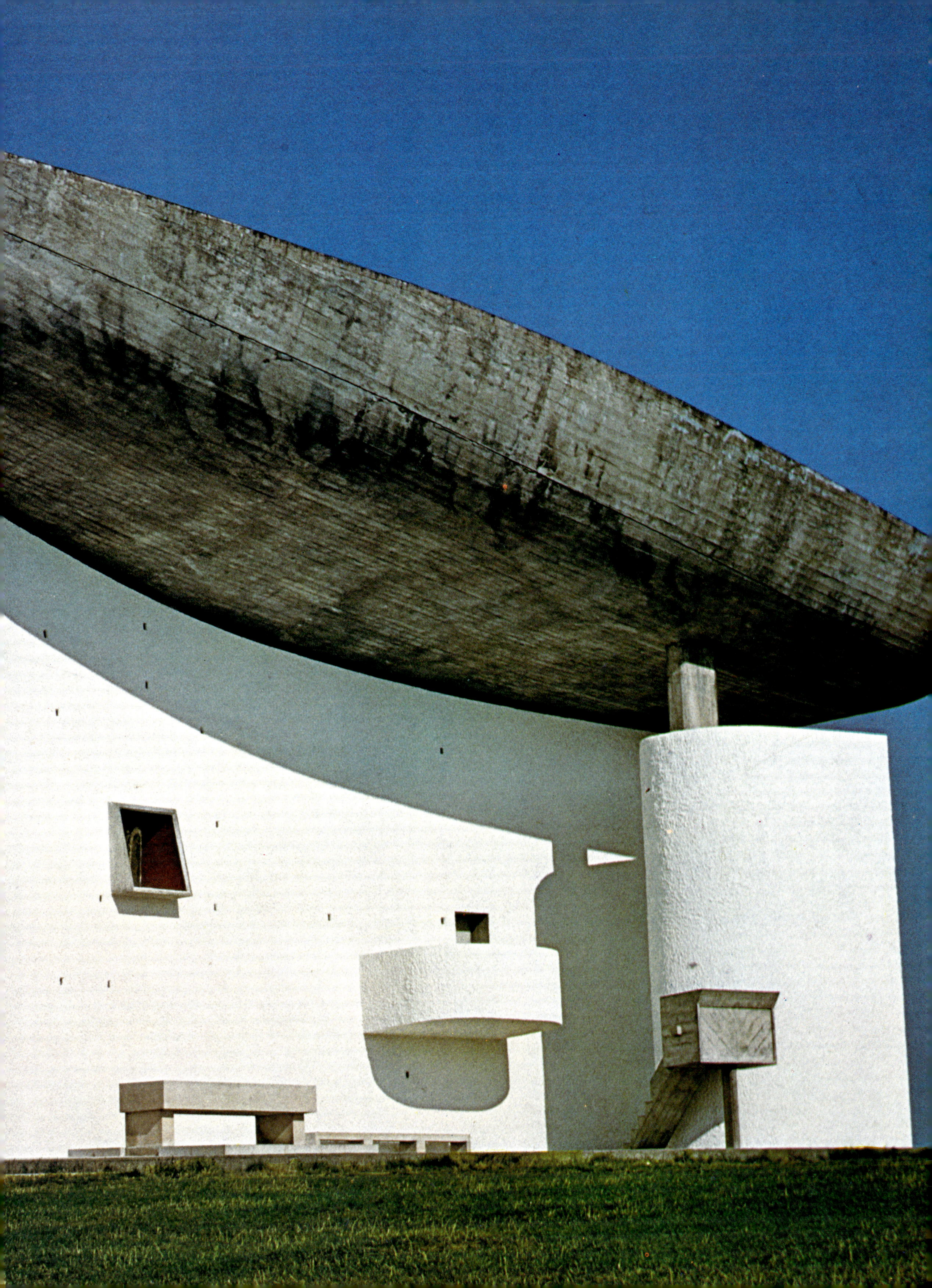

Preceding page, the Chapel of Notre-Dame-du-Haut at Ronchamp, built by Le Corbusier during the early 1950s. The previous chapel was destroyed by artillery during World War II, but some of its stones were used in the new building. Le Corbusier's detractors labeled the chapel "baroque"—a charge which infuriated the architect, who prided himself on his mathematical precision.

Above, the southern façade of the chapel, with its upswept prowlike corner (facing page). The windows with their embrasures are widely splayed either inward (north wall, below right) or outward (south wall, below left) and filter a constantly varying light into the nave.

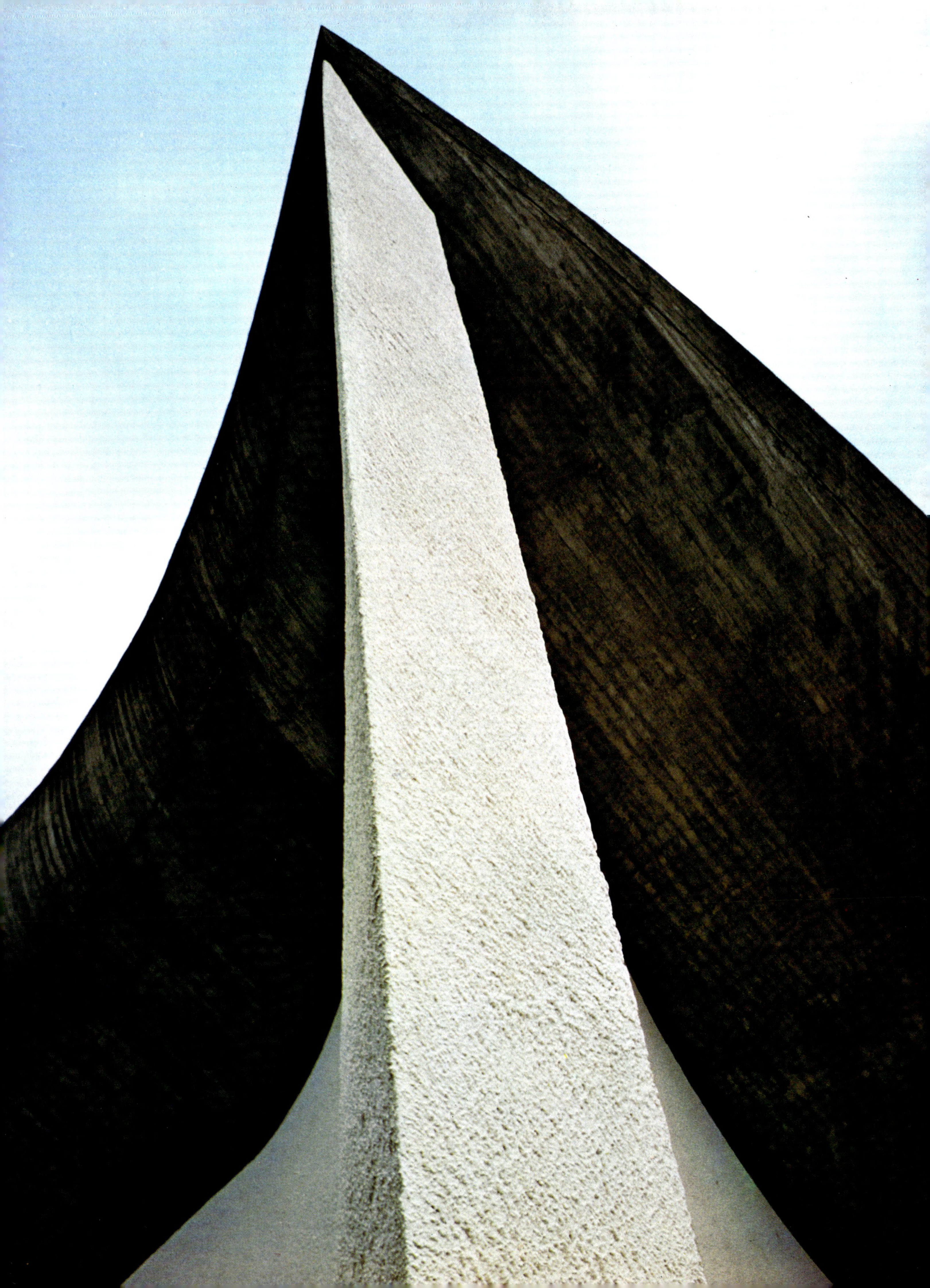

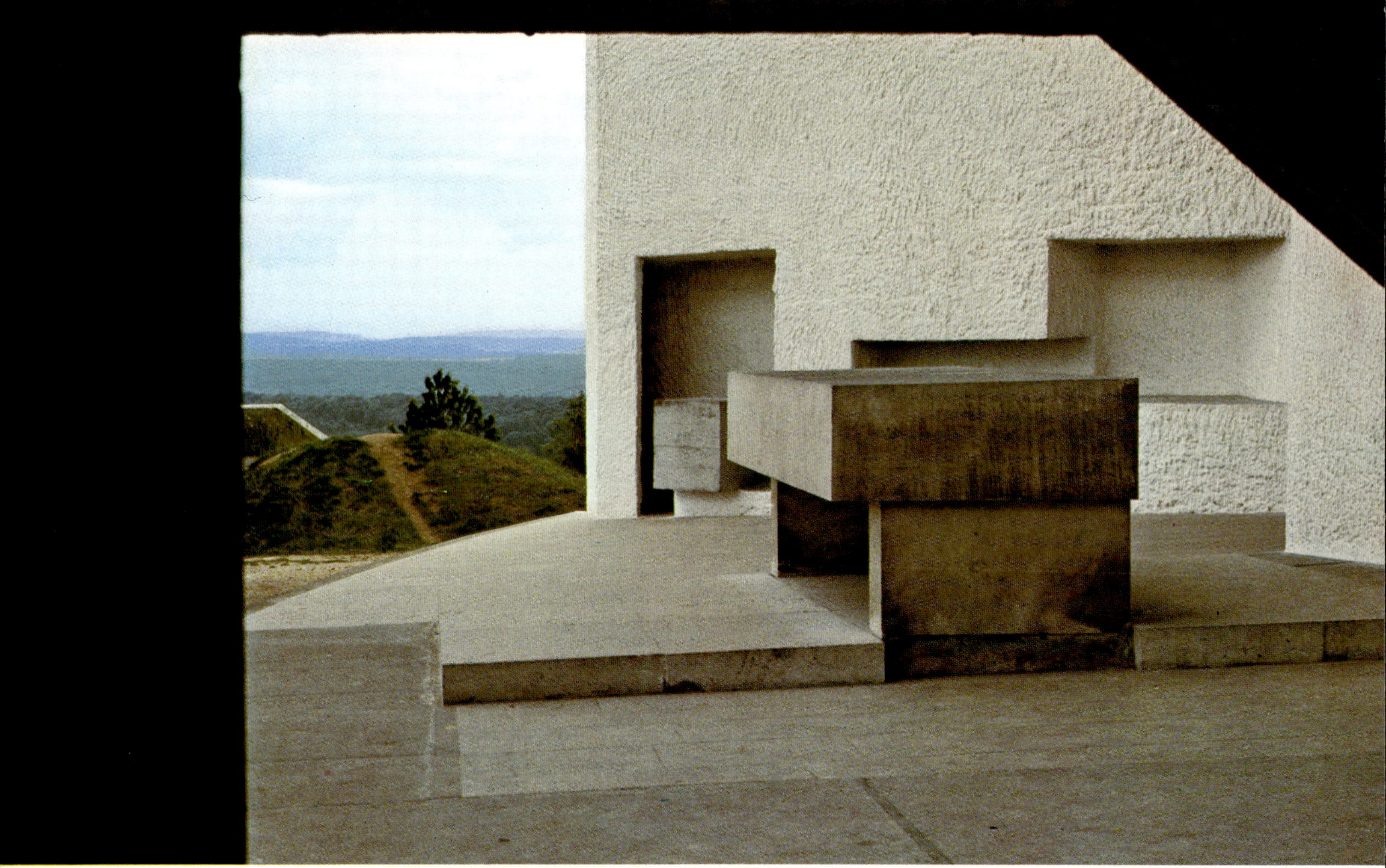

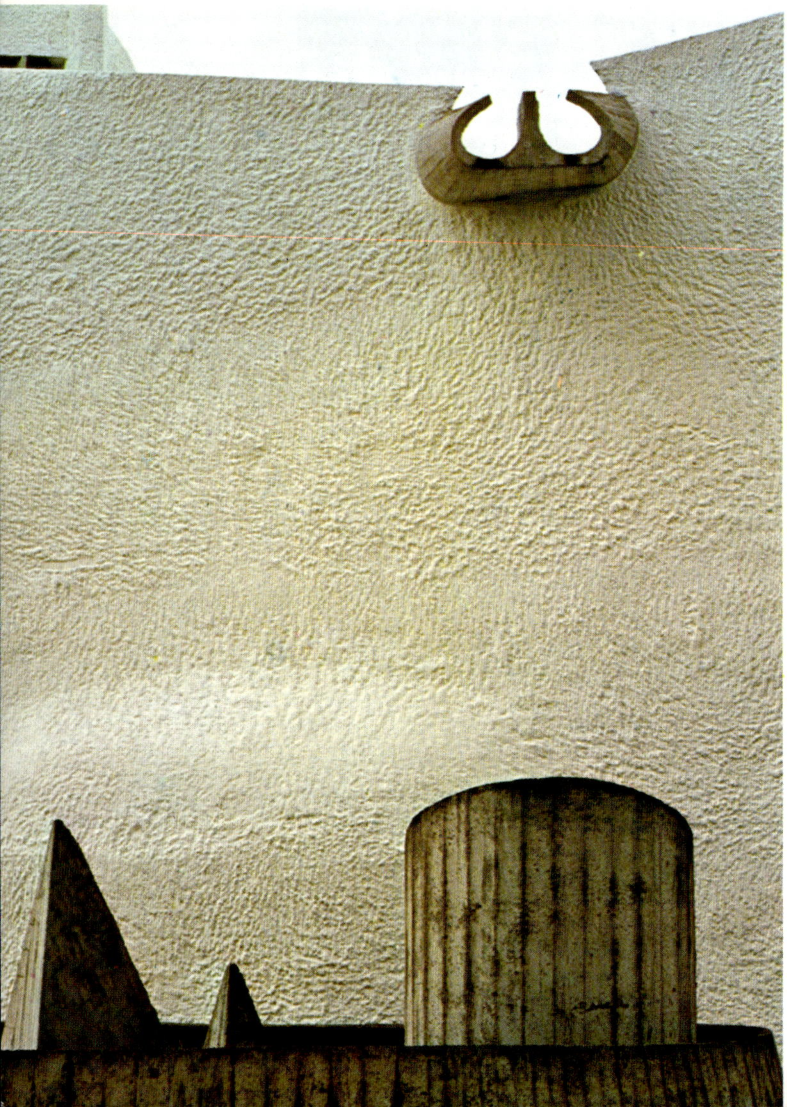

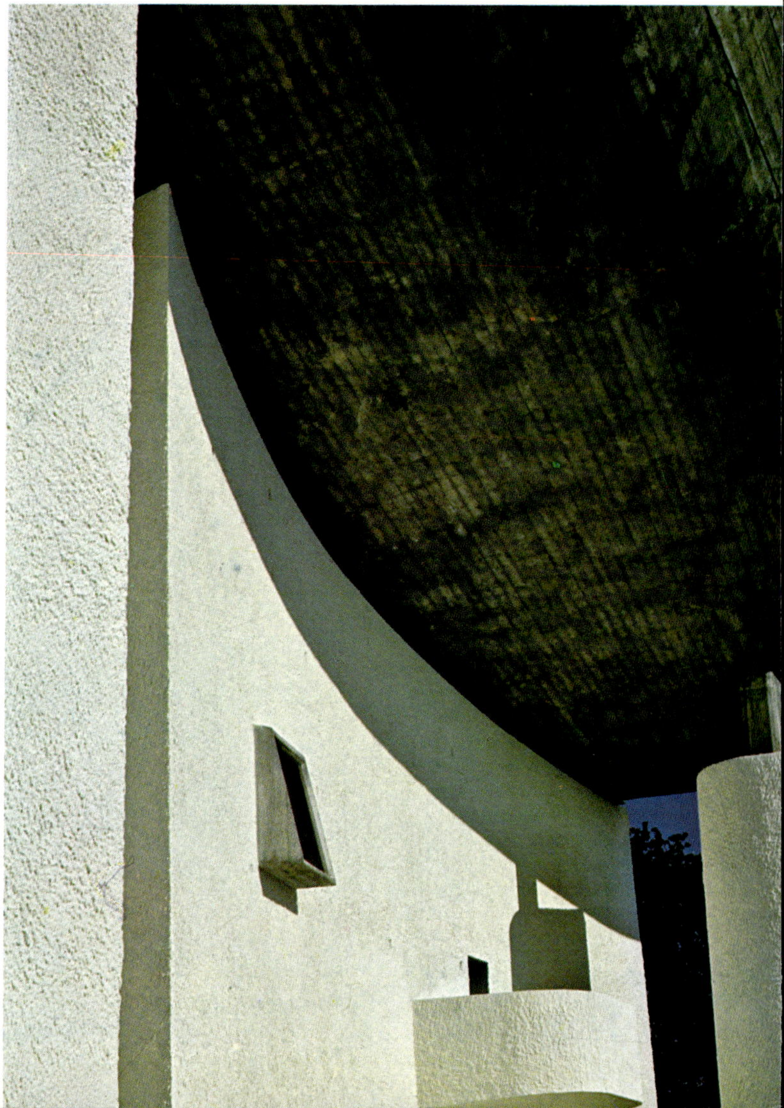

Left, the austere block of the outside altar. Le Corbusier designed the chapel so that mass could be celebrated both in the small, restful interior of the chapel and outside, with pilgrims sitting on the grass—as though the church itself were the apse of an immense temple roofed by the sky.

Below, far left, a rainwater spout and catchment basin.

Below left, a view of an exterior pulpit, which is accessible from within the chapel.

Right, top and center, two views from the north. Despite the originality of the chapel, several influences are suggested: the Mediterranean quality of the white volumes enhanced by sunlight; Le Corbusier's earlier tendency toward "functional" architecture, with its clear surfaces and pure volumes; and the primitive flavor in many of the details.

Below right, the "light catchers" of one of the side chapels, designed to carefully apportion the captured light that illuminates the altar within the tower.

"The key is light," wrote Le Corbusier. Within the chapel a magical play of light is created by the windows with their widely splayed embrasures. To the south and east (above left and far right), the roof is almost invisibly supported on columns, leaving a narrow blade of light separating it from the wall so that the roof appears to hover weightlessly.

Above, far left and right, the south wall, studded with small windows that filter the light as if through the leaves of an enchanted forest. Le Corbusier eschewed traditional stained glass for the chapel, preferring to paint the windows with his own designs and inscriptions. This interior façade of the chapel, which seems so freshly conceived, was actually designed according to the Modulor, a system of proportional measures invented by the architect. Exact mathematical and geometric ratios govern the relationship of each aperture to the others and of all of them to the wall as a whole.

Light within the chapel takes many forms.

Left, an altar in one of the side chapels, bathed in light from the tower above.

Facing page, votive candles, arranged with geometric simplicity, flickering before a venerated statue of the Virgin that was rescued from the ruins of the previous chapel. On some of the windows are the words of the Ave Maria, painted by Le Corbusier himself.

Following page, the great "prow" of the chapel. The chapel itself marvelously illustrates Le Corbusier's belief in architecture as "the skillful, correct, and magnificent interplay of volumes, put together in light."

la mer

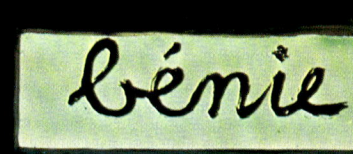

bénie entre toutes les femmes

marie

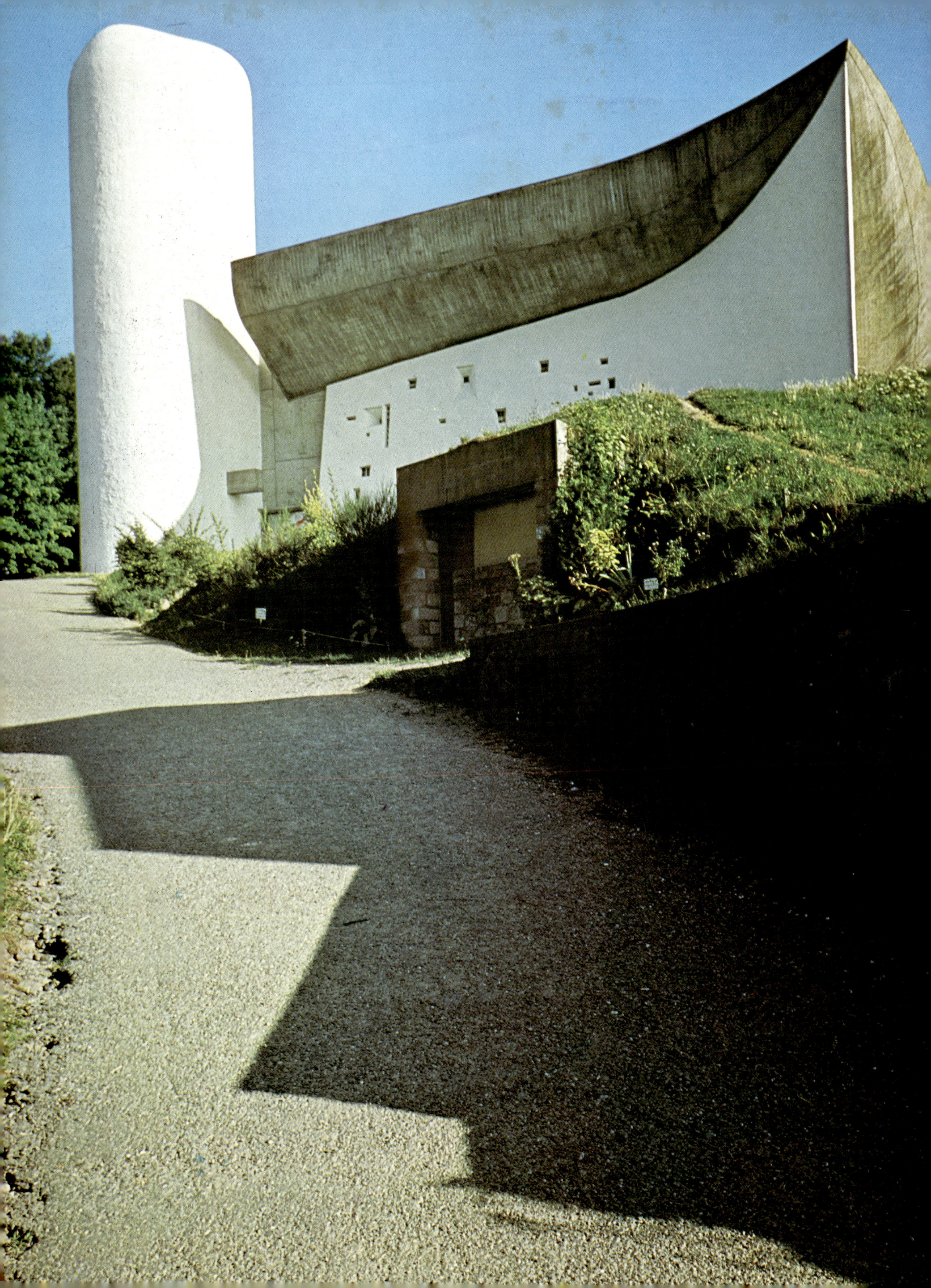

Chapel at Ronchamp France

In 1950, the French architect Le Corbusier received a commission to rebuild the Chapel of Notre-Dame-du-Haut on a hill near Ronchamp, a village in the Franche-Comté area of France, close to the Swiss border. This hill had long been considered sacred, having been associated first with pagan and then Christian worship over the centuries. But its chapel had been blasted by artillery during the liberation of France at the end of World War II, and all the projects submitted for its reconstruction had been rejected as overambitious and too costly. Le Corbusier, it was hoped, might be able to design a suitable sanctuary that would harmonize with the surrounding landscape.

Le Corbusier, then already sixty-three, undertook the project with his customary tenacity. The resultant bold, unorthodox design, with its full-blown curvilinear forms and dramatic use of color and sense of space, is without doubt one of the few great religious structures of our time. However, the completed Chapel at Ronchamp met with as much hostility as admiration. Le Corbusier was particularly incensed by the charge of "baroquism." To be identified with a style he vehemently disliked—after a lifetime of dedication to "all-embracing mathematics," to meticulous precision, and to constant research and adjustment—that was the supreme insult!

Such criticism, however, was nothing new. Throughout his career, he had been subjected to a continual barrage of accusations of architectural heresy, "vandal-

Above, Le Corbusier at his worktable in the private studio within his office in Auteuil—a cubicle that he called "the study for patient research."

Right, the ground plan, transverse section, and façade of the Chapel at Ronchamp.

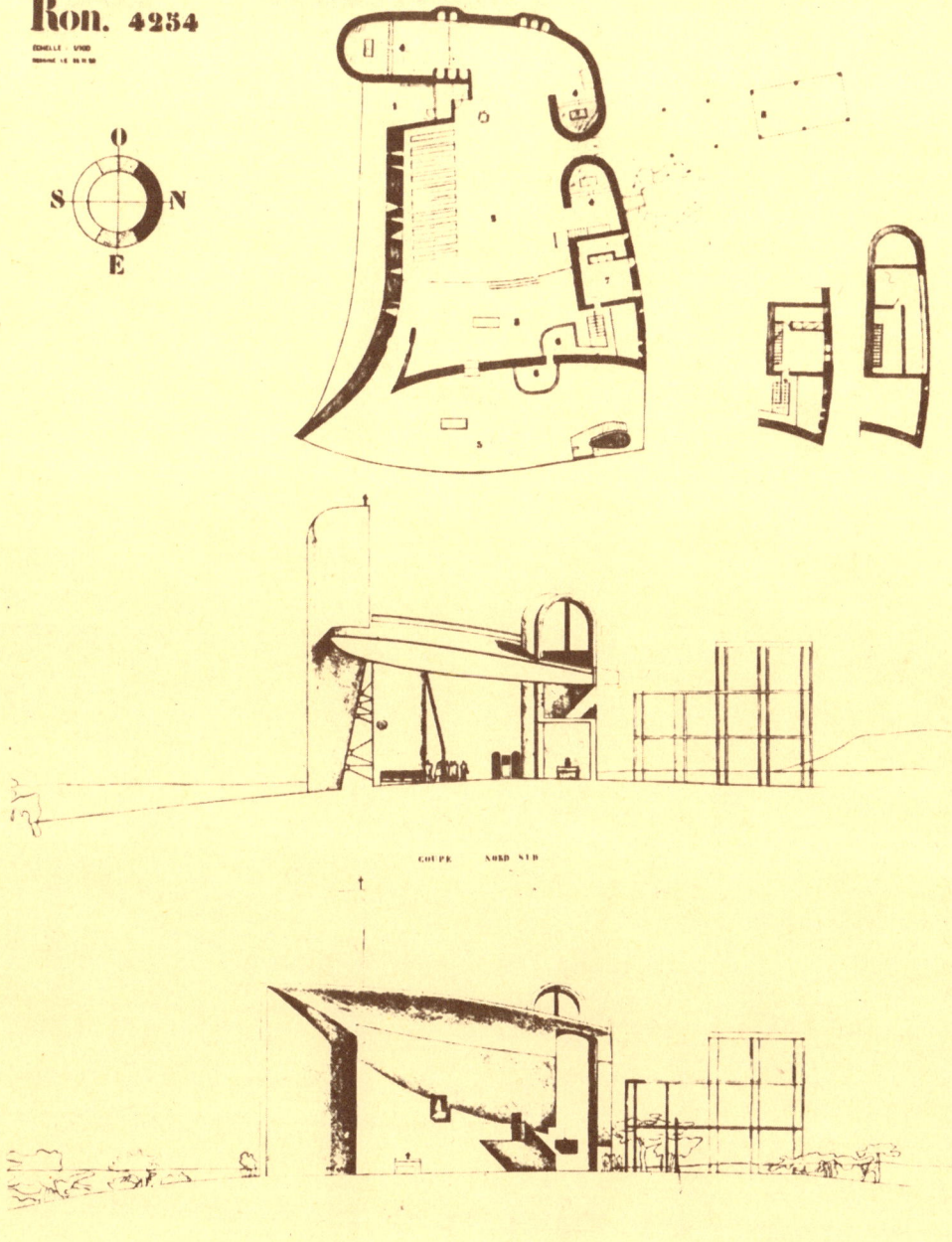

ism," megalomania, and contempt for historic and artistic tradition. But his genius, like that of Michelangelo, thrived on conflict. Indeed, Le Corbusier has sometimes been dubbed the Michelangelo of his age. Not only did he share Michelangelo's fiery temperament, but Le Corbusier can be said to have changed the direction of the twentieth century, as Michelangelo is recognized as having influenced the entire course of the Renaissance.

Le Corbusier was an accomplished painter as well as a brilliant architect. He was also one of the first social critics to recognize the totally new requirements of modern life after World War I. At the beginning of his career, he was particularly attentive to the growing complexity of urban life and the "functional" architecture it necessitated. He popularized the mechanistic notion of the house as *une machine à habiter* ("a machine to live in") emphasizing simplicity and efficiency. He was one of the architects—among them Walter Gropius and Ludwig Mies van der Rohe—who, in a wave of postwar experimentation, stripped architecture of its historical deceits and superfluities, and whose unadorned cubic forms became known as the International style. Yet, later in his career, Le Corbusier increasingly valued the plastic possibilities of architecture. The Chapel at Ronchamp is probably the climax of this sculptural development.

One day in June 1950, the architect spent three hours on the hill at Ronchamp. He familiarized himself with the ground and the horizons and became, in his own words, "permeated" with them. The ruins of the old chapel were on the grassy crown of the hill, reached by a steep and winding dirt track. To the west stretched the plain of the Saône River; to the north lay a small valley and a village; to the east, the Ballons d'Alsace; and to the south, the last spurs of the Vosges Mountains sloping down into a valley. As he surveyed the landscape, Le Corbusier had a vision of the chapel created by a team of master craftsmen, all working together on the lonely, windswept hill. The idea would eventually become reality. For five years his group of designers and artisans would share the rewards and the frustrations of constructing the new hilltop chapel.

Le Corbusier's first step was to make meticulous drawings of the surrounding landscape. As a painter, he believed in the importance of preliminary drawings as a means of unlocking—in his own words—"the visual echo in the realm of shape." His design for the chapel was above all a response to the landscape. For Le Corbusier, it was "a phenomenon of visual acoustics"—a counterpoint to the line of hills and a celebration of the blue of the sky and the play of the clouds.

The finished chapel is a massive sculpture which stands out against the wide horizon and is visible for miles from the surrounding hills and green woodlands. Like a twentieth-century Stonehenge, it appears elemental and natural, with an expansive, uncramped dignity. The majestic upward sweep of the roof unifies the elements of its composition and creates an air of almost dramatic inevitability.

Yet, as if in defiance of its mass, the chapel has an appearance of weightlessness. The whitewashed walls seem made of papier-mâché, and the upswept roof,

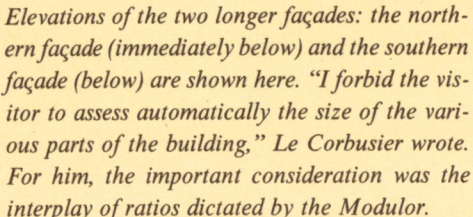

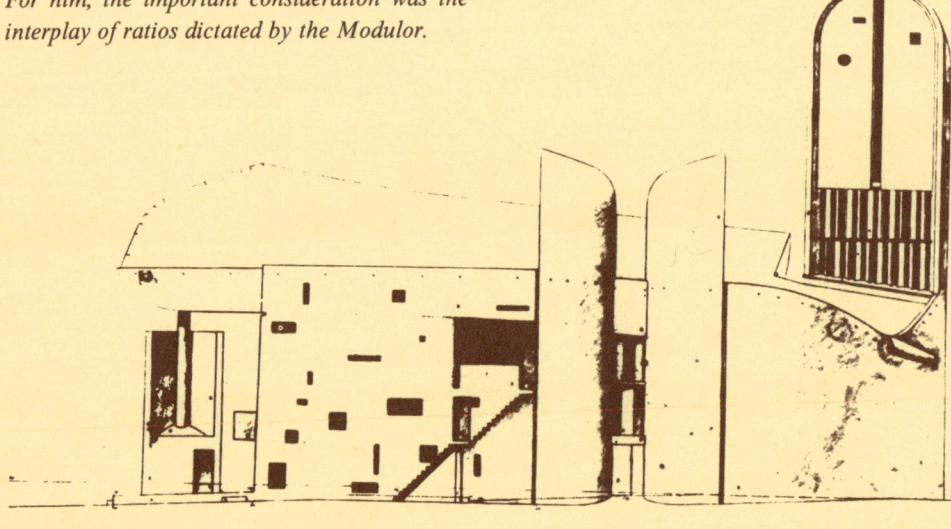

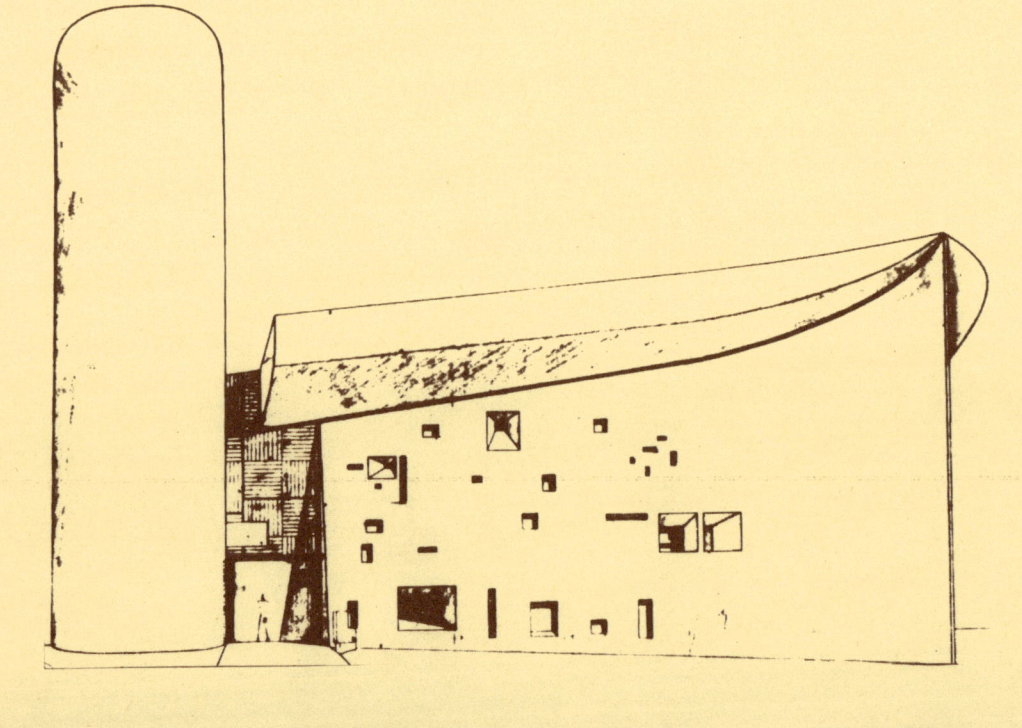

Elevations of the two longer façades: the northern façade (immediately below) and the southern façade (below) are shown here. "I forbid the visitor to assess automatically the size of the various parts of the building," Le Corbusier wrote. For him, the important consideration was the interplay of ratios dictated by the Modulor.

invisibly supported a few inches above the walls on columns, appears to hover substantially but weightlessly. Le Corbusier modeled the roof after the shell of a horseshoe crab he had picked up while walking with his friend, the sculptor Tino Nivola, along a beach on Long Island, New York. For months the shell occupied the place of honor on his drawing board.

Aside from the beauty of the structure, Ronchamp, as a whole, is also one of the truly remarkable modern architectural spaces. With its precise relationship of formal elements, around and through which space flows freely, it is a supreme example of what Le Corbusier called "ineffable space."

Le Corbusier assembled a small book describing the creation of the Chapel at Ronchamp. In it is a poem called "The Key," which emphasizes the importance of understanding his use of light in any interpretation of the building:

The key is light
and light illuminates shapes
and shapes have an emotional power.

On the following page, Le Corbusier goes still further—"Observe the shadows, learn the game"—and suggests that the reader turn the pictures upside down or sideways to become better aware of the play of light. By his poetic logic, the eye-varying light is music: "Precise shadows ... enchanting arabesques ... counterpoint and fugue. Great music."

Below, an axonometric perspective of the chapel, with the roof "removed."

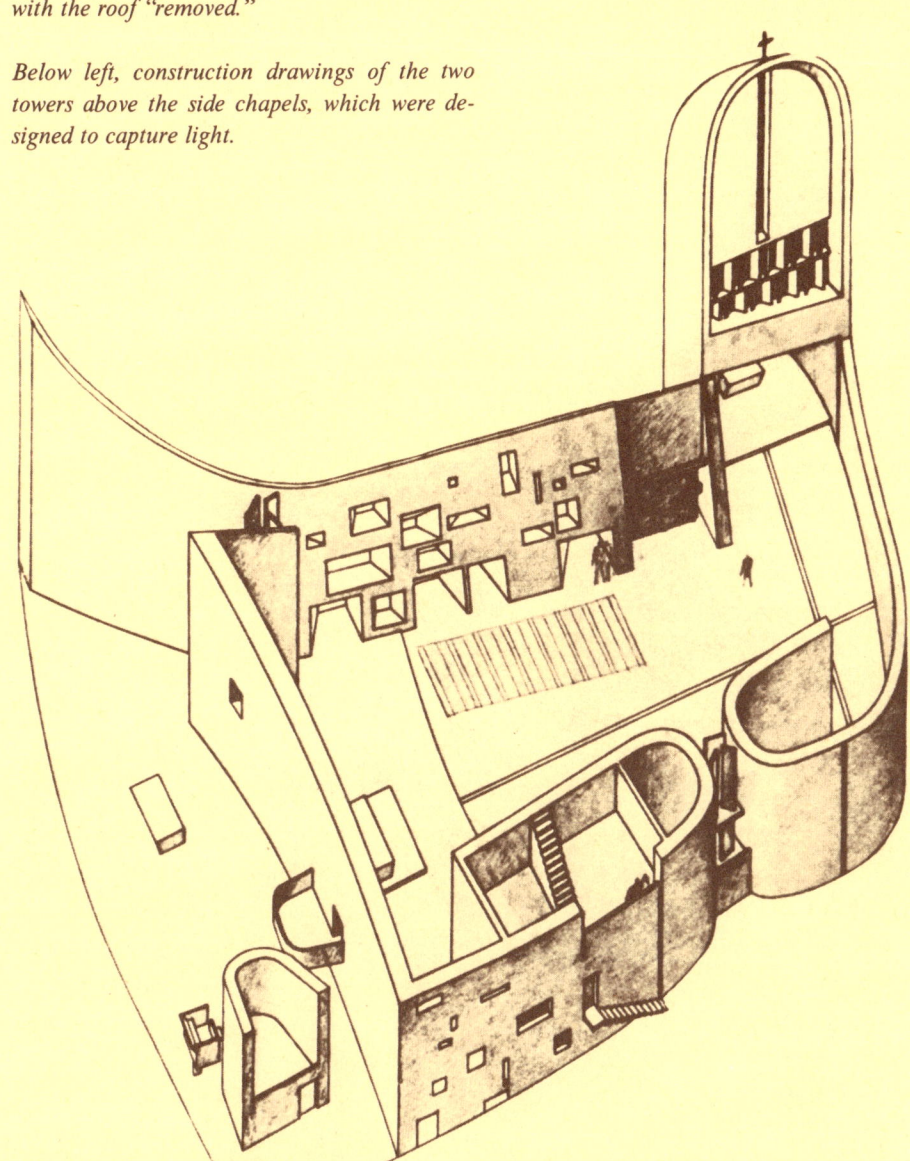

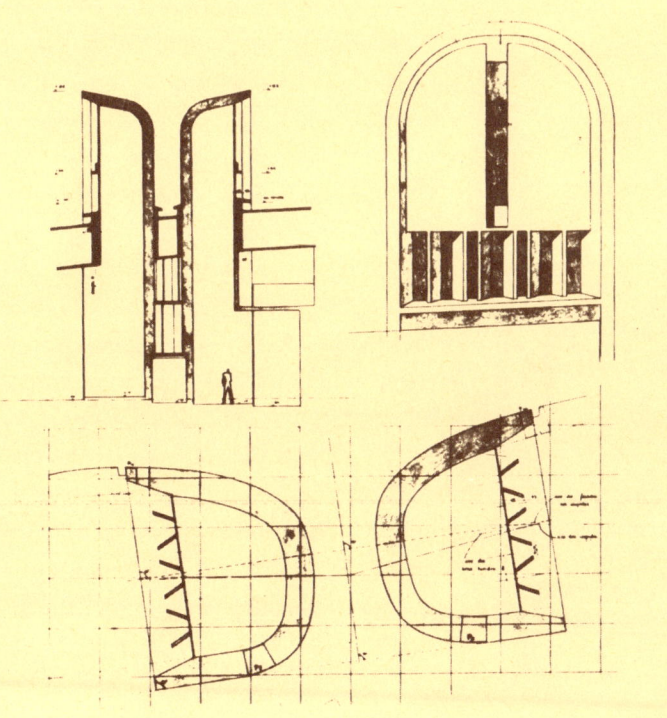

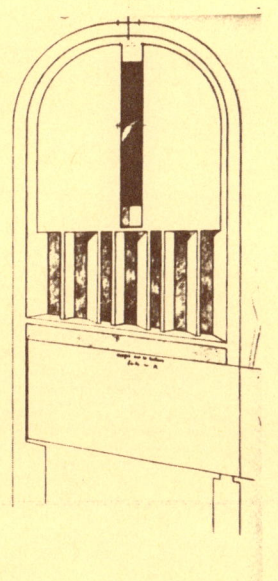

Below left, construction drawings of the two towers above the side chapels, which were designed to capture light.

It is easy to see what the architect meant. Outside, the light gives form to the brilliant white of the walls and defines the varied pattern of the window openings that throw huge shadows across the unbroken expanses. The light picks out the colors of the glazed, painted steel of the pivoting door. It also projects the colors of the windows—decorated with designs and inscriptions painted by the architect himself—deep into the interior of the chapel. Other windows, particularly on the north wall, diffuse the light, giving the chapel a luminous, almost mystical aura.

Le Corbusier's sense of light also contributes in other ways to the special mood of the interior. The narrow glazed strip of light between the roof and the walls lights the underside of the roof, blotting out its supports, so that—like the dome of Hagia Sophia in Istanbul—the heavy span appears to be suspended in the air. The three towers of the side chapels—like three stone nuns searching the horizons—catch the light at different times of the day and filter it down onto the altars below. Most spectacular is the northeast tower, with red walls which bathe the altar beneath in a magical red glow.

As far as possible, the materials used in the chapel were left in their natural state: stone and cement paving; wood benches; *béton brut* for the ceilings (raw concrete still bearing the marks of the wooden form work into which it was poured); wood-block flooring; a cast-iron altar rail; altars of dressed stone from Burgundy; and a simple bronze cross. This use of materials implied a respect for their primitive, essential state, a recognition of their innate sculptural properties, an emphasis on construction rather than on finish. To Le Corbusier, raw materials were beautiful in their honesty, in much the same way that the depiction of a nonidealized human form may be.

Le Corbusier's construction techniques were innovative. The walls—"absurdly but practically thick," he called them—were formed of gridlike supporting frames and stone from the original chapel, overlaid with steel meshing and sprayed with cement. The crab-shell roof is literally a shell, formed of two thin membranes of reinforced concrete separated by a space of more than six feet and protected by several coats of waterproofing.

The few decorative touches—a wall of liturgical purple, stove-enameled murals, a pivoting statue of the Madonna—are simple and unobtrusive. There is an exterior as well as interior pulpit, so that services can be held outside on the grassy hill for the pilgrims who visit the chapel. Le Corbusier also envisioned a skeletal bell tower that would transmit electronic music, but it was never actually built.

When dedicating the chapel, Le Corbusier stated that he had wanted to create a place of silence, of prayer, of peace, of spiritual joy. As an atheist and nonconformist, he admitted elsewhere that the requirements of religion had little effect on his design for the chapel. Its form, he wrote, was an answer to the "psychophysiology of the feelings." However, through his sincere intuitive belief in some sort of cosmic truth and natural law and his integrity as an artist, he created the Chapel of Notre-Dame-du-Haut—one of the most religiously convincing buildings of the twentieth century.

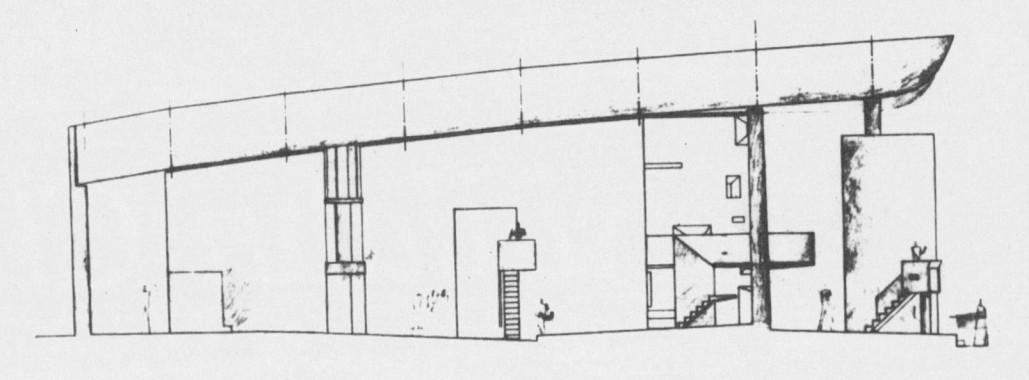

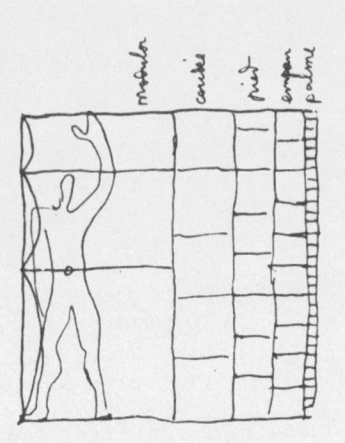

Above, a longitudinal section through the chapel. Left, a sketch by Le Corbusier of the Modulor, the system he used to work out the proportions of his later buildings.

Below, two paintings by Le Corbusier. A painter as well as an architect, he used the compositional skills he had developed as a painter in designing the chapel. He also painted the windows and the enormous entrance door.

Taivallahti Church

Finland

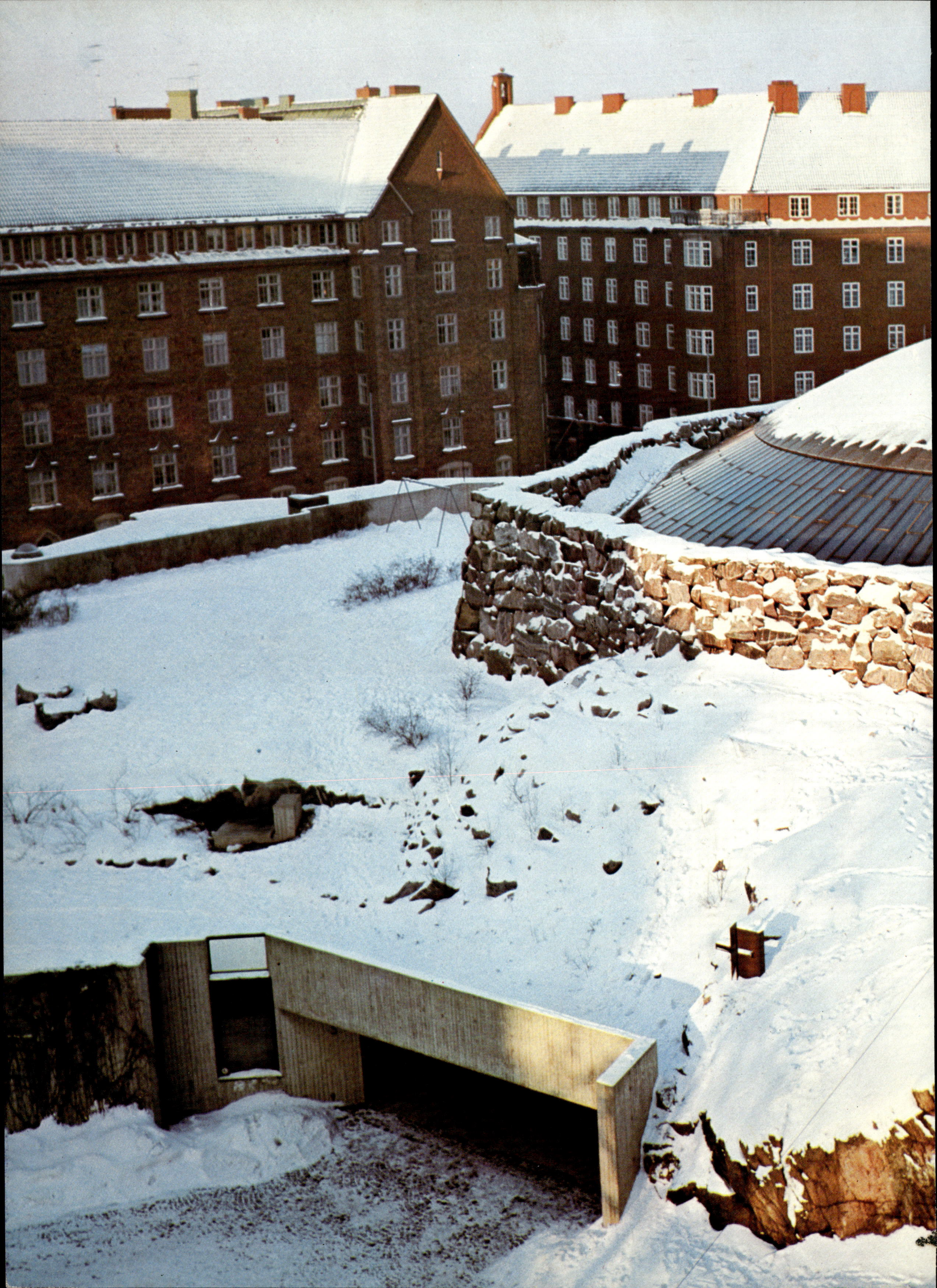

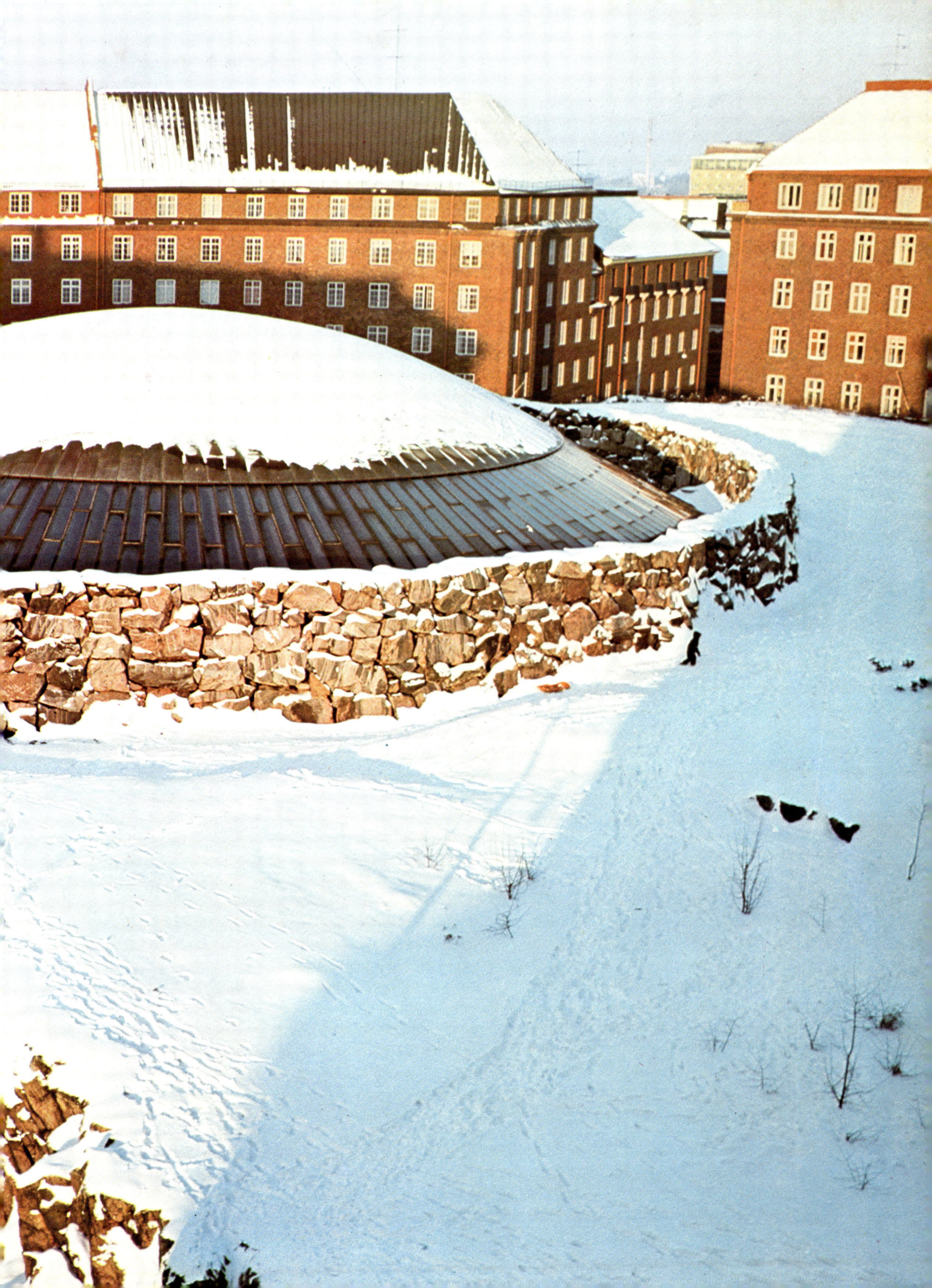

Preceding page, the snow-covered dome of the church, rising above its rocky base. It is separated from the surrounding park by a wall built of stones quarried from the site.

At night, the dome (above left) eerily resembles a flying saucer set down in the city of Helsinki. Modern materials are used here in conjunction with natural elements such as the roughly hewn stones that define the character—both functional and primitive—of the structure.

Above right, a detail of the strip of windows that runs around the base of the dome.

Left and right, the entrance of the church. The doors are entirely of glass. Where the bare rock is not left exposed, the walls are of concrete, or "reconstituted rock," as it has been called.

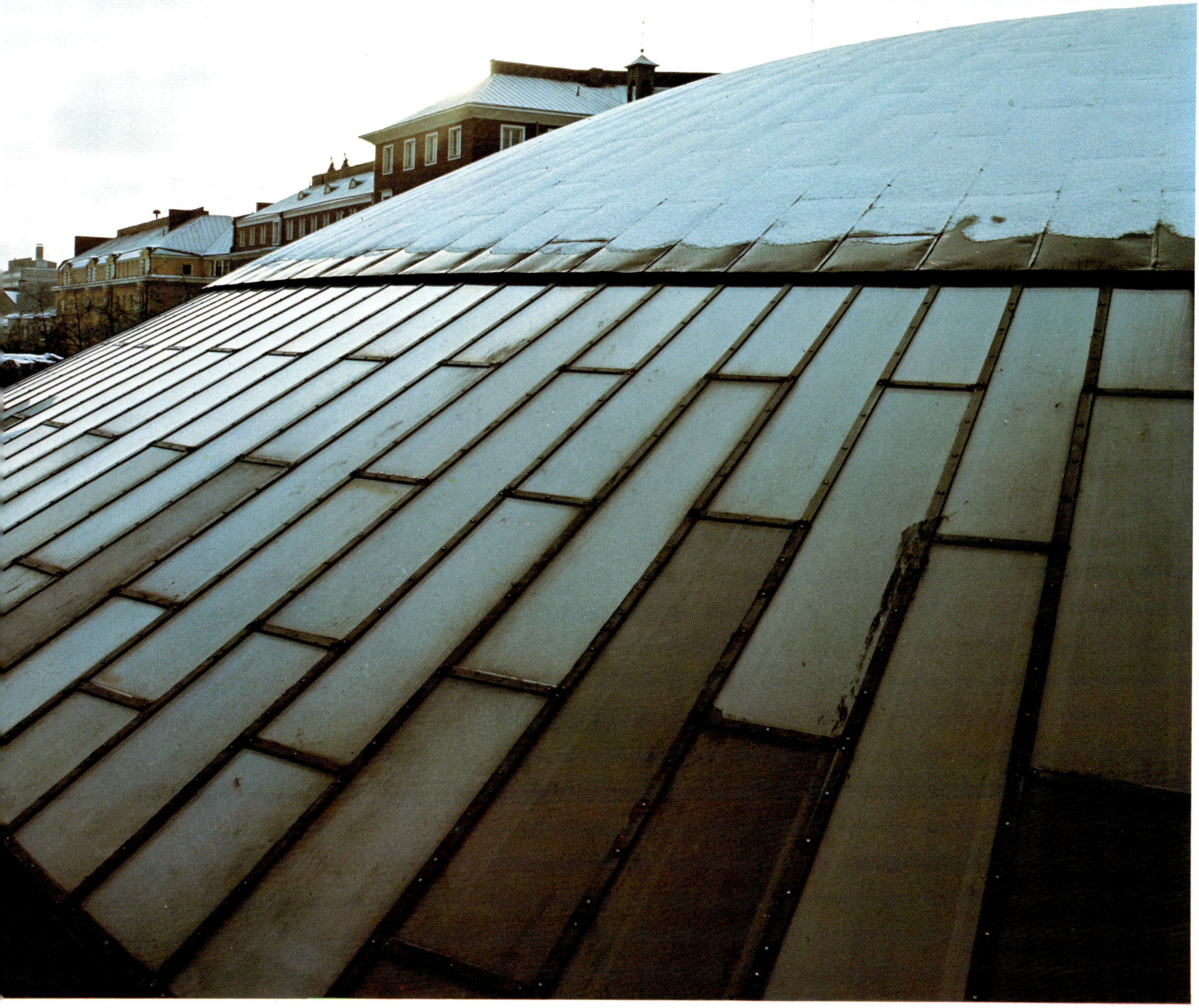

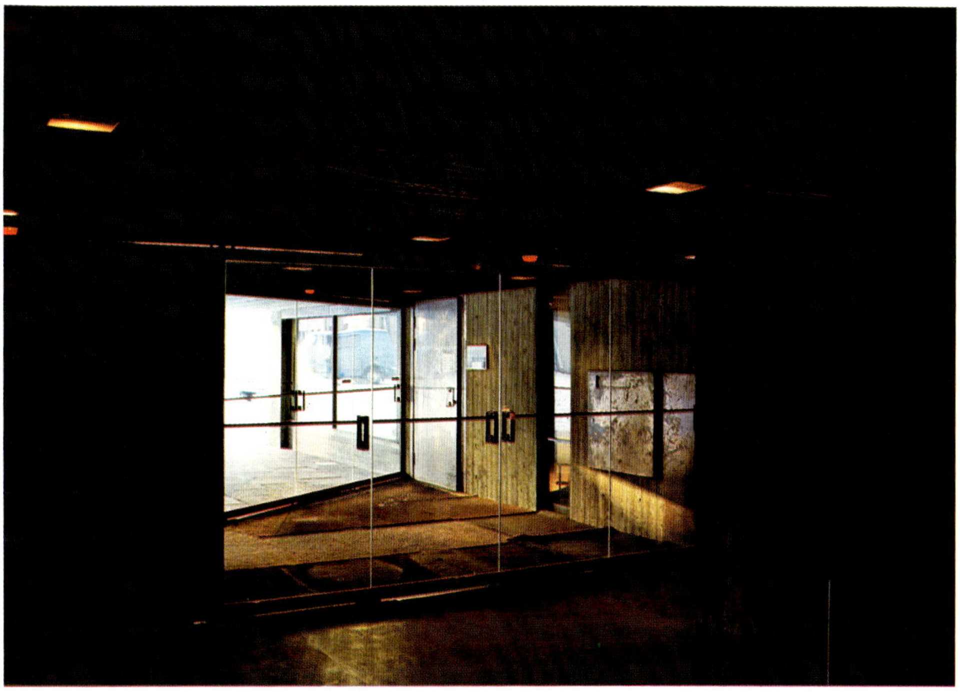

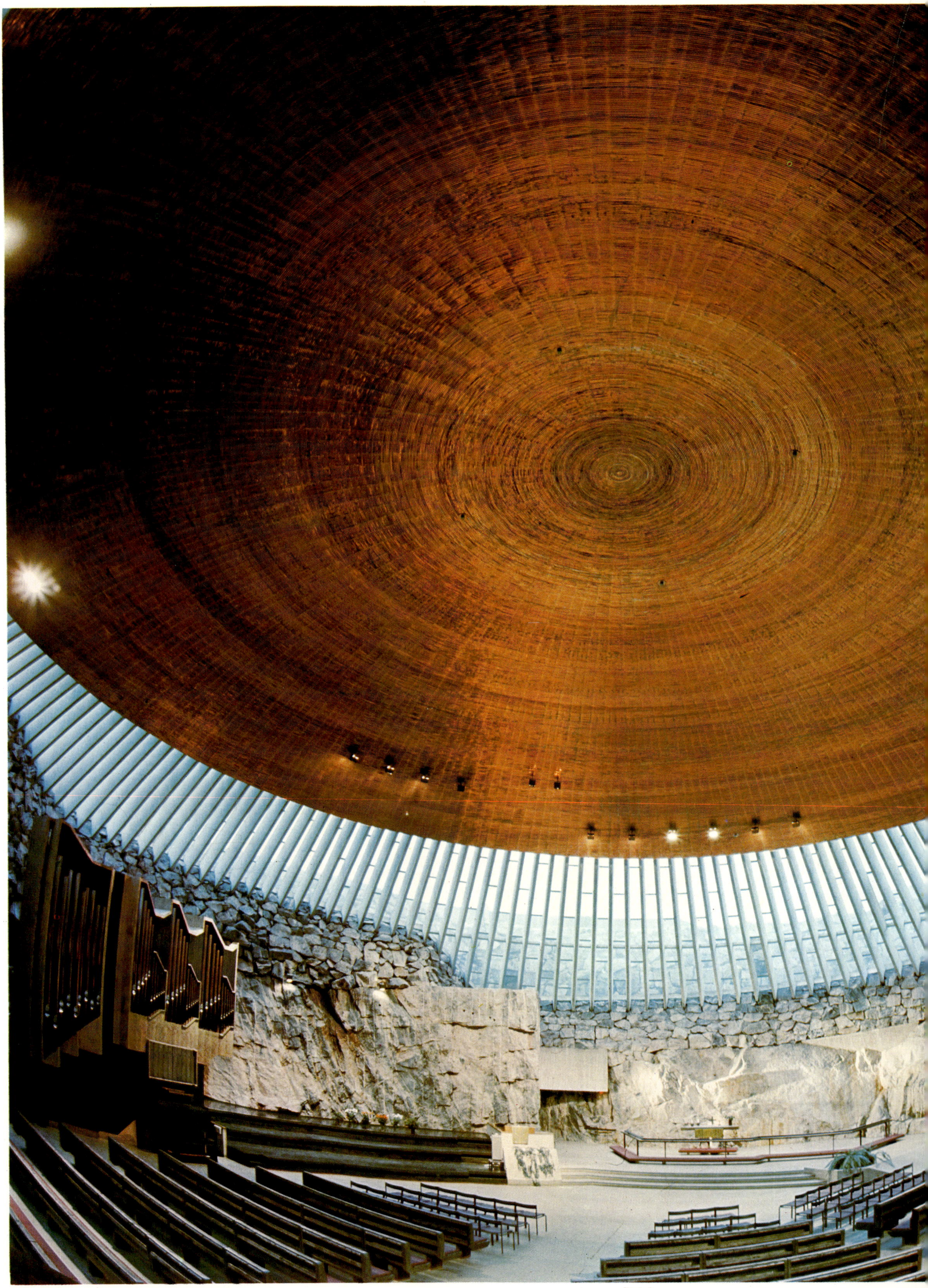

Left, Taivallahti's spacious interior, with a view of the altar. The body of the church is hewn out of the great rock that filled the center of the square. The architects were thus able to preserve a piece of nature in the midst of a city, while creating a place for prayer that is protected, luminous, and beautiful. The dimensions of the church allow it to serve as a concert or convention hall. Seen from within, the immense geometric dome is in striking contrast to the romantically "natural" rock walls below. One hundred eighty prestressed concrete beams support the roof.

Above, in the foreground, the stone font, and, in the distance, the church organ.

Below, the simple pews and the altar.

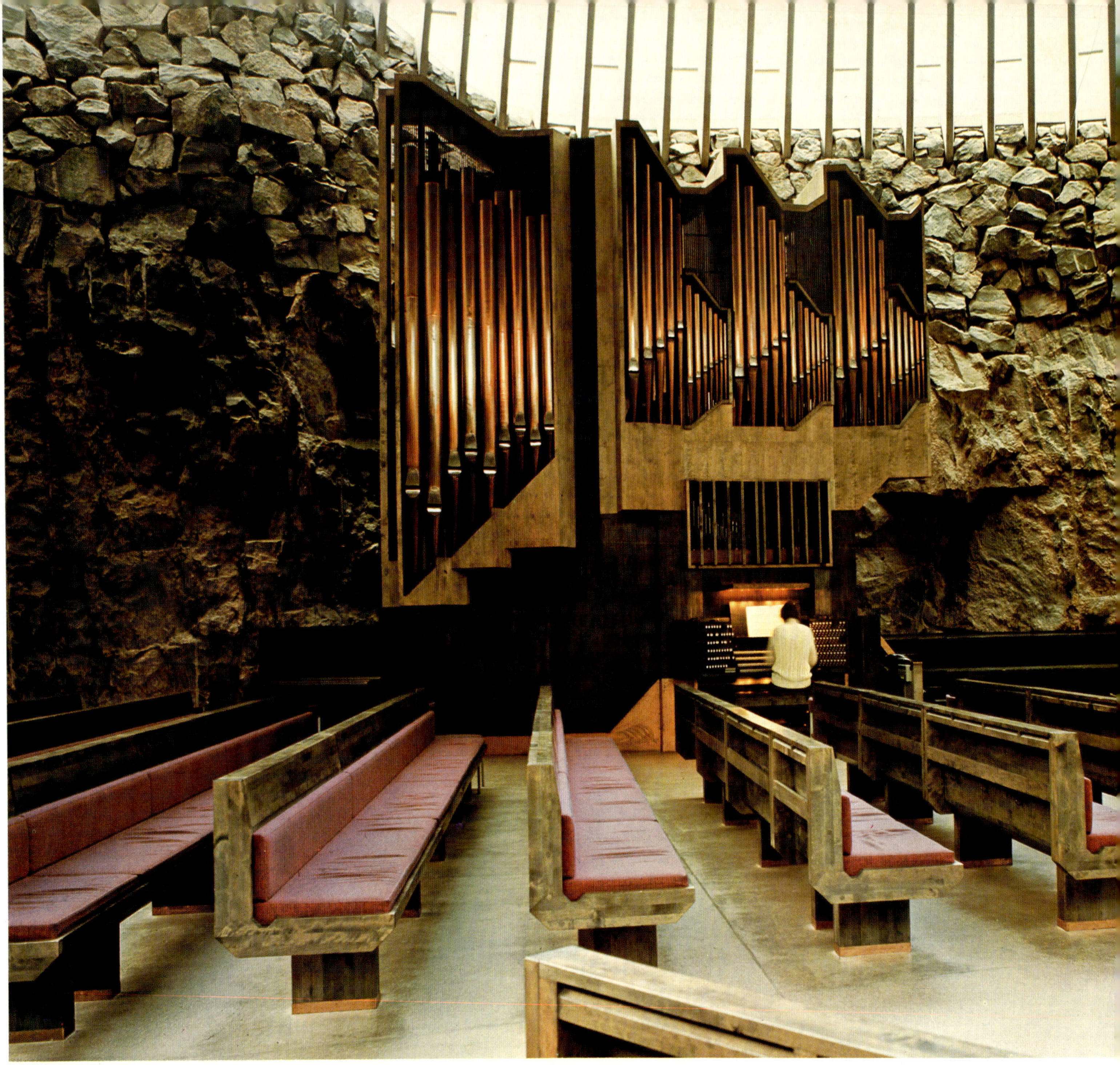
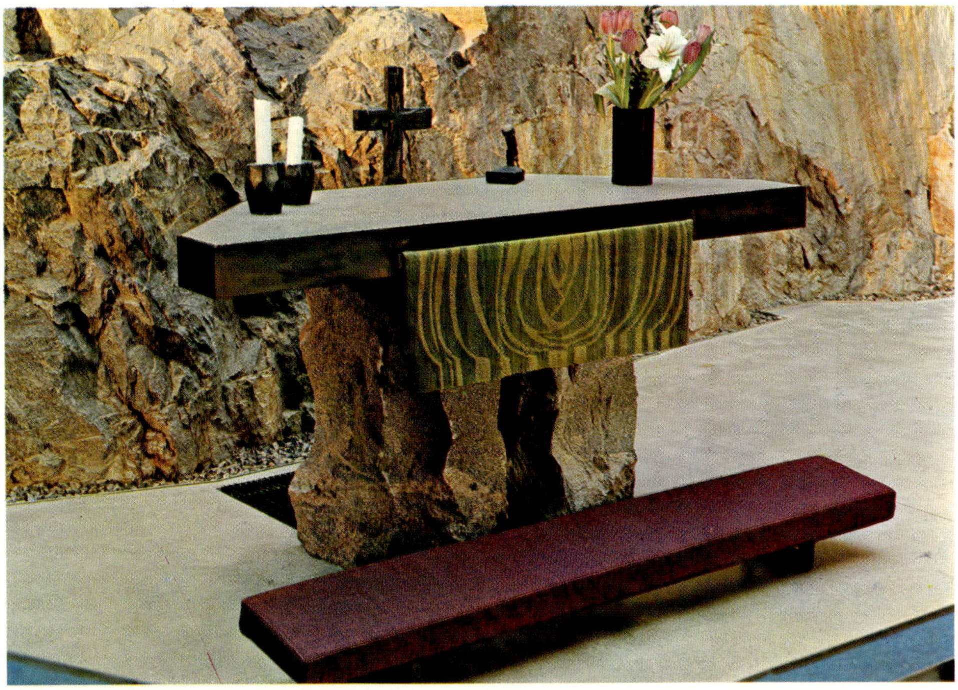
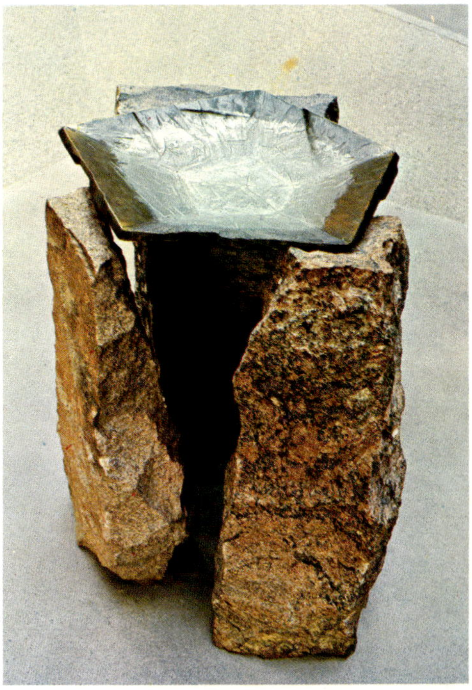

Above left, the organ, set close against one roughly carved wall.

Above and below right, the angular copper gallery in the rear of the church seems to focus the church toward the altar. Its gleaming surface evokes a sense of modernity within a basically primitive setting.

Left and far left, the font and the altar, whose bases are formed from stones from the excavation site.

As in many modern works, materials of contrasting textures are dramatically juxtaposed at Taivallahti. The photographs on this page show the effects achieved by the combinations of copper, coated aluminum, glass, and stone. Stone—both quarried and applied in the form of concrete—is the common denominator of the building.

Following page, the copper dome, which hangs suspended over the church, reflecting light from the broad band of windows into the interior space.

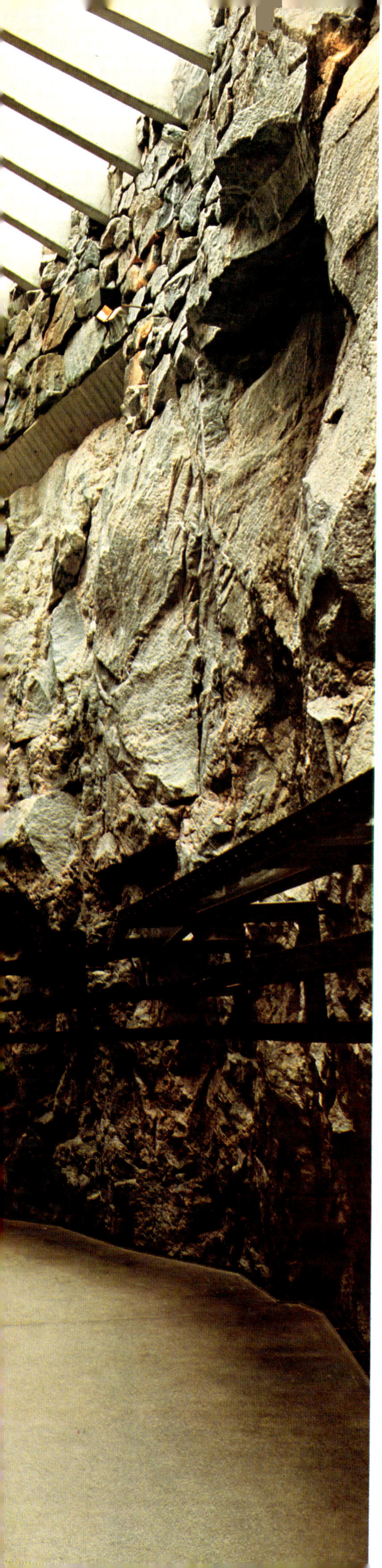
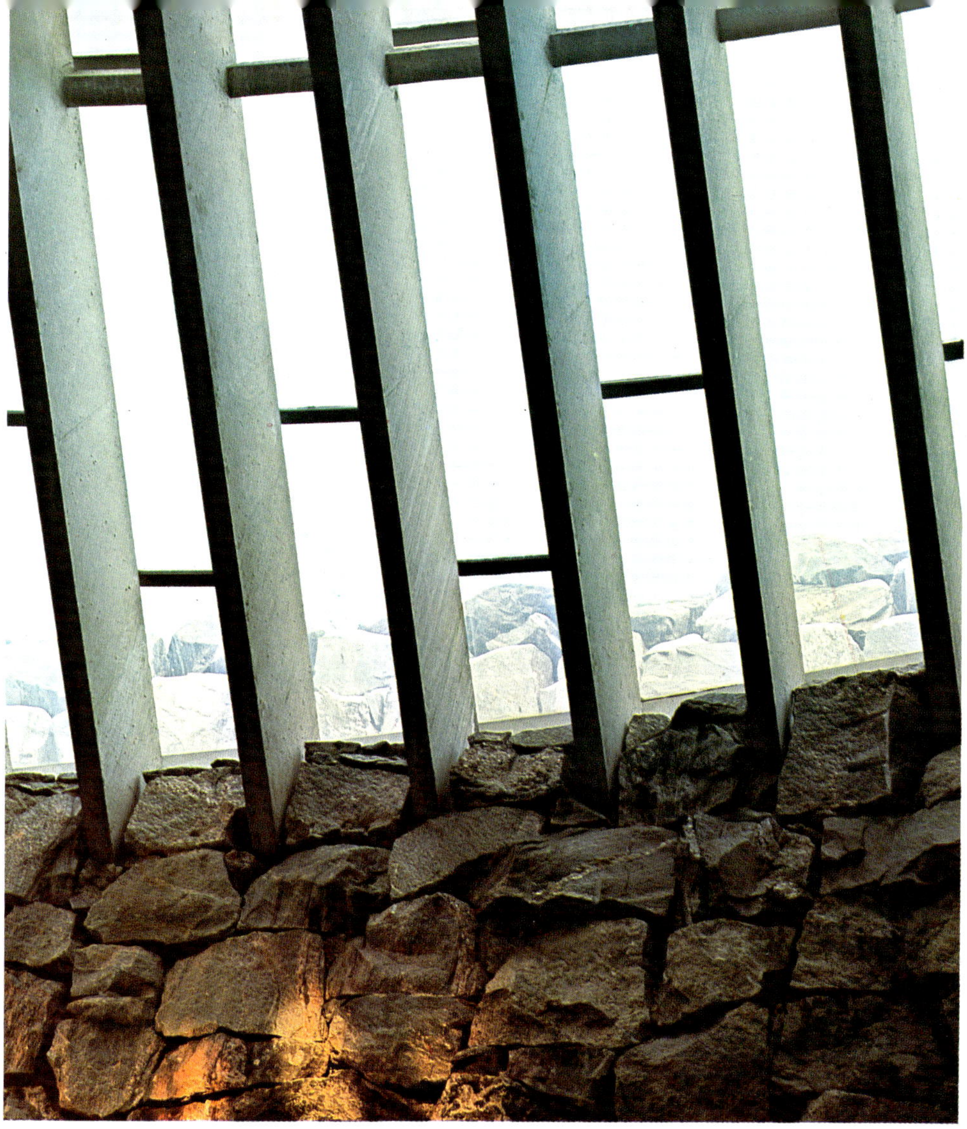
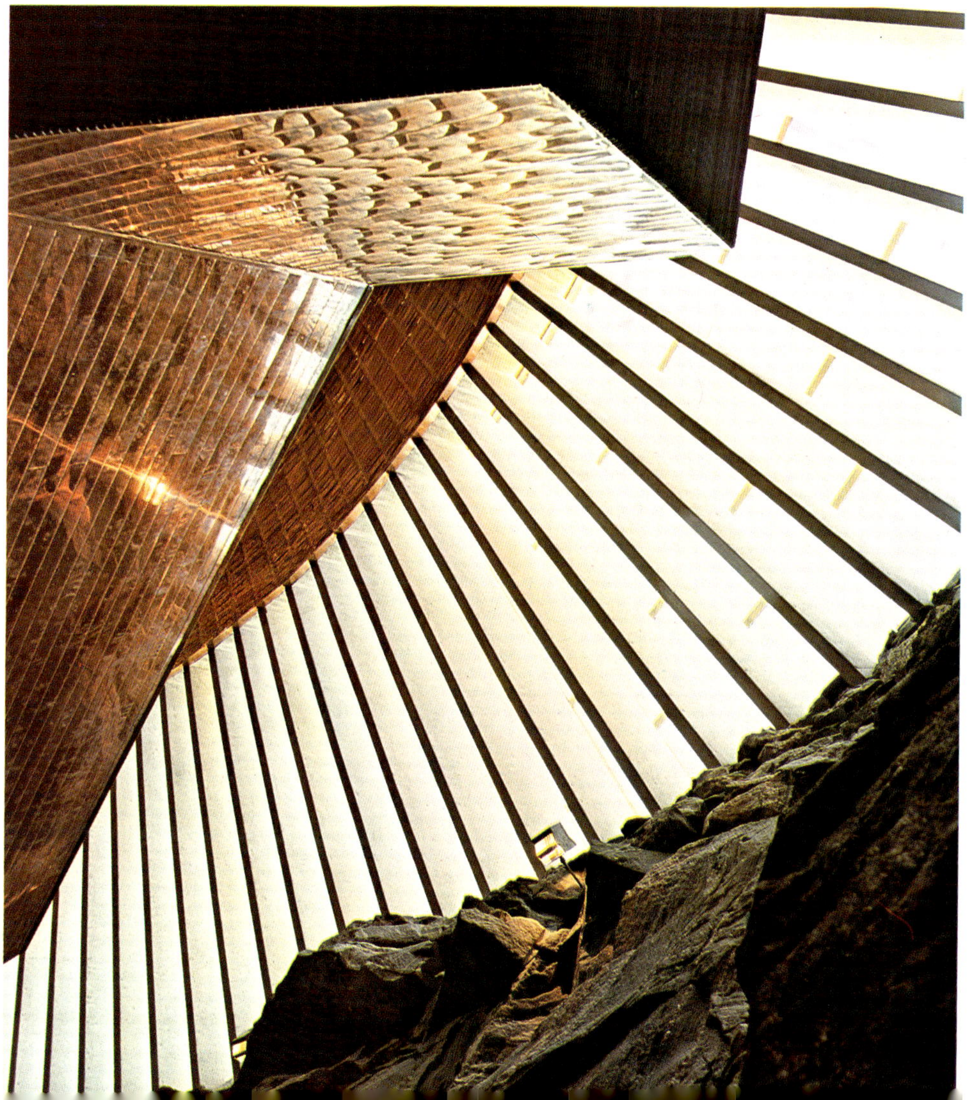

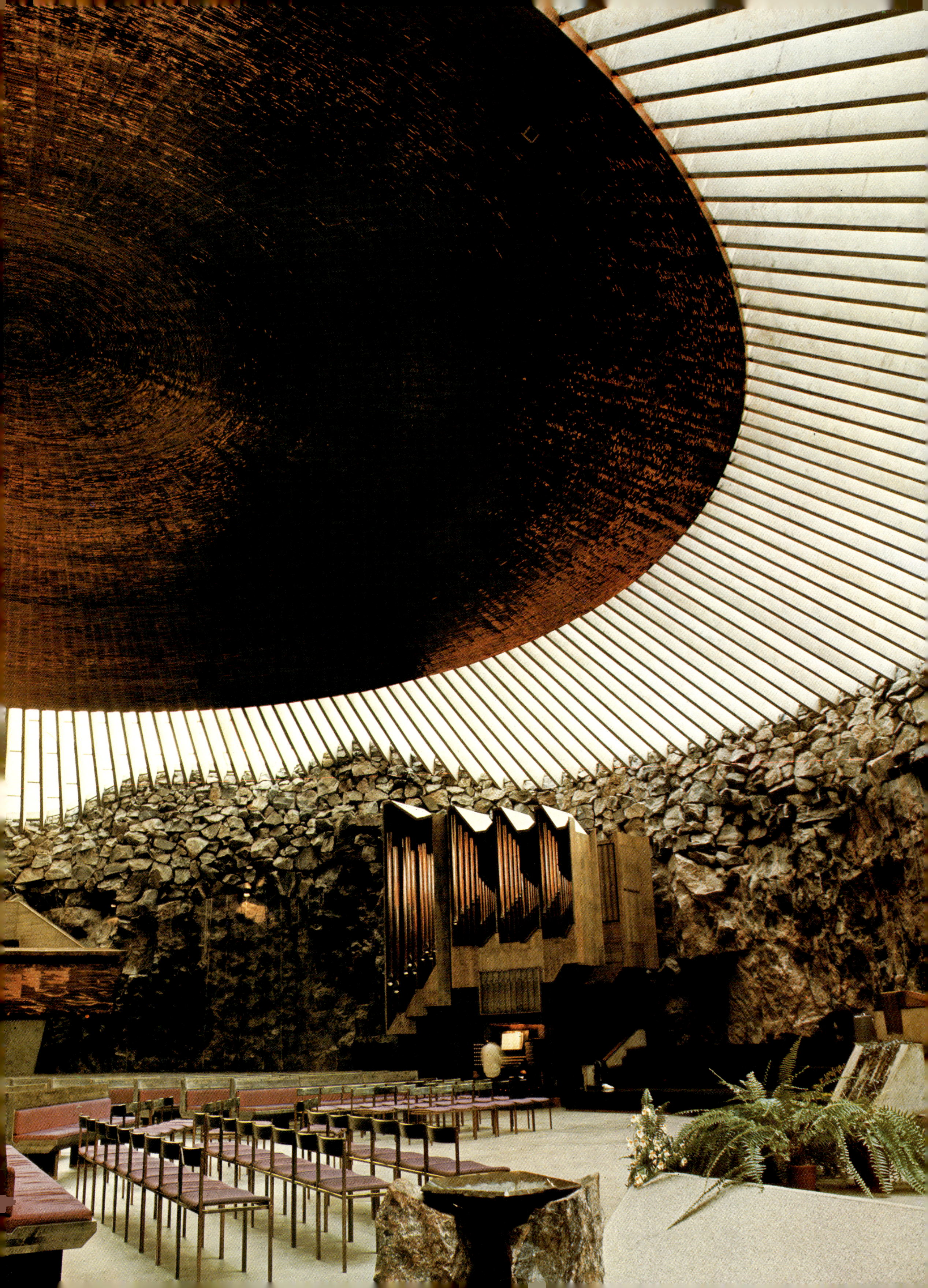

Taivallahti Church Finland

Architecture is no longer the art of building churches. Of course, churches are still being built, but the age is gone when a chronicler could write: "The world, as if dressed for a new life, is putting on a white mantle of cathedrals." The cathedrals of today are airports, refineries, and superhighways, huge sports stadiums and office towers, dams, and satellite cities. They are built in a style called Functional, which was born out of the technology of mass production and the constraints of modern economics.

Exceptions to this rule do, of course, exist. Modern architecture has produced some memorable churches that combine contemporary methods of construction with contemporary ideas about religion. One example is the starkly modern, domed Church of Taivallahti in Helsinki's Temppeliaukio ("Temple Hill") district.

The original plan was to build a large imposing church on the site. However, an architectural competition held in 1932, followed by a second one in 1936, produced no clear winning designs. The selection committee eventually decided on a plan that called for a church fronted by an almost skyscraperlike tower. Preliminary excavation began in the fall of 1939, but the work was interrupted almost immediately by the outbreak of war.

More than twenty years passed before the committee resumed its duties, and by that time, their original plan for a church seemed inappropriate. In the intervening years, Finland had become even more of a socialist and secular society. Although ninety-five percent of the Finnish people are Christians, only four percent claim to attend church regularly. A new church, therefore, would also have to function as a community center, auditorium, and concert hall.

In August 1960, the church committee announced yet another competition. This time, they specified that the church was to serve the needs of the community at large as well as the parish, while preserving to the greatest possible extent the character of the public park in which it was to be situated.

In January 1961, from a field of sixty-seven entries, they chose the plan submitted by a pair of young and talented architects, the brothers Timo and Tuomo Suomalainen. Their proposal, entitled *Kivikirkko* ("Stone Church"), was outstanding for its elegant simplicity and for the masterful way it resolved the numerous

Right, the architects of Taivallahti, Timo and Tuomo Suomalainen.

Below and far right, photographs of the early stages of the excavation of the church.

architectural problems posed by the competition committee.

Those problems were, in fact, formidable. First, the site chosen for the church was a circular space, surrounded by blocks of unprepossessing buildings. Second, in the center of the space was an enormous, irregular rock that rose to a height of forty feet above street level. To dynamite the rock away was out of the question, for in this urban neighborhood the rock was a precious contact with nature, a stretch of open ground in the center of the city. It was equally unthinkable, though, to relegate the church to a corner of the site.

The Suomalainens had a bold plan. They would leave the rock intact as far as possible, hollow out an opening for the church in the center of the rock, and cover the excavation with a large aerial dome. They would then connect the church proper with tunnels to the parish meeting rooms, the vicarage, and other secondary buildings which would be set into the sides of the rock in a way that would preserve its general outline. As the architects themselves said: "The special nature of the location led to the idea of making the church out of the rock outcrop itself and to add extra forms and structures as naturally as possible."

Almost immediately, there were difficulties. The architects were asked to make some changes in their original design. These involved removing the projected bell tower and reducing the secondary buildings by two-thirds of their planned size. And still, the finance committee argued incessantly about the cost of the construction. Seven years passed before the Suomalainens were able to get the work underway. Construction, or more properly excavation, finally began on February 14, 1968. Less than two years later, on September 28, 1969, Taivallahti Church was consecrated.

It is not entirely accurate to speak of the church as having been "built." Perhaps a more appropriate term would be "architecture by removal," an idea usually associated with certain Indian temples or funerary monuments in Egypt and Persia. To hollow out the space, blasting holes were drilled adjacent to existing faults in the rock. The rock was then dynamited along these natural cracks, so that there would be as little evidence of drilling and dynamiting as possible. However, any marks resulting from the process were left visible. The granite walls of the excavation were also left natural and unfinished, without any stone dressing or plaster. As the architects noted: "Marks from the digging were avoided as much as possible, but not artificially masked, since it was our

Clockwise from left: the excavation in its later stages; the casting of the foundation wall; the supports for the prefabricated beams; and the wooden form upon which the dome was cast. Because of the irregularity of the rim, the supporting beams for the dome are all of varying lengths.

idea that the system of construction should remain easily visible."

The church, therefore, has none of the finished surfaces to be found in a conventional building—there is just very roughly worked rock. The architects allowed an eighteen-inch margin of error between the intended alignment of the walls on the plans and the location of the actual rock face. (In an ordinary building, the comparable margin of error might be a quarter of an inch.) The walls and floors, of course, have no insulation, neither thermal nor acoustic. The primeval rock itself isolates, protects, warms, and enfolds so that the church has the oddly comforting feeling of a subterranean lair.

Excavating Taivallahti was only half the work. The other half involved planning, engineering, and installing the roof. The creation of the dome proved to be an impressive technical feat, as well as an ingenious solution to the aesthetic problem of converting a raw cavity into a harmonious and habitable architectural space.

First, one hundred eighty beams of prestressed concrete were set, like the spokes of a wheel, around the perimeter of the hole, at a slight angle from the horizontal. Then, a shallow concrete dome—the hub of this dish-shaped wheel—was cast in the center. This seemingly simple operation turned out to be a complex problem for the engineers working on the church. The dome was to be both rather broad—an average of seventy-five feet across—and rather flat. It was also irregular, for the rim of the wheel was the edge of the excavation. Thus, each of the precast spokes was a slightly different length from the next.

To calculate the requirements of the dome, a model of the structure was built. The model was subjected to representations of the stresses that the actual dome would be expected to bear. These experiments gave the engineers the information they needed to design the roof of the church.

The outer ring of double-glazed skylights lies above the prefabricated beams, while the thin concrete shell in the center is covered inside and out with copper. From below, the copper and glass dome appears to hover dramatically above the space. The architects knew that a support with a bright light on either side appears a good deal more slender than it actually is. In fact, the concrete beams are already remarkably thin; on sunny days, they seem to disappear.

The ring of windows encircling the ceiling is, in the architects' words:

The decisive part of the design. The most "weightless" part of the church.

Several views of the erection of the beams and the casting of the cement used for the center of the dome are shown here. The prestressed concrete beams support a thin concrete shell, which was covered outside with a copper roof, and support an acoustic copper ceiling inside the church.

152 • Individual Creations

Through it the heavy freeform of the stone wall joins the mathematical form of the dome, and the hall space opens upward toward the open space outside.

From the exterior, only the upper part of the dome, covered in a gradually aging copper, is visible to passers-by. The great ring of glass is hidden by a wall of stone, quarried from the site, which follows the contour of the excavation. The wall minimizes the church's intrusion upon its natural surroundings, and it also keeps parkgoers away from the dome and its skylights.

Such a fusion of modern and primitive materials is a bold and elegant achievement. It is this subtle union of past and present that makes Taivallahti's roughly carved, unadorned center so immediately inviting. The expansive copper dome looms overhead like a giant sun, reflecting the light that enters through the windows at its base. The harsh granite dramatically contrasts with the play of light overhead. Glass against metal, metal against stone, stone against glass—juxtapositions of texture everywhere give the church a vital, natural atmosphere.

In planning their church, the Suomalainen brothers paid strict attention to the secular as well as the religious needs of the community. Therefore, they designed the building itself to function not only as a church but also as an auditorium for concerts or conferences. The church has a choir loft, as well as space for an orchestra. There is a control room for recording, for radio and television transmissions, and for simultaneous translations. Enclosed in its primeval rock, Taivallahti is equipped to meet the needs of a contemporary urban community.

Apart from pews, an organ, a font, and a small cross on the altar, there are few traditional ecclesiastical accouterments within Taivallahti. In keeping with the overall principle of its design, stones from the site were used for various details, such as the supports of the altar and the font. The simple altar and pews, low to the ground, accentuate the height of the great coppery dish that hangs overhead—as do the rising pipes of the organ, which nestle so close to the wall that they seem to be some sort of natural outcropping.

Taivallahti has been seen as a visual metaphor for the place of the church in modern society. Stripped of its traditional façades and furnishings, at ease with a sophisticated modern technology, yet carved deep into rock, it is a space in the heart of the city where people may gather to worship and reflect.

Above and right, the interior of the church during construction, showing the scaffolding supporting the work. Once construction was underway, Taivallahti Church took only a year and a half to complete.

Guggenheim Museum

U.S.A.

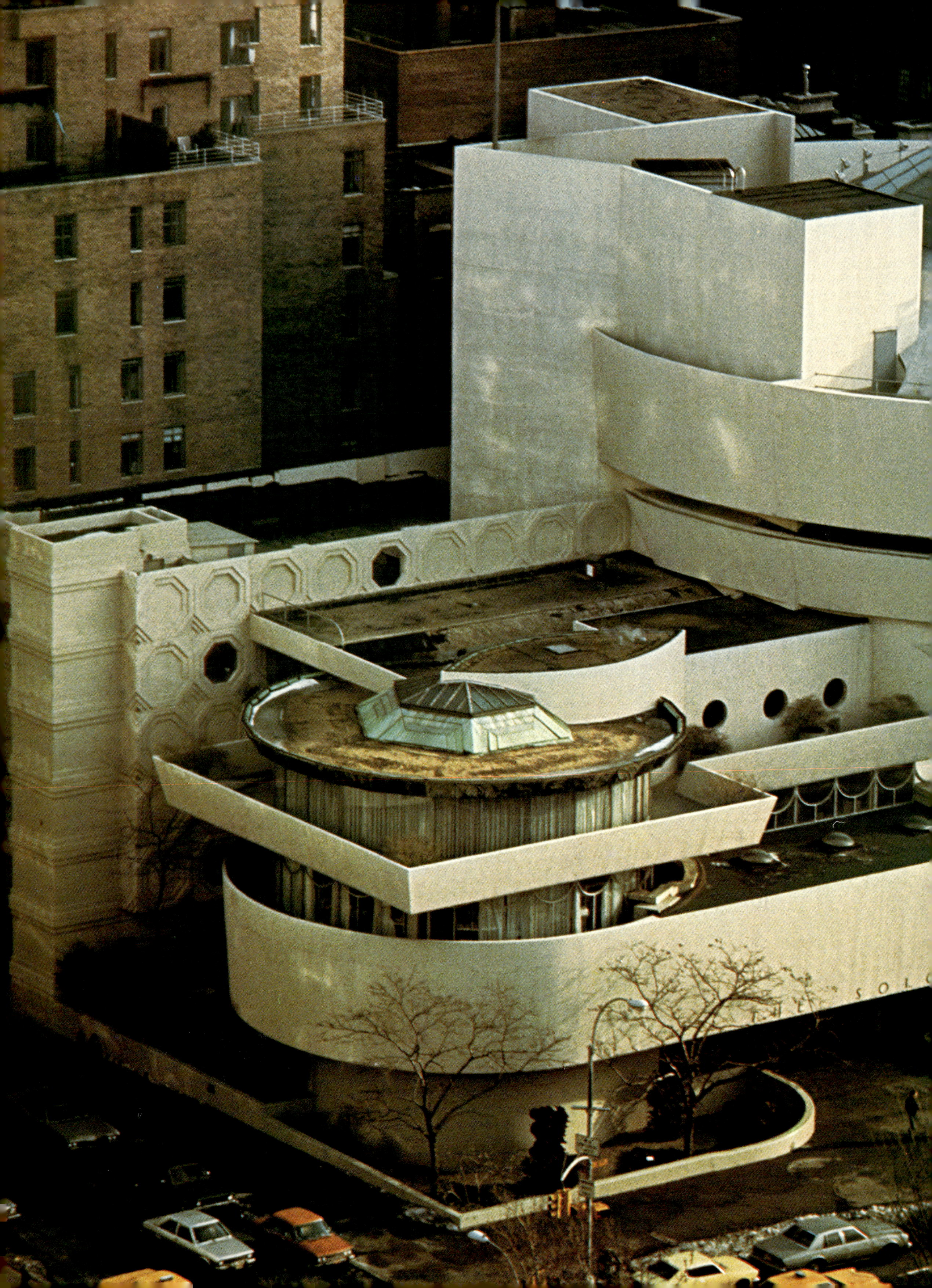

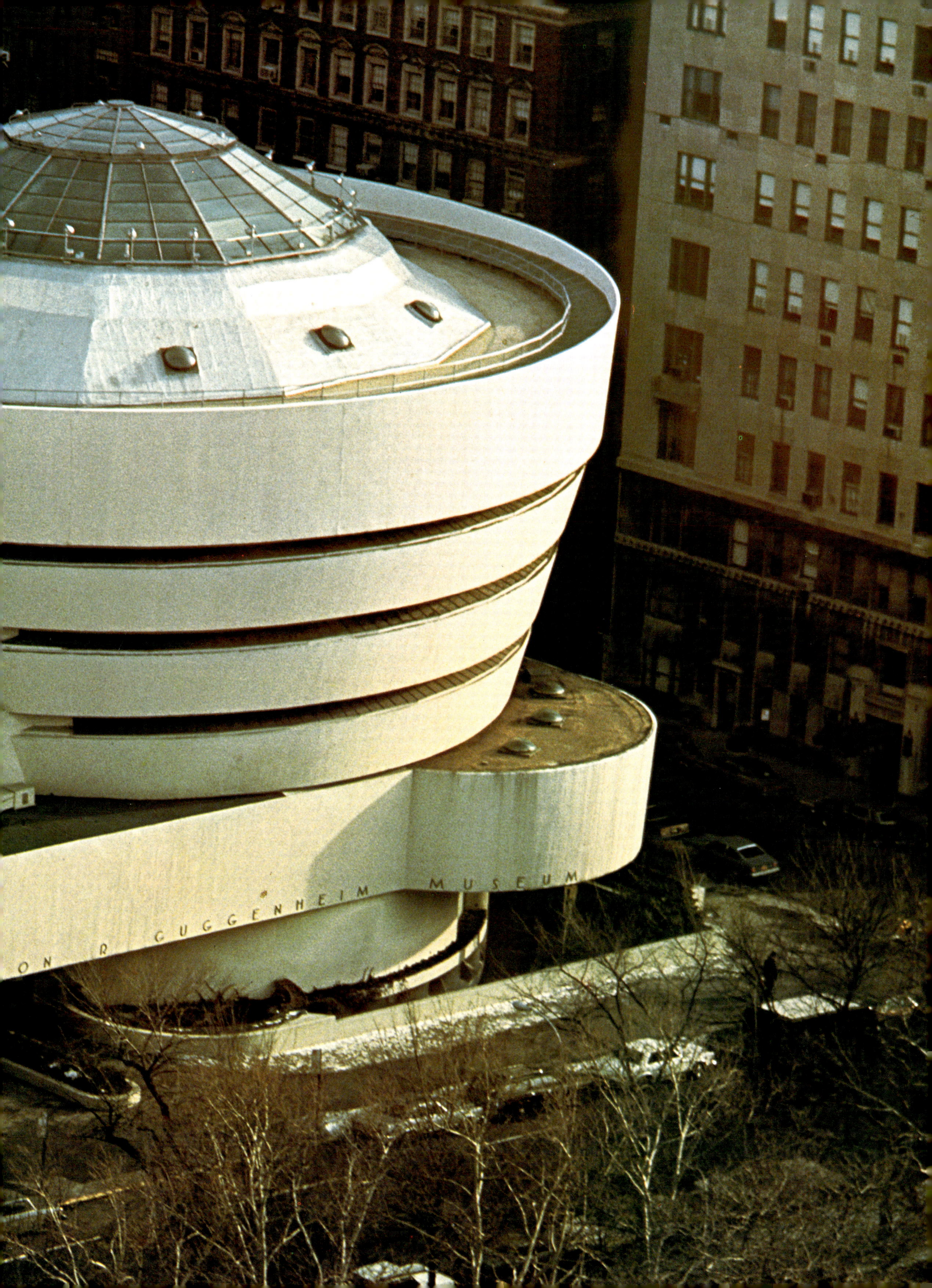
GUGGENHEIM MUSEUM

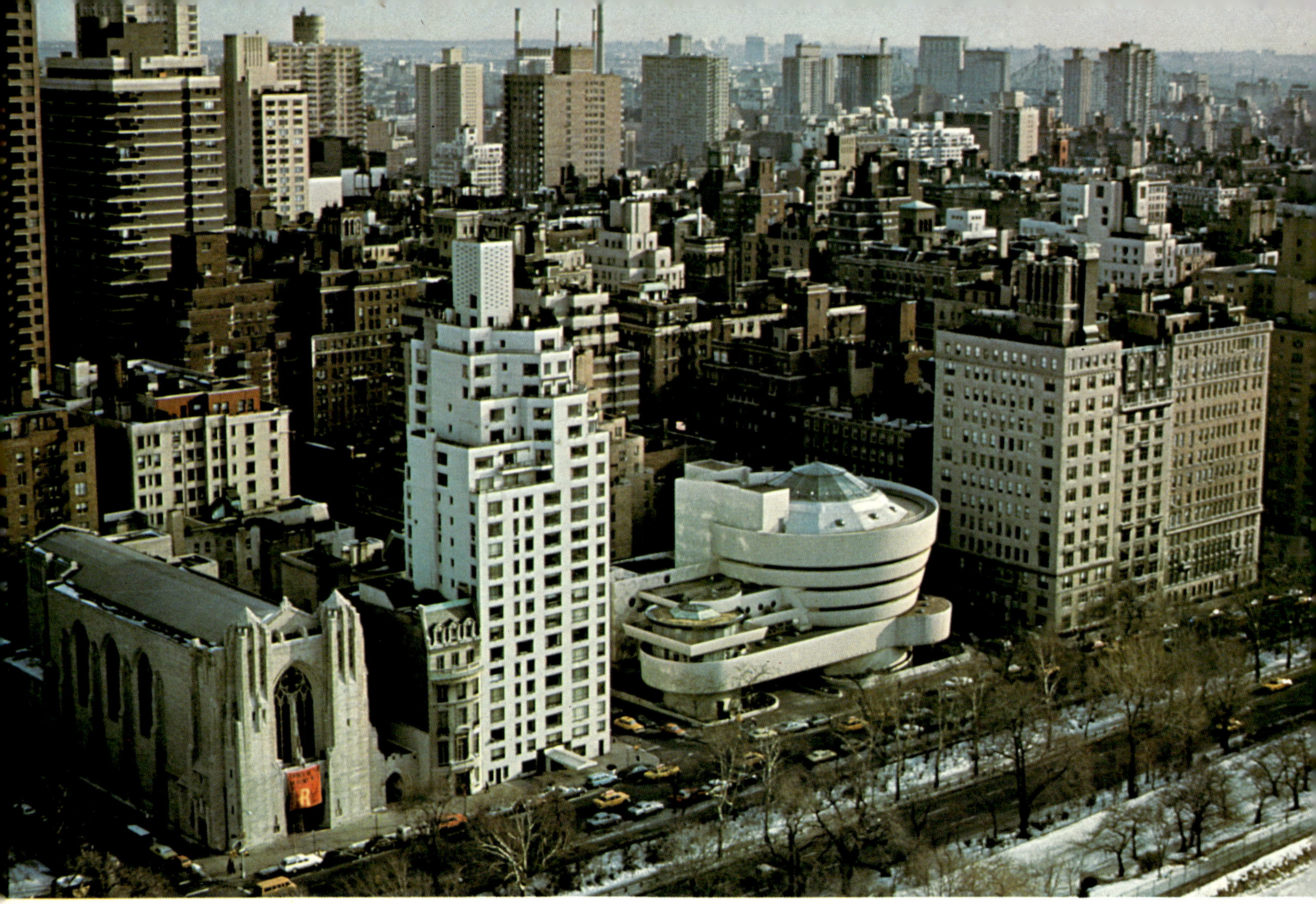

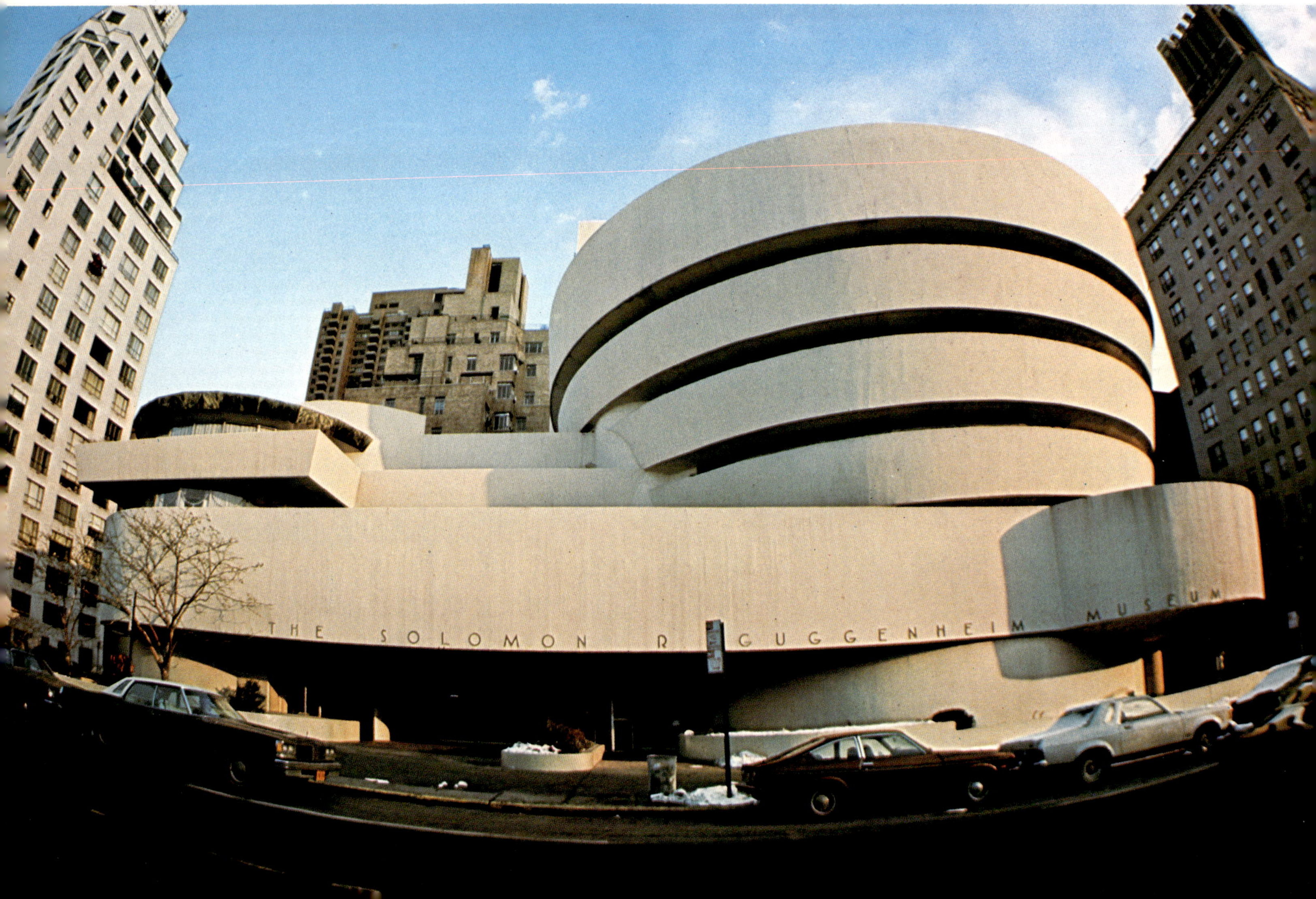
THE SOLOMON R GUGGENHEIM MUSEUM

Preceding page, the Guggenheim Museum, seen from above with its huge skylight. It is one of Frank Lloyd Wright's last major works and is also among his least decorated—perhaps because he wanted nothing to distract from its spiral design. Wright considered the spiral to be the ultimate and most coherent form for the "organic architecture" of which he was the undisputed master.

Above left, the Guggenheim in its setting on Fifth Avenue. The museum stands out in sharp contrast to the buildings around it. In Wright's view this was proof of its greatness. In fact, his concrete spiral makes the surrounding structures look archaic—as though they are intruders upon a landscape to which only the museum itself is native.

Left, above, and right, a sense of the "energy" and mass of the huge spiral, which might seem precariously balanced were it not for the solidarity of the huge slab upon which it rests.

The interior space of the museum is entirely fluid, as Wright envisioned it, and functions along the lines of his original idea. As visitors enter, they are taken to the top of the ramp by the elevator, whose columnlike shaft breaks the curve of the ramps (left and above). As visitors make their way down the spiraling ramp, they can view the modern paintings which are hung on the walls. Most of the museum's daytime illumination comes from the huge central skylight (below), which is reflected in a pool on the ground floor (facing page).

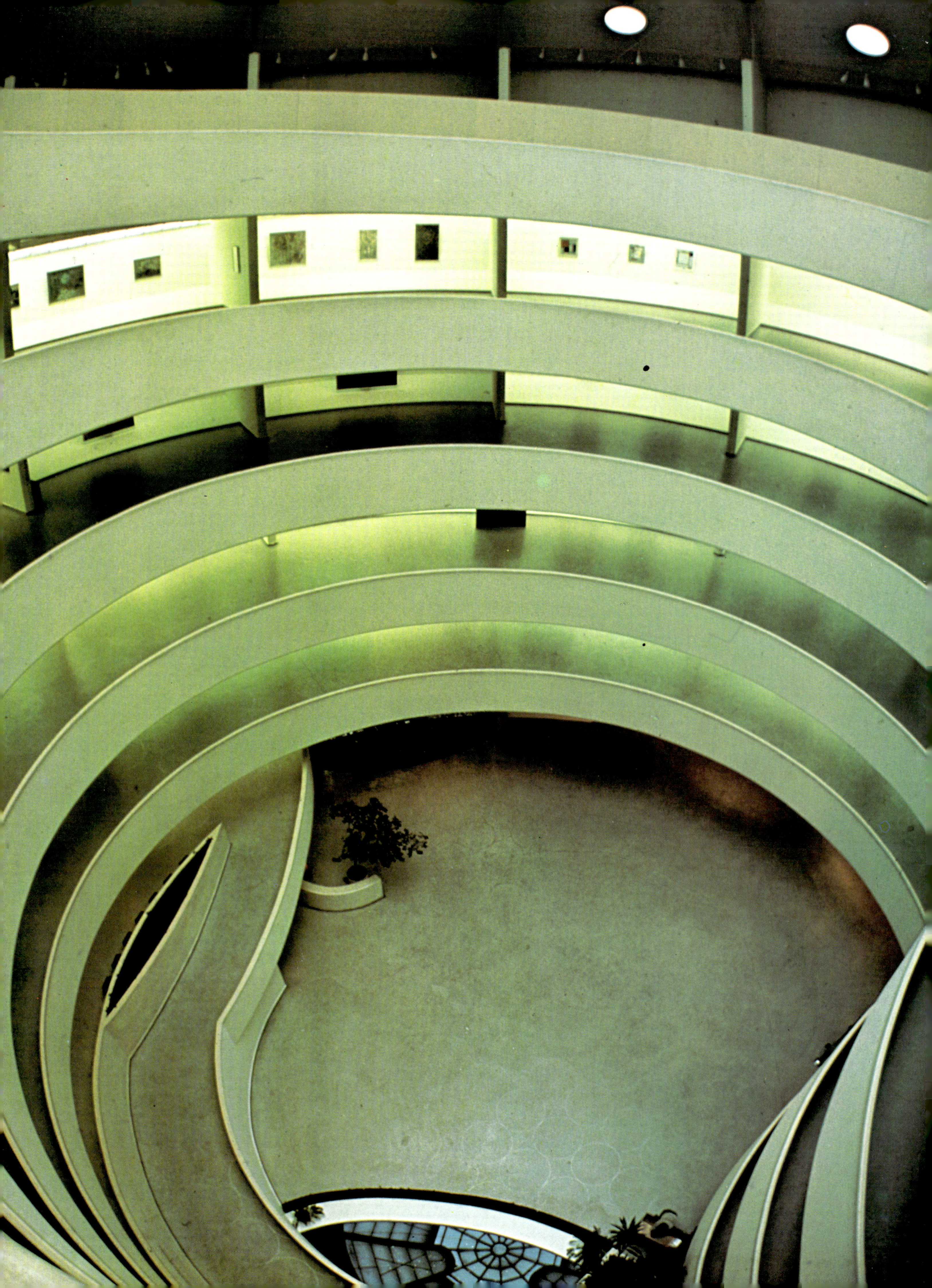

Wright's spiral design has proved to be somewhat impractical for a picture gallery. The visitor has to stand on a sloping floor and look at flat paintings hung against curved walls—a sometimes discomforting experience. Some critics have suggested that the architect must have hated modern art to have housed it in such an unsympathetic atmosphere, but it is more likely that Wright was so enthralled with the form that he paid little attention to the function it was to serve. However, he did justify his design on functional grounds. Walking down the linear ramp was supposed to be less tiring than wandering through the maze of a conventional gallery, although some visitors find it just as tiring—and dizzying as well. The Guggenheim is among the best-known and most popular museums of modern art in the world, although the building itself may well be the prime attraction for most visitors.

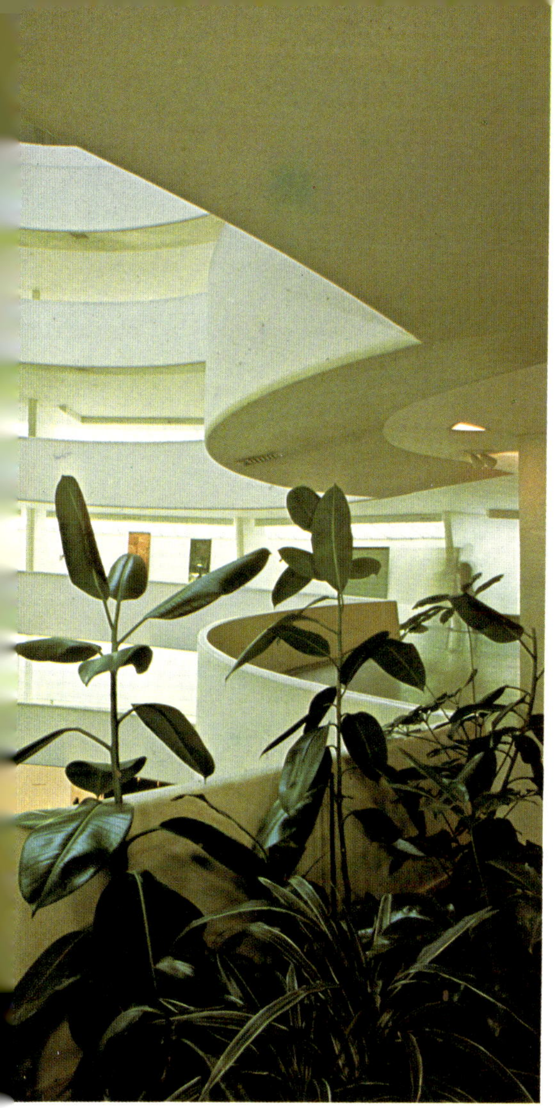
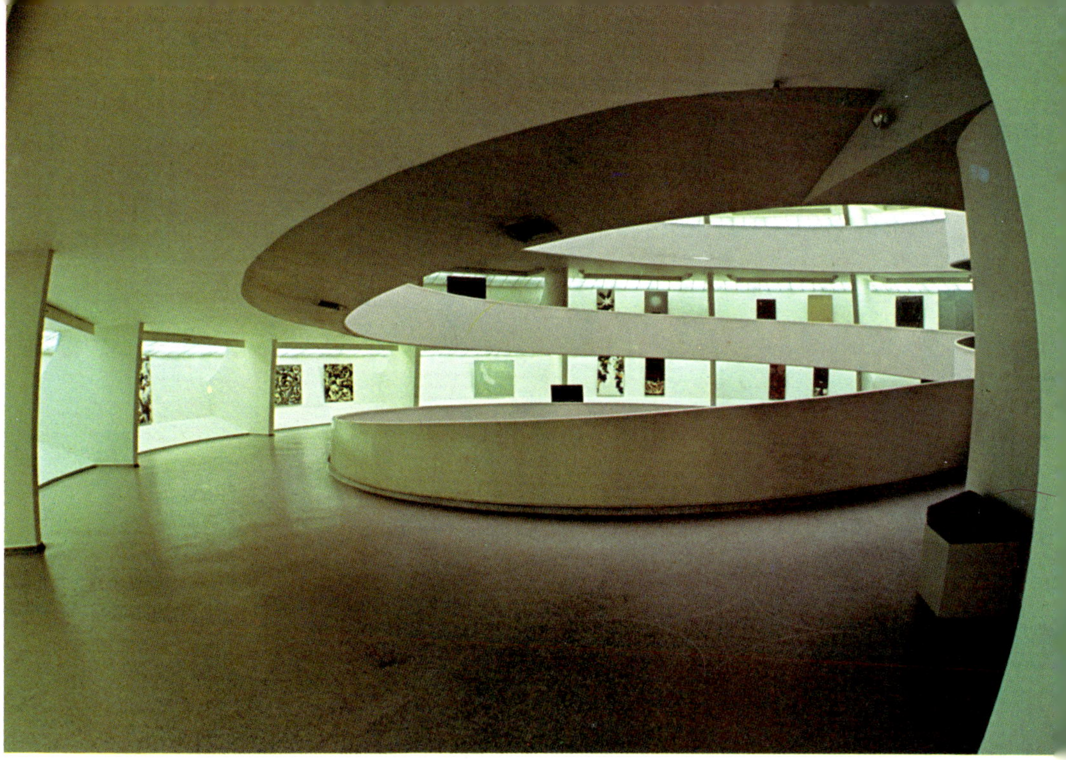
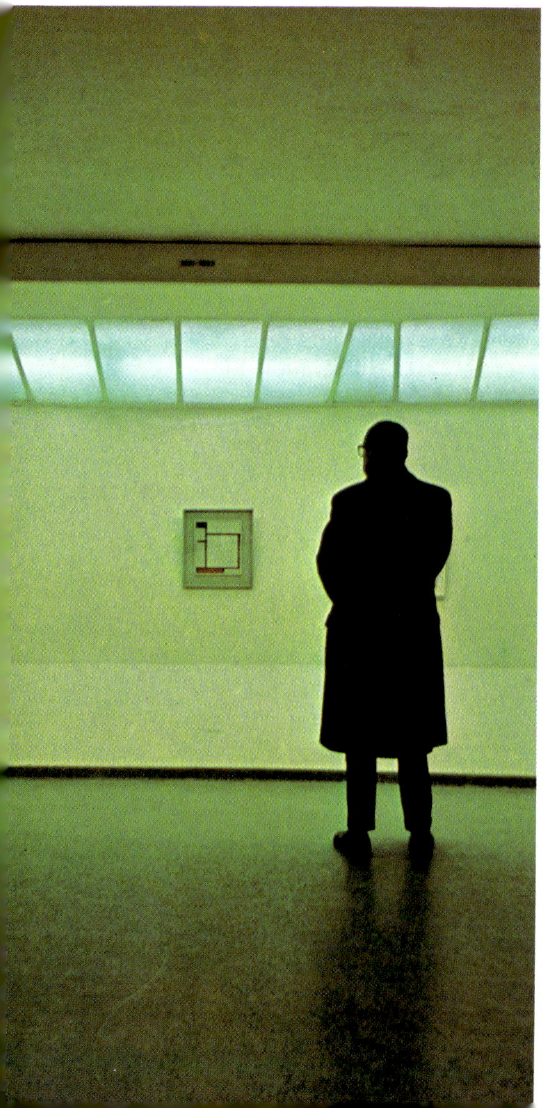
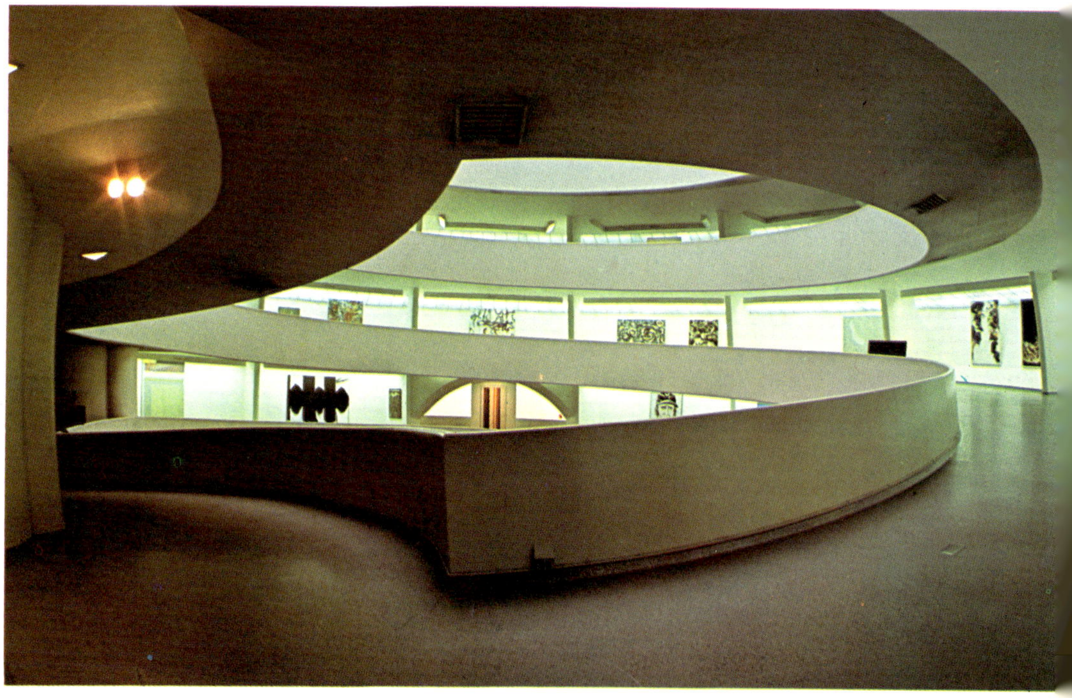
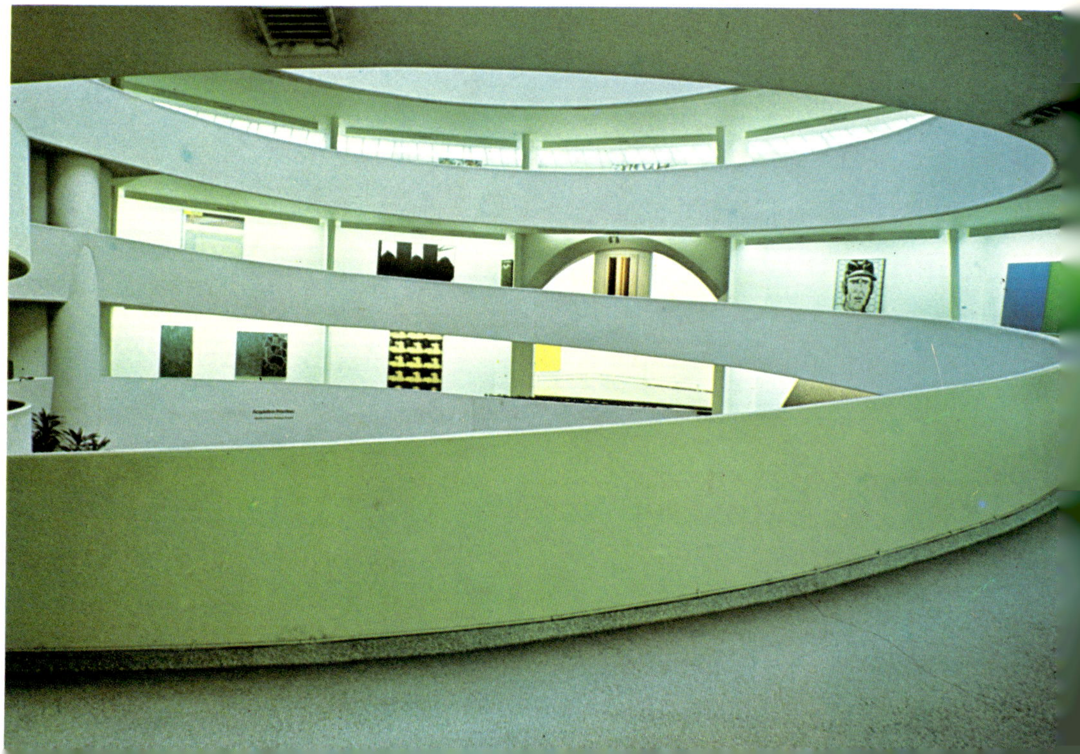

The museum reflects Wright's characteristic attention to the integrity and continuity of his interiors and the fusion of each element into the overall design.

Above and left, an arch overlooking a side gallery.

Below, the leaf-shaped reflecting pool that rests inside the ground floor curve of the ramp. The foliage at the edge of the pool seems to grow naturally out of the concrete of the ramp.

Curved forms dominate the spaces devoted to the museum's subsidiary activities—the small auditorium (above left), the book sales stand (center left), the restaurant (below left), and an ancillary gallery (below).

Following page, the Guggenheim—perhaps the only museum in the world in which all the galleries can be seen at a single glance.

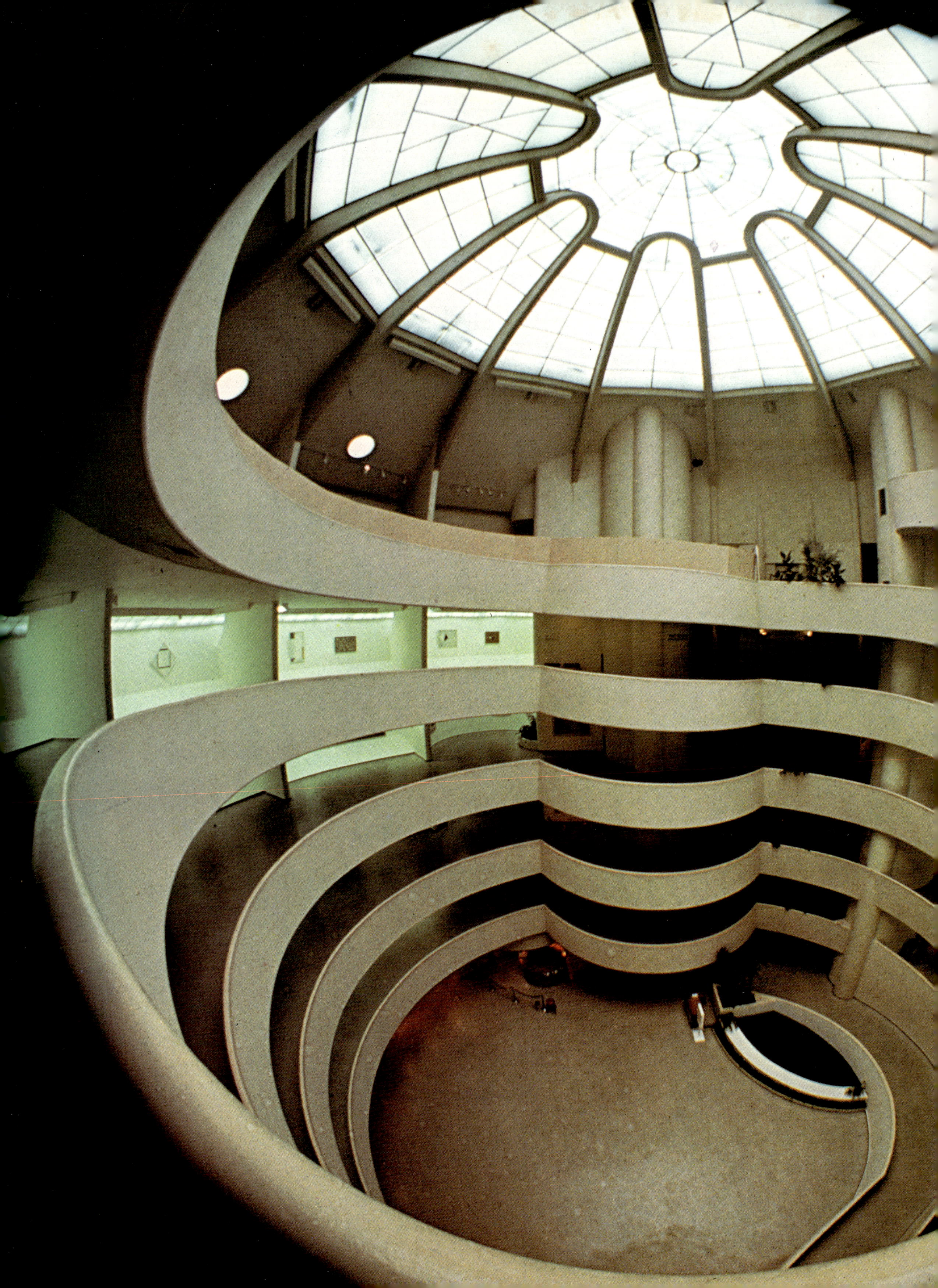

Guggenheim Museum U.S.A.

In 1932, New York's Museum of Modern Art assembled what was clearly meant to be a definitive exhibition of modern architecture. It presented the work of Frank Lloyd Wright along with that of Le Corbusier and Ludwig Mies van der Rohe and Walter Gropius, two leaders of Germany's revolutionary design school, the Bauhaus. On that occasion, Wright exuberantly commented, "I warn you, that having made an excellent start, I fully intend not only to be the greatest architect that has ever been but also the greatest of all future architects."

Wright's candid endorsement of his own work was understandable, if somewhat extravagant. When his three coexhibitors were still in grade school, he was already designing remarkably innovative houses, any one of which could have established his pre-eminence among contemporary architects. With the help of a band of devoted assistants, Wright had created dozens of them, year after year. By 1932, Wright's work had become highly individualistic—often with hints of the expressionism that later was to suffuse his design for the Guggenheim Museum.

Wright's own training had been limited to a few years' work in the studios of some well-known Chicago architects, during which time he had risen to become chief designer for Louis Sullivan, the father of the modern skyscraper. Though Wright respected Sullivan—he was fond of calling him *lieber meister* ("dear master")—their relationship was abruptly dissolved when the master discovered that his young protégé had begun to secretively design buildings for clients of his own, in violation of their contract.

Frank Lloyd Wright's childhood had been shaped by a transplanted New England heritage of liberal Protestantism and an acceptance of the "natural philosophy" that was expressed in the writings of Walt Whitman and Henry David Thoreau. In the spirited and energetic atmosphere of the times, it is perhaps not surprising that Wright also developed that insistence upon absolute freedom of mind which marks the true pioneer as well as the renowned artist, which is why he often seemed more concerned with finding the proper form to embody an idea than with pleasing his clients. To Wright, the artistic integrity of his work was far more important than its utilitarian function. Once, when the owner of one of his houses called to say that rain was dripping on him from a crack in the ceiling, Wright is said to have suggested that the man move his chair.

Both Wright's genius and his obstinacy came to play their roles in his design for the Guggenheim Museum in New York City. In the early 1940's Solomon R. Guggenheim, who was committed to fostering the development of modern painting, found himself in need of more space to house a growing collection of pictures. Quite justifiably, but perhaps ingenuously, he decided that a museum of modern art ought to be the work of a leading modern architect. Ironically, he turned to Wright, a man known to have little empathy for twentieth-century painting, and commissioned him to design the new museum. Wright's creation is one of the most original buildings in the world, a museum with its own place in the history of art. Yet, as a picture gallery, it is a failure. Ultimately, the only thing it displays well is itself.

One of the first problems—in Wright's view—was the location of the proposed building. The foundation had selected a corner site on Fifth Avenue, facing Cen-

Below, one of the masterly perspective drawings that Wright's studio produced to illustrate the project.

Above, Frank Lloyd Wright's first house and studio in Oak Park, Illinois. Left, the architect with some of his many student-collaborators.

tral Park. If there was one thing that Frank Lloyd Wright detested, it was the big city—not New York in particular, but the very concept of city. "The city," he used to say, quoting Ralph Waldo Emerson, "makes man sociable and loquacious... and artificial." Wright's feelings were well known; nevertheless, the commission was offered and accepted by the architect.

The administrators of the museum may have been unaware of—or refused to acknowledge—Wright's growing rejection of the conventional square and rectangular forms of city buildings and blocks. In his continual search for natural forms appropriate to human needs—forms that he described as "organic architecture," opening out onto the world rather than insulating people from it—Wright had begun to explore the possibilities of the triangle, the polygon (recalling the forms of mineral crystals), and even the circle. For some time, he had been ready to take the logical step from the circle to the spiral, the form of conch shells, "plastic and continuous"— for the spiral, or more properly a helix, is simply a circle carried into the third dimension, a circle of movement, an infinite line. In fact, many years earlier, Wright had wanted to build a great spiral that would give concrete form to his vision. In 1927, he proposed turning the top of Sugarloaf Mountain in Maryland into a spiral ramp that would take cars up to an observatory at the peak. In the 1930s, however, Wright returned to more conventional forms, thus his helical spiral dream was not realized until he convinced Solomon Guggenheim that an inverted conical spiral would make a magnificent museum.

Progress on the building was slow, but the delays were not attributable to Wright. The preliminary design, a fantastic perspective drawing that shows the original project—the architect always made meticulous studies for his proposals—was presented in 1943. Guggenheim's approval was secured in 1944, but construction was not scheduled to begin until the war was over. It was delayed by the death of Solomon Guggenheim in 1949, then again until 1956 by the New York City building codes, as well as by some disagreements between the architect and the directors of the Guggenheim foundation. Work was not finally completed on the museum until after Wright's death.

The museum is essentially a long ramp which starts at ground level and spirals upward in five concentric turns, continually growing wider so that it opens out toward the top. Within the spiral is a vast central space, illuminated primarily by a huge skylight. At the first floor level, the main spiral is joined with a smaller, round building, used for readings, lectures, and offices. A broad horizontal rectilinear base structure connects both elements and also relates the museum as a whole to its rectilinear environment of city blocks and conventional buildings.

The startling effect of the Guggenheim is accentuated by its apparent simplicity. Outside, there is little more than the lettering of the name of the museum to break the smoothness of its concrete walls. This starkness is unusual in Wright's work, for many of his buildings are so highly decorated that their carefully designed spatial structures are barely discernible.

Wright was fond of quoting Lao-tse, who twenty-five centuries earlier had stated that "the reality of a vessel is the space which it encloses." The Guggenheim Museum may be the architect's clearest demonstration of the somewhat contradictory way in which he interpreted these words. Wright said he could not understand the inability of his colleagues to differentiate between urban and rural architecture. He proclaimed his lack of patience for architects who unthinkingly transposed the boxlike structures suitable for cities into country landscapes. He abhorred the unnaturalness of "urban" buildings that took no account of their rural surroundings, those whose closed interior spaces communicated with the outside only through the small windows punched in their walls. Remaining true to his view of life itself as fluid, continuous, and integrated, Wright wrote about wanting to design structures that would harmonize with their surroundings, using materials that were natural to the environment in which they were to stand. In the Guggenheim Museum, he certainly achieved a perfectly continuous, self-contained organic form where the flowing spiral shapes both the outside structure and the space within. If here Wright can be faulted for all but ignoring his urban neighbors, at least he almost makes them look as though *they* are the ones that are out of place.

In defense of his stunningly original design, Wright declared that he was not merely playing a game with forms: He believed that the helix was really the best shape for a picture gallery. He claimed that the conventional manner of displaying paintings in one dreary room after another distracts the attention of visitors by making them concerned with the condition of their feet rather than with the masterpieces on the walls. According to Wright, this museum fatigue was an inevitable consequence of wrong-headed architecture. At the Guggenheim, visitors would enter on the ground floor and be carried by elevator up to the top, where they would begin to slowly wind down along the spiral. Any weariness would be counteracted by the natural form of the shell, which would gently "spiral" visitors down to the first floor. As they descended, they would be able to study the paintings hung along the outward-leaning walls. In this way, each work of art would be viewed at an angle—as Wright believed the artist himself had seen it on the easel.

There was considerable controversy over the design. Some raised the objection that very large rectangular canvases could not tolerate the sloping floors and curved walls. A reply of sorts in *The Architectural Forum* that "the rectangular frame of a painting has more to do with the frame than with the painting" is true enough, but most canvases are still stretched on rectangular frames before being painted. However, this objection is really unimportant. The curve of the walls is gradual enough to allow all but tremendously oversized canvases to hang comfortably.

The spiral defines a magnificent space and has become a compulsory stop on even the most cursory tours of New York. The Guggenheim often impresses visitors more than the better-known and more prestigious Museum of Modern Art,

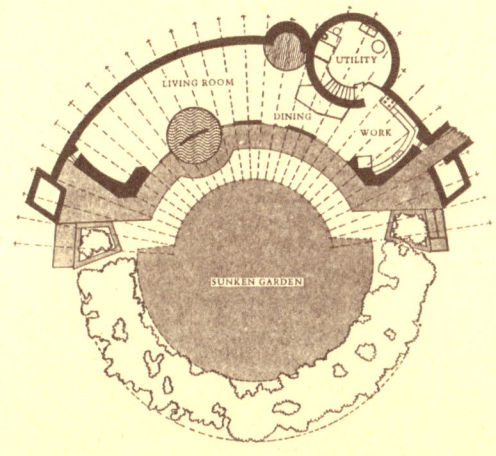

Above, plan of the Jacobs House designed in 1943, which reflects Wright's interest in circular buildings. Right, the first version of the Guggenheim, higher than the final design.

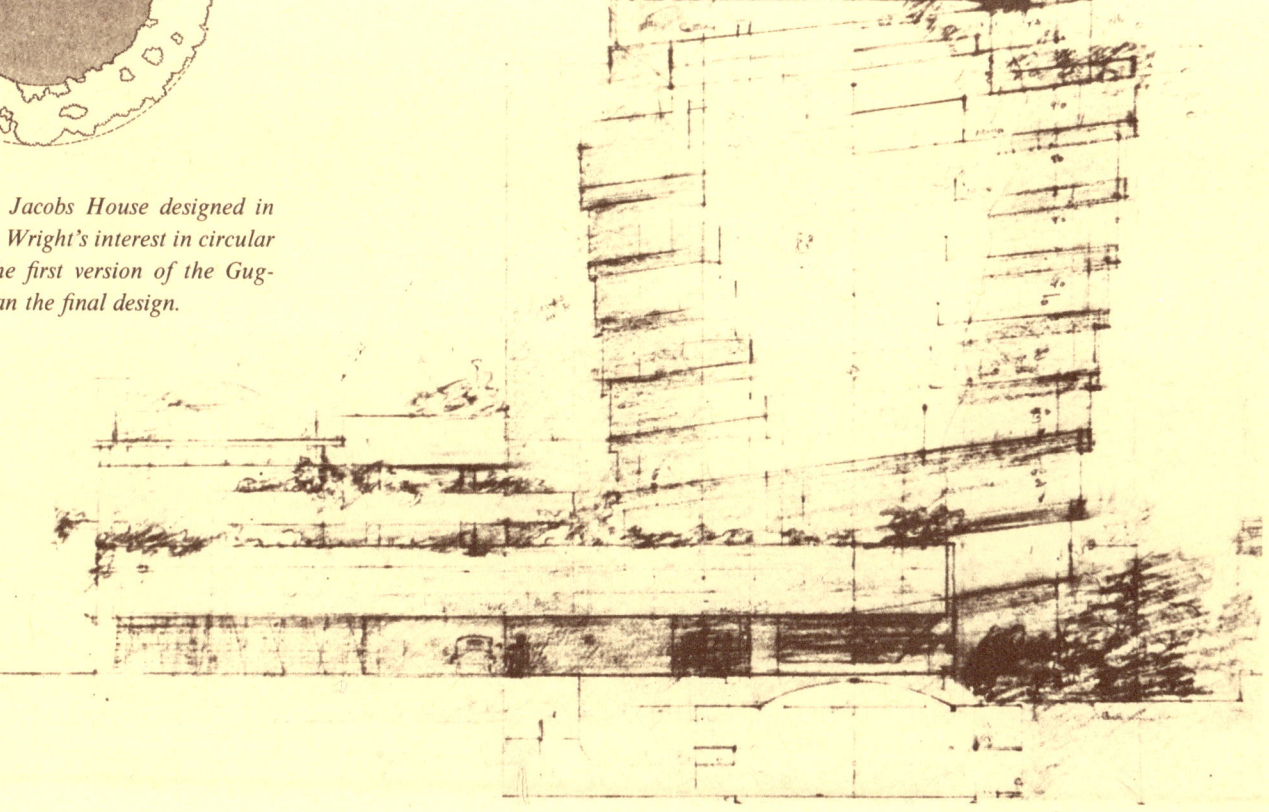

partly because it is on a more human scale. It is a continuous structure, far ahead of its time, and while it was under construction—and remaining upright in apparent defiance of gravity—Wright would smirk happily and say of his colleagues, "They'll spend years trying to work it out." But as a museum, it is a challenge. Visitors must make their way down a ramp at an angle, studying paintings hung on a wall that both curves and slopes. Wright's original idea of hanging the pictures as they were painted was never carried out—the paintings are customarily suspended perpendicular to the ground to alleviate additional discomfort to the viewer.

It is easy to conclude that Wright did not hold the Guggenheim collection in very high esteem. One of Wright's resentful ex-disciples has even suggested that the architect created the museum in order to annihilate the pictures. By his own admission, Wright did not appreciate modern painting; he certainly knew little about it and may well have cared less about the collection than about his spiral. Certainly, one of Wright's strongest convictions was that the true artist knows that his own creations must come first.

A building that functions well, as Wright ceaselessly reminded us, is not everything. A house is not a machine; it is above all a way of giving tangible and intelligible form to ideas, hopes, and illusions—to human life. In this sense the Guggenheim Museum is a success. It suggests how exciting the world could be and how many beautiful things it offers—if only every individual would be fully, freely, and enthusiastically himself and would choose personal integrity over the trappings of success. Most important, the museum underlines that crucial distinction between the merely interesting—gratuitous forms created simply to arouse astonishment—and the truly beautiful.

Above, left and right, two sketches showing how the museum was to function. Wright's professed intention was to revolutionize museum design.

Left, a perspective drawing made in 1949, showing the museum at night. Here it looks a bit like the flying saucer that some critics labeled it. The proposed attached apartment house in the background was never built.